THOMAS DEKKER

THOMAS DEKKER

A STUDY

BY

MARY LELAND HUNT, Ph.D.

New York

RUSSELL & RUSSELL

1964

COLUMBIA UNIVERSITY STUDIES IN ENGLISH

FIRST PUBLISHED IN 1911
REISSUED, 1964, BY RUSSELL & RUSSELL, INC.
L. C. CATALOG CARD NO: 64—15039

PRINTED IN THE UNITED STATES OF AMERICA

TO MY MOTHER

PREFACE

This study, tentative and incomplete as it is, would have no reason for existence if there had been any previous attempt to give a unified account of Dekker's life and personality, and if much of the criticism of the man and writer had not been distorted by an imperfect chronology or a partial knowledge of the facts. The object, then, has been to collect scattered material, including that furnished by Dekker himself, which has been much neglected, to arrange that material in chronological order, and to arrive at an understanding of the man. If the endeavor to understand has been colored by personal feeling, the reader is entreated to remember that a happy comradeship of three years is bound to leave some trace behind.

My indebtedness to scholars in the field of Elizabethan literature requires a word. The best outline of Dekker's life is to be found in the "Dictionary of National Biography" by A. H. Bullen, which in most respects agrees with that of Fleay. Memoirs of varying value are prefixed to Shepherd's edition of Dekker's "Dramatic Works," to Grosart's edition of the "Nondramatic Works," and to the Mermaid edition of the "Best Plays." The plays are discussed in all extended accounts of the Elizabethan drama, especially by Ward, who implicitly and explicitly ranks them low, and by Schelling in the somewhat scattered fashion required by his scheme. The growing tendency towards appreciation is marked in the "Cambridge History of English Literature" by an admirable article on a portion of Dekker's prose and by a sympathetic account of his life and plays, the latter however not overburdened with facts. Swinburne's essay, with all its need of shading and positive deduction, remains the best comprehensive view of Dekker's writings. Much gratitude is also due to students of special aspects of Dekker's work, notably to Mr. C. H. Herford and Mr. R. A. Small; nor should the names of Mr. E. E. Stoll and Mr. F. E. Pierce be forgotten. Mr. Greg's edition of "Henslowe's Diary," text and commentary, has been very helpful.

But my deepest obligations are to Professor Ashley Horace Thorndike, of Columbia University, to whom I owe, besides mention of the subject, much assistance, generously given and infinitely stimulating, whether by way of criticism or suggestion, and whose methods, gained first from his writings and afterwards in the lecture room, I have tried to follow, however inadequately.

I desire also to express my cordial thanks to Professor Charles M. Hathaway, Jr., of the United States Naval Academy, who kindly read the manuscript, and from his special knowledge of Dekker gave me the benefit of many a helpful criticism; to Dr. E. H. Wright, of Columbia University, who carefully read my study; and to Dr. Carl Van Doren, also of Columbia University, who secured some valuable Dekker material from the British Museum that would otherwise have been inaccessible.

M. L. H.

NEW YORK CITY,
August 10, 1911.

CONTENTS

CHAPTER   PAGE

I. INTRODUCTION I
The point of view. Dekker in part his own biographer. His
trustworthiness. His *Grove of Bay Trees* a record of enthusiasms. His affection for Nash. His early intellectual environment.

II. EARLY LIFE 11
Birth-place. Birth-date. Education and reading. A possible
campaign in the Low Countries. Democracy. Habits. Tastes.

III. THE EARLIEST PLAYS 28
*Old Fortunatus. The Whore of Babylon. The Weakest Goeth
to the Wall.*

IV. WITH HENSLOWE, 1598-1600 47
The character of the connection. Number of plays. Pay. Col-
laborators. Subjects of lost plays. *Canaan's Calamity. The
Sun's Darling. The Shoemaker's Holiday. Patient Grissill.*

V. THE QUARREL WITH JONSON. THE CLOSE OF THE
HENSLOWE PERIOD, 1601-1602 64
An interrupted play. Jonson's *Poetaster. Satiromastix. Sir
Thomas Wyatt.* Dekker the man between 1598 and 1602: his
poverty, his friendships.

VI. THE INFLUENCE OF MIDDLETON 86
The Magnificent Entertainment. Ode. New features in Dekker's
plays. Realistic comedy in England, 1598-1604. Middleton.
*The Honest Whore. Westward Ho. Northward Ho. The
Roaring Girl* (out of chronological order).

VII. THE PERIOD OF PROSE 115
Dedications and prefaces. *The Bachelor's Banquet. The Won-
derful Year. The Double P. P. News from Hell. A Knight's
Conjuring. The Seven Deadly Sins of London. Jests to Make
You Merry. The Dead Term. The Bellman of London. Lan-
thorn and Candlelight.* Rowlands. *A Strange Horse-race* (out
of chronological order). *The Raven's Almanac. Work for
Armorers. The Gull's Hornbook. Four Birds of Noah's Ark.*

VIII. 1610-1619: PLAYS: IMPRISONMENT 147
Complaint of hard times. *If It be not Good, the Devil is in
It. The Virgin Martyr. Match Me in London. Troja Nova*

xi

xii

Triumphans. Imprisonment. Letters to Alleyn. *Of a Prison.*
Geffray Mynshul. *Dekker his Dream.*

IX. THE LAST YEARS 177
Return to play-writing. *The Witch of Edmonton. The Wonder
of a Kingdom. The Noble Soldier. Penny-wise, Pound-foolish.
A Rod for Runaways. Britannia's Honor. London's Tempe.*
A lyric. A *Prison* narrative.

X. CONCLUSION 198
BIBLIOGRAPHICAL NOTE 205
INDEX 208

NOTE

References to the plays are for the greater part to Shepherd's four-volume edition of "The Dramatic Works of Thomas Dekker," published by Pearson, 1873; referred to under P., with the number of the volume and the page. Exceptions are named in full.

All references to "Patient Grissill" and, with two exceptions, to the prose are to Grosart's five-volume edition of "The Non-dramatic Works of Thomas Dekker," 1884; referred to under G., with the number of the volume and the page. The two pamphlets not included in this collection are named in full.

Fleay's article on Dekker in his "Biographical Chronicle of the English Drama" is indicated by Chr.

Except in a few cases that will be readily understood, spelling and, where it has seemed desirable, punctuation and the use of capitals have been modernized. Dates are expressed in the new style.

THOMAS DEKKER

A STUDY

CHAPTER I

INTRODUCTION

We do not know the month, possibly not the year, in which Thomas Dekker was born; we know still less about the date when he died; and we are not certain that he was ever married. But we know many facts more important than these.

We know, for instance, that he was a man of letters, who lived by his pen and in no other way, a consistent follower of the Muses, "pure maids but poor ones,"[1] as he says in his punning fashion. As early as 1604 he gaily spoke of himself as one "whose crest is a pen and inkhorn;"[2] and five or six years later, in another epistle, after dividing writers into two classes, those whose books are not worth so much brown paper, and those who, "being free of Wit's merchant-venturers," make, for gain only, some five or six voyages to the press every new moon, and who "spit nothing but ink and speak nothing but poem," he continues: "I would keep company with neither of these two mad-men if I could avoid them, yet I take the last to be the wisest and less dangerous: for sithence all the arrows that men shoot in the world fly to two marks only, either pleasure or profit, he is not much to be condemned that, having no more acres to live upon than those that lie in his head, is every hour hammering out one piece or other out of this rusty Iron age, sithence the golden and silver globes of the

---

[1] *Epis.-Ded., A Knight's Conjuring,* ed. E. F. Rimbault, Spen. Soc. Pub., Vol. 5.

[2] *Epis.-Ded., The Wonderful Year,* G., I, 76.

world are so locked up that a scholar can hardly be suffered to behold them."[3]

Again, we know, with few intervals, what Dekker, the man of letters, was doing from January, 1598, down to 1632, when, in a merry little song of appreciation, we hear his voice for the last time.

We know, besides, certain definite facts about the inner life of the man: what he liked and disliked, what he loved and hated; for his essentially lyrical temperament constantly repeats its utterances in personal prose and in dramatic verse, and when specific thoughts and emotions come constantly to the surface, their opposites never, we may assume that they were permanent. Some of them are well known: his pity for maimed soldiers, for poor scholars, for the victims of usurers; his horror of cruelty; the democracy of his outlook that at times included even women in its scope. We likewise know his love of books and music, his liking for law, and his passion for poetry and religion.

We often know his mood at the time of writing or printing, for to most of his prose pieces and to some of his plays are prefixed dedications or prefaces or both, which, though frequently veiled under whimsical language, are full of personality, and are, besides, often of special significance when taken in connection with the known facts of his life—a trustworthy record, for they show anger when we know from other sources that he had reason to feel anger; depression and pain, when we know, again from other sources, that the circumstances of his life might well arouse these emotions; fatigue and boredom, when he might naturally have had such feelings. We may therefore be sure that his more usual note of gayety and buoyancy is an honest expression of joy in life and work, and equally sure that his religious faith was just what he affirms it to be. However silent other dramatists may be upon the question of the destiny of the soul, Dekker makes his position perfectly clear in both prose and verse. He writes in a typical passage:

[3] *Epis.-Ded., Lanthorn and Candlelight,* G., III, 178–179.

3

"You see, therefore, how dreadful a fellow Death is, making fools even of wise men, and cowards of the most valiant; yea, in such a base slavery hath it bound men's senses that they have no power to look higher than their own roofs, but seems by their Turkish and barbarous actions to believe that there is no felicity after this life, and that, like beasts, their souls shall perish with their bodies."[4]

This religion did not fail him in the one tragic period of his life, and it is present in most of his works, from the young austerity of "Fortunatus" to the wise and sweet humanity— when all the world was bigoted—of "The Witch of Edmonton." Whatever his life may have been and however much his writings may have conceded to low popular tastes, he believed always that it was base to do evil, and, in a half-pagan age, that there was a happy future for the innocent and good. To him religion and poetry were the main facts of life—a creed that never shows the way to wealth although it may to a sort of beatitude. Curiously enough, Whipple, who was much impressed by Dekker's "wretchedness," felt forced to apply to him, fittingly as I think, his own words spoken of Fortunatus, "all felicity up to the brims."

In the contemporary records of Elizabethan literature, the name of Dekker does not appear until January, 1598, but our certain knowledge of some of his experiences and ideals goes back to earlier days. During those stirring years of England when to glory of adventure and glory of war was added the thrill of new shaping forces in literature, he was young and keenly sensitive to what was going on about him, both to the outburst of love for country and queen that followed the defeat of the Armada, and to the dramatic influences that between 1587 and 1598 were transforming the traditions of the stage; and he was alive to the new melodies then in the air. They were the same forces and melodies that at about the same time were influencing Shakespere, older than Dekker, but not, like the younger man, born and brought up in London where they were exhibited and felt earliest. His enthusiasms may easily be gathered from allusion, reference, and imitation in his plays, but on one occasion he spoke out directly. In

[4] *The Wonderful Year*, G., I, 145.

1607 he wrote "A Knight's Conjuring," altered from his "News from Hell," published the preceding year, a sequel to Nash's "Pierce Penniless, His Supplication to the Devil." Among the changes is an added chapter on the abode of the blest, *"fortunatae insulae."* From this I quote almost the whole of the passage about the bay-trees, partly for the purpose just indicated and partly to show, at the outset, Dekker's attitude, constant and life-long, towards poetry. It was written when he was approximately thirty-five years old.

"Beyond all these places is there a grove, which stands by itself like an island; for a stream that makes music in the running clasps it round about like a hoop girdle of crystal: laurels grow so thick on all the banks of it that lightning itself, if it came thither, hath no power to pierce through them. It seems, without, a desolate and unfrequented wood, for those within are retired into themselves, but from them came forth such harmonious sounds that birds build nests only in the trees there to teach tunes to their young ones prettily. This is called the Grove of Bay trees, and to this consort-room resort none but the children of Phoebus, poets and musicians: the one creates the ditty and gives it the life or number, the other lends it voice and makes it speak music. When these happy spirits sit asunder, their bodies are like so many stars, and when they join together in several troops, they show like so many heavenly constellations. Full of pleasant bowers and quaint arbours is all this walk. In one of which, old Chaucer, reverend for priority, blithe in cheer, buxom in his speeches and benign in his haviour, is circled round with all the makers or poets of his time, their hands leaning on one another's shoulders, and their eyes fixed seriously upon his, whilst their ears are all tied to his tongue by the golden chains of his numbers; for here, like Evander's mother, they spake all in verse; no Attic eloquence is so sweet: their language is so pleasing to the gods that they utter their oracles in none other.

"Grave Spenser was no sooner entered into this chapel of Apollo but these elder fathers of the divine fury gave him a laurel and sung his welcome: Chaucer called him his son and placed him at his right hand. All of them, at a sign given by the whole choir of the muses that brought him thither, closing up their lips in silence and tuning all their ears for attention, to hear him sing out the rest of his Faerie Queene's praises.

"In another company sat learned Watson, industrious Kyd, ingenious Atchlow, and, though he had been a player moulded out of their pens, yet because he had been their lover and a register to the Muses, inimitable Bentley: these were likewise carousing to one another at the holy well, some of them singing pæans to Apollo, some of them hymns to the rest of the gods, whilst Marlowe, Greene, and Peele had got under the shades of a large vine, laughing to see Nash, that was but newly come to their college, still haunted with the sharp and satirical spirit that followed him here upon earth: for Nash inveighed bitterly, as he had wont to do, against dry-fisted patrons, accusing them of his untimely death, because if they had given his muse that cherishment which she most worthily deserved, he had been fed to his dying day on fat capons, burnt sack and sugar and not so desperately have ventured his life and shortened his days by keeping company with pickle herrings. . . . He had no sooner spoken this, but in comes Chettle sweating and blowing by reason of his fatness; to welcome whom, because he was of old acquaintance, all rose up and fell presently on their knees, to drink a health to all the lovers of Helicon: in doing which they made such a mad noise that all this conjuring, which is past, being but a dream, I suddenly started up, and am now awake."[5]

There are three groups, it will be noticed; the first painted with a hand that is reverent yet true, the second with less sympathy, the third in so intimate and genial a way as to make one feel that here the writer is on familiar ground.

Dekker, then, loved Chaucer; indeed Chaucer is one of the few English poets quoted by him, for into his " Strange Horse Race" he brings the Franklin's description of winter in modernized dress,[6] and he elsewhere refers to Chaucer's Kentish connection,[7] and to the "Canterbury Tales."[8] And he loved Chaucer's son, "grave Spenser," so rich in the affection of his contemporaries. He had already shown his admiration for " The Faerie Queene " by borrowing its nomenclature in the drama that celebrates the greatness of Elizabeth, and it is possible that from the same source he learned some of the sweetness of his poetry.

The members of the second group are not important, so far as we know, in Dekker's history, not even Kyd, for although, like other playwrights, he frequently quotes " Jeronimo, go by," and sometimes alludes to the older " Hamlet," his genius did not greatly occupy itself with violence, ghosts, or bloodshed, and his only revenge tragedy, left unfinished, could have had nothing of the Kydian type about it. The rest of the group may have been added as a sort of tribute to the memory of Nash, who in his writings affectionately mentions all three.[9]

[5] *A Knight's Conjuring*, 74–77.
[6] G., III, 336–337.
[7] *A Rod for Runaways*, G., IV, 302, margin.
[8] *Northward Ho*, P., III, 52.
[9] See Rimbault's notes on *A Knight's Conjuring*, 98–99.

Very different is the case with the third group, every member of which contributed something to Dekker's style or subject matter. Chettle may be an exception, yet with him the external relationship was probably the closest of all, for they collaborated for some five years; Chettle later wrote a well-known verse about his affection for the younger man;[10] and the latter once borrowed money to help release his friend from imprisonment.[11] This third group possesses a homogeneousness exhibited by neither of the others. Whether Dekker knew the men in the flesh or not, he had seen their plays and read their prose, and had found much that was congenial. Looking at the group from this point of view, one misses the name of Lyly; but to the bohemians Lyly had never belonged, either in his tastes or in the circumstances of his life; and besides, it may well be that at the time of writing Dekker had not heard of his death, which took place after years of comparative obscurity, in November, 1606. Dekker seldom mentions or alludes to any of his works: "Mother Bombie" once or twice,[12] "Love's Metamorphosis" in "Patient Grissill";[13] and "Arcadian and Euphuized gentlewomen" in "The Gull's Hornbook."[14] This is the more strange because Lyly's influence upon his first known play is so powerful as to result in imitation, and it helped to fix permanently the characterization and the style of some of his most delightful comedy. Possibly, though this seems doubtful, that influence was already so pervasive when Dekker began to write that he did not recognize its origin. It is not necessary, however, to account for Lyly's absence from those happy spirits, for Dekker was not consciously drawing up a list of "the authors that have influenced me."

Although Dekker's creed was too stern to allow his unreservedly admitting to those Elysian fields any class except babes who had lived too briefly to learn sin of their parents, it did not keep him from giving to Marlowe, Greene, Peele, and

[10] See below, p. 84.
[11] See below, p. 79.
[12] *The Witch of Edmonton*, P., IV, 404.
[13] G., V, 127.
[14] G., II, 254.

Nash, very comfortable places there. Of the group of four, Marlowe, as might be expected, was by far the most important to Dekker; and though "Tamburlaine" is mentioned in his works more often perhaps than any other play and some of its details are copied in his dramas, yet "Doctor Faustus" more deeply impressed itself upon his religious nature. A very wonderful day it must have been when the younger poet heard for the first time the inspired apostrophe to Helena and listened to the heart-wringing despair of a soul lost while "Christ's blood streamed in the firmament." All his life Dekker was greatly concerned with the struggle between good and evil. In "The Honest Whore," it is the right and wrong impulses in the human heart, humanly swayed by other personalities; but in "Old Fortunatus" it takes the Marlowe form; so also in "The Virgin Martyr," and, to some extent, in "If It be not Good."[15] Of course Dekker, like every other dramatist after Marlowe, felt the liberating power of his verse, but though he was moved to emulate it at times, his happiest work came to be distinguished by a simplicity and clarity very unlike Marlowe's sonorous periods.

Very different it was, too, from Peele's "luxury and allurement of words," yet who but Peele remotely suggested the melody of such a passage as this?

> "There can I shew thee
> The ball of gold that set all Troy on fire;
> There shalt thou see the scarf of Cupid's mother
> Snatcht from the soft moist ivory of her arm,
> To wrap about Adonis' wounded thigh;
> There shalt thou see a wheel of Titan's car
> Which dropt from heaven when Phaeton fired the world:
> I'll give thee (if thou wilt) two silver doves
> Composed by magic to divide the air,
> Who, as they fly, shall clap their silver wings,
> And give strange music to the elements;
> I'll give thee else the fan of Proserpine,
> Which in reward for a sweet Thracian song
> The black-brow'd Empress threw to Orpheus,
> Being come to fetch Eurydice from hell."[16]

[15] See discussion of the plays in question.
[16] *Old Fortunatus*, P., I, 110.

8

Possibly Dekker felt the witchery of Peele's "Old Wives' Tale," both the genial homeliness of the opening scene and some of the details. If Peele used the echo dialogue in his folk-lore play, so does Dekker in his own folk-lore plays, " Old Fortunatus " and " If It be not Good ; " and to Peele's Golden Head from whose beard gold may be combed corresponds Dekker's Golden Head in " If It be not Good," that sheds from its " brows and hair " a golden shower, although one is of fairy origin and the other of infernal. Greene too used magic, but perhaps Dekker was more interested in his gentle and faithful women, so true to life in many ways as to constitute a novelty on the English stage of that early time ; for between Margaret, the keeper's lass of Fressingfield, engaged with her cream-bowls and occupied in " running cheeses," and Jane waiting upon customers in her shop, the stage offers no heroine whose humble occupation is so much a part of her attractiveness.

Whether the prose of Greene[17] or Nash more strongly influenced Dekker's pamphlets, it would be hard to say. " News from Hell " was written in imitation of Nash, and it was from Nash that he derived the fantastic style in which too many of the prefaces and dedications were composed, although no man then living could at will put his ideas into clearer, more direct, and more idiomatic prose ; this gift appears in " The Bachelor's Banquet " and " The Wonderful Year," written some time before " News from Hell." But Dekker had a special admiration for Nash, both as man and as writer. In " A Knight's Conjuring," he describes him as " a mad Greek that had drunk of the holy water and was full of the divine fury."[18] In " News from Hell," he affirms that the book was written " even out of my love to Pierce Pennyless because he hath been always a companion to scholars ; "[19] and a little farther on is found the well-known tribute:

" And thou into whose soul, if ever there were a Pythagorean metempsychosis, the raptures of that fiery and inconfinable Italian spirit were boun-

[17] Greene's lost *Exhortation of London unto her Children* suggests an interesting comparison with Dekker's London pamphlets.

[18] *p.* 13.

[19] G., II, 94–95.

teously and boundlessly infused, thou sometimes Secretary to Pierce Penniless and Master of his requests, ingenious, ingenuous, fluent, facetious, T. Nash: from whose abundant pen honey flowed to thy friends and mortal aconite to thy enemies: thou that madest the Doctor a flat Dunce, and beat'st him at his two tall sundry weapons, poetry and oratory: sharpest satire, luculent poet, elegant orator, get leave for thy ghost to come from her abiding and to dwell with me a while, till she hath caroused to me in her own wonted full measures of wit that my plump brains may swell and burst into bitter invectives against the Lieutenant of Limbo if he cashier Pierce Penniless with dead pay."[20]

Dekker further showed his interest in "T. Nash" by continuing in "The Gull's Hornbook" and in "Satiromastix" the controversy as to the relative merits of long and short hair \
waged between Nash and Richard Harvey,[21] and by versifying in his "Canaan's Calamity" a subject that Nash had written upon.[22]   Perhaps, too, his stinging description of Samuel Rowlands as likely to be "taken for a Beadle of Bridewell"[23] arose from his knowledge of a literary theft practised by Rowlands upon Nash.   Middleton, who also loved Nash, refers distinctly to something of the sort in "Father Hubbard's Tale."[24]

It has seemed desirable to dwell upon these enthusiasms of Dekker's youth. How happy we might be if Shakespere had left behind anything so intimate and self-revealing! There were other influences—Shakespere included—but they were among the living in 1607. There were also fashions in prose and poetry prevailing in Dekker's youth that he never showed any inclination to follow: the euphuistic novel, the sonnet sequence of feigned love, the long and dreary poem of passion, and the "snarling satire."

The poets of the third group, except Chettle, were producing their best work between 1587 and 1593, and Marlowe's

[20] G., II, 102–103.
[21] See R. A. Small, *Stage-Quarrel*, 124.
[22] See below, p. 52.
[23] See below, pp. 135–136.
[24] See Bullen's *Middleton*, VIII, 62–63, for the text and for Bullen's note which incorporates Malone's suggestion as to "that humorous theft."
    When Dekker speaks of Nash's "keeping company with pickle herrings," he surely is not referring to the banquet that killed Greene, as Dyce queries and Rimbault affirms, but to the brilliant pamphlet entitled *Lenten Stuff*, in which Nash pays such eloquent tribute to the red herring of Yarmouth.

complete output falls between those narrow limits. Dekker, as a Londoner, early experienced the delights of contemporary drama. In that little city of some 125,000 inhabitants, genius must have elbowed genius. He may have seen "grave Spenser," and whether or not he was acquainted with the other poets and playwrights, it could not have been difficult for him to get glimpses of them at the theatres, or at the ordinary or the tavern to which they resorted, or at the stationers' stalls where the new books might be seen and handled. It seems certain that he knew Nash, who was, it might be added, nearest his own age, and who, in 1597, was working upon his share in "The Isle of Dogs" for the manager for whom Dekker was writing by January of the following year and very likely earlier. Judging only from Dekker's own utterances in prose and verse, we shall hardly go wrong, then, if we think of him, at about 1593 or 1594, as that happiest of mortals, a poet, young and conscious of his powers, curious and reverent of genius in others, proud of his country and the tongue it spoke,

"Whose language now dare more than any can,"[25]

idealistic in his scorn for wealth and his ardor for wisdom and poetry, and endowed with a gay humor that must have served, later at least, as a sort of screen between a gentle nature and the sharp points of mere existence. And he had the peculiar happiness of living in a world that, in spite of much brutality and coarseness, was all hunger and thirst after the fulness of life, all passion for beauty and poetical expression.

[25] See below, p. 84, for the whole ode.

CHAPTER II

EARLY LIFE

According to his own testimony, Thomas Dekker was born and brought up in London. "O thou beautifullest daughter of two united monarchies," he cried in 1606, "from thy womb received I my being, from thy breasts my nourishment";[1] and, nineteen years later, "O London! thou mother of my life, nurse of my being, a hard-hearted son might I be counted if here I should not dissolve all into tears, to hear thee pouring forth thy passionate condolements."[2] But this ardent son of London hardly needed to proclaim his loyalty in such specific terms: six[3] of his prose works are directly concerned with the great city,—its sufferings, its vices, it glories, its manners, and its monuments; and about half of his extant plays make London the real scene of action, with details of shops and apprentices, streets and public buildings—the sort of loyalty, the sort of local color that one acquires most easily in youth. Curiously, too, his most extended passage in praise of the country[4] was written to heighten the contrast when he discovered that sin might flourish more easily outside the city than within. One[5] of the pamphlets is little more than a fervent dialogue of reciprocal praise and blame between London and Westminster, in which the latter often affectionately apostrophises her elder: "O my dearest playfellow";[6] "O thou darling of Great Britain, thy princes call thee their treasurer, and thou

---

[1] *Induction, The Seven Deadly Sins,* G., II, 13.

[2] *A Rod for Runaways,* G., IV, 285.

[3] *The Wonderful Year, The Seven Deadly Sins of London, Jests to Make You Merry*—the greater part, *The Dead Term, The Gull's Hornbook, A Rod for Runaways.*

[4] See the opening pages of *The Bellman of London,* G., III.

[5] *The Dead Term,* G., IV.

[6] *Idem,* 21.

11

art so ";[7] " Thou provident mistress over so many families ";[8]
"O thou the best and only huswife of this island ";[9] "O
thou charitable reliever and receiver of distressed strangers."[10]

The date of Dekker's birth is not as certain as the place, but
the available evidence points to 1572. He was "old" in 1628:

> "For my heart danceth sprightly when I see
> (Old as I am) our English gallantry."[11]

In 1631 he wrote, "I have been a priest in Apollo's temple
many years; my voice is decaying with my age."[12] He is more
specific in the dedication prefixed to "English Villanies:"
"This is no sermon but an epistle-dedicatory, which dedicates
those discoveries and my three-score years devotedly yours in
my best service." Now "English Villanies" was the new title
given in 1632 to the seventh edition of a popular rogue-book
first published as "Lanthorn and Candlelight ";[13] in 1638
another edition was brought out under the title of 1632. The
1632 edition is very rare; not even Fleay had seen a copy of it,
and the quotation is extracted from the 1638 edition; but he is
doubtless right in assuming that the dedication was added[13a]
when the title was changed—in 1632. In any case 1638 is
plainly out of the question, for that would make Dekker about
twenty years old when in 1598 he was ranked by Meres as
among those most excellent in tragedy. Dekker's habit, sometimes unpoetically exercised,[14] of giving the exact figures in
specific cases makes it practically certain to me that the "three-
score" is here to be taken on its face value. A slight piece of
contemporary evidence hitherto unnoticed in this connection
makes it clear that he was born later than 1570, but probably

---

[7] *The Dead Term*, G., IV, 14.

[8] *Idem*, 28.

[9] *Idem*, 32.

[10] *Idem*, 36.

[11] From the lost tract entitled *Wars, Wars, Wars*.

[12] *Dedication, Match Me in London*, P., IV, 133.

[13] First printed in 1608, reprinted (twice) in 1609, in 1612, 1616, 1620,
1632, 1638.

[13a] The 1620 edition has no personal dedication.

[14] See, for example, *The Whore of Babylon*, P., II, 257.

not much later. In 1610 Samuel Rowlands, in "Martin Mark-all," an angry attack upon Dekker,[15] accused him of employing, in "Lanthorn and Candlelight," "old words used forty years ago, before he was born."[16] While the phrase "forty years" may conceivably be a round number, it is far more likely that it was applied to one somewhat younger than forty than to one known to be of just that age, for it is Dekker's comparative youth that is contemptuously referred to. There is nothing in the known facts of his life that makes 1572 an unlikely date.

Nothing is known of Dekker's parents. A Thomas Dekker was buried in St. Saviour's, Southwark, in 1594, and his widow was living in Maid Lane, Southwark, in 1596. Although the name was too common[17] for its occurrence to establish a relationship, the spelling is in favor of the poet for he was very particular to spell his name in just one way, whether as a signature to the few notes, receipts, and letters, that have come down to us, or on the title-pages of the pageants that he prepared for the press; and with this spelling agrees, for the most part, the name attached to his prose work and to his uncollaborated plays. However hazardous it may be to offer a guess as to the family of a genius, this at least may be said: Dekker's early tastes seem to have been refined and his writings appear to indicate that he was brought up among books; in his personal utterances, he speaks of himself with dignified reserve—too great indeed for the purposes of biography, a letter to Alleyn from prison, for example, complaining of nothing but the "barbarousness" of his associates;[18] after his death he was bracketed with Ford as a gentleman[19] by actors of the company which had presented one of his plays.

[15] For further discussion of *Martin Mark-all*, see below, p. 136.

Collier was mistaken in assuming that *Lanthorn and Candlelight* was the reply; on the contrary, it furnished the occasion for Rowland's attack; for, in his *Martin Mark-all*, he takes to himself the humorous description of a certain "usurper" found in Dekker's preface to *Lanthorn and Candlelight*, 1609. The mistake has been handed on in *The Rogues and Vagabonds of Shakespeare's Youth*, E. E. Text Soc., 1869.

[16] *Works* ed. by the Hunterian Club, II, 36.

[17] *Chr.*, followed by Ward and Bullen.

[18] See below, p. 166, for the letter in question.

[19] On the title-page of *The Sun's Darling*.

14

Although it is not known how or where he was educated, he
seems to have had learning and reading enough to enable him
to use rightly if somewhat loosely the name of scholar, which
he cherished only less than that of poet. Grosart, whose edi-
torial labors have brought him much into Dekker's society,
sees "traces of scholarly culture in his most hasty produc-
tions."[20] Over against his name, on the title-page of a copy
of "Troja Nova Triumphans" in the British Museum, is
written in a contemporary hand, "marchant-tailor," but
Grosart's investigations have found no shred of evidence connecting him with that famous school.[21] Nor, though he sometimes speaks of the universities and has a prayer for "the two
universities" in "The Four Birds of Noah's Ark,"[22] and an
allusion to Cambridge now and then,[23] is there any probability
that he was ever in attendance upon either. But as in his
writings he uses Latin and classical mythology easily and
abundantly and as he undertook the translation of Dedekind's
Latin poem "Grobianus,"[24] he would seem to have had at least
a grammar-school education or its equivalent, for Latin then
constitued the bulk of such discipline. He was fond of pre-
fixing Latin mottoes to his plays,[25] pageants,[26] and prose;[27]
some of his pamphlets close in the same way,[28] and there is
considerable Latin in their body[28] and on their margins.[28] In
"The Whore of Babylon" his disputants use scholastic Latin;[29]
in the same play Elizabeth quotes Virgil;[30] in another, a
mourning lover reads Seneca in his study.[31] The "short and

[20] Memorial-Introduction, G., V, p. xiii.
[21] Mem.-Intro., G., V, pp. x–xi.
[22] G., V, 54.
[23] The Dead Term, G., IV, 82; Sir Thomas Wyatt, P., III, 96–97.
[24] See below, p. 142.
[25] See title-pages of The Whore of Babylon, Satiromastix, If It be not
Good, Match Me in London, The Wonder of a Kingdom.
[26] See title-pages of The Magnificent Entertainment, Britannia's Honor,
London's Tempe.
[27] See title-pages of The Wonderful Year, The Seven Deadly Sins of
London, News from Hell, A Strange Horse-race, etc.
[28] As above.
[29] P., II, 240–1.
[30] Idem, 220.
[31] 1 Honest Whore, P., II, 57.

pithy sentences"[32] appended to "The Four Birds of Noah's
Ark" are mostly drawn from the Church Fathers, and some of
the same authorities are used later in the prose parts of his
"Dream."[33] If one may judge from the authors[34] quoted,
named, and alluded to, and from the free use of classical
mythology, the range of Dekker's reading in Latin was wide;
in Jonson's eyes, it was, of course, inaccurate and unscholarly.

There are some indications that Dekker had "less Greek":
in "The Gull's Hornbook," for example, he uses Greek characters for a single word;[34a] he quotes what Aristophanes said
"in his Frog";[35] in two plays he gives Greek names to some
of his characters;[36] and he occasionally speaks of "Homer,
Hesiod, Euripides, and some other mad Greeks"[37] as if he
were acquainted with them in their own speech.

As he translated the fifteenth-century French satire "Les
Quinze Joyes de Mariage,"[38] it may be assumed that he read
French. Although in his plays his pretended French doctors
speak the jargon generally employed on the stage to arouse
laughter, he uses French phrases now and then, and in a
pageant called "Britannia's Honor," there is a little speech of
very easy French addressed to Henrietta Maria.[39] His writings show little evidence of an acquaintance with Italian or
Spanish, but he uses a few phrases from each language now
and then,[40] and employs appropriate names in the plays that

[32] G., V, 103–108.
[33] G., III, 25–54.
[34] Without attempting to give a complete list, for this paragraph on
Dekker's Latin is superficial, one may say that the names of Horace,
Virgil, Ovid, and Martial probably occur most frequently. In A Strange
Horse-race are quoted, with marginal mention of their names, Pliny,
Suetonius, Tacitus, Virgil, Plutarch, Paracelsus, Aesop, Ovid, Horace. G.,
III, 317–320 and 348–362.
[34a] G., II, 227.
[35] To the Reader, The Wonderful Year, G., I, 79.
[36] The Whore of Babylon, Satiromastix.
[37] To the Reader, The Wonderful Year, G., I, 81.
[38] See below, p. 124.
[39] P., IV, 101.
[40] As in Northward Ho, P., III, 60–61; and in Old Fortunatus, P., I, 136.

have their scene in either Italy or Spain.[41] But for dramatic
purposes, his favorite modern language was Dutch. In "The
Shoemaker's Holiday," "the Dutch talk," writes Ward,[42] "is
very racy and at least as full of idiom as that of Dirk Hat-
teraick in Scott's masterpiece." There is considerable Dutch
in Dekker's share in "The Weakest Goeth to the Wall," also,
and somewhat less in "Northward Ho."[43] Next to Dutch, in
his plays at least, Dekker liked Welsh.[44] His is the most
idiomatic as well as the most entertaining Welsh-English on
the Elizabethan stage; in "Patient Grissill" Keltic words are
mixed with the broken English.[45]

It would be idle to try to estimate the extent of Dekker's
reading, the more so as he is in the habit of alluding to books
and their characters indirectly, humorously, even punningly.
When he describes one of the seven deadly sins of London as
"the Gaveston of the time,"[46] I suspect that he is thinking of
Marlowe's "Edward the Second," although that may not be
the case. When he writes of an old prisoner: "In his face
were the Ruins of youth, in his garments of Time; in both the
Triumphs of poverty,"[47] it is very possible that his phrase was
conditioned by the memory of a poem by Spenser, but one
cannot be sure. Among the writers, not elsewhere noted, that
he actually mentions by name, however, are Stow,[48] with his
"chronicle of decimo sexto," "huge Holinshed,"[49] Machiavelli,[50] and Sir John Harington, to whom he dedicated "The

---

[41] *The Honest Whore, The Wonder of a Kingdom, Match Me in London,*
and *If It be not Good.*

[42] *A History of English Dramatic Literature,* II, 457.

[43] There is Dutch talk in *The Roaring Girl* and an identifying Dutch phrase
in *Sir Thomas Wyatt;* and a little Dutch speech by Hans the waiter in
Westward Ho.

[44] There is a Welsh pair in *Patient Grissill,* a Welshman in *Satiromastix,*
and another in *Northward Ho.*

[45] For a comparison of Dekker's dialect with Shakespere's, see W. Bang's
Dekker-Studien, Englische Studien, band 28, 226–7.

[46] *The Seven Deadly Sins of London,* G., II, 58.

[47] *The Misery of a Prison and a Prisoner,* G., II, 338.

[48] *The Gull's Hornbook,* G., II, 236 ; *The Wonderful Year,* G., I, 96.

[49] *The Wonderful Year,* G., I, 96.

[50] *Work for Armorers,* G., IV, 131.

Dead Term."⁵¹ He seems to have been familiar with " Piers
Plowman,"⁵² " Sir John Mandeville's Travels,"⁵³ and Jourdan's
account of the Bermudas.⁵⁴ He liked folk and fairy lore, for
they form the groundwork of two of his plays and doubtless
also of the lost " Fairy Knight."⁵⁵ He tells us that he greatly
enjoyed history: " O histories! you sovereign balms to the
bodies of the dead, that preserve them more fresh than if they
were alive, keep the fames of princes from perishing when
marble monuments cannot save their bones from being rotten,
you faithful intelligencers between kingdoms and kingdoms,
you truest councillors to kings, even in their greatest
dangers."⁵⁶ But the book that Dekker knew best and quoted
most frequently was the Bible. A eulogy of it opens " The
Seven Deadly Sins of London."⁵⁷ In his " Dream "⁵⁸ he gives
chapter and verse and the whole poem is full of biblical phrasing. From the same source is derived much of the simplicity
and the rhythm, soft or fervent, of his book of prayers,⁵⁹ and,
more subtly, of his language elsewhere. He sometimes uses its
phraseology, too, for half humorous purposes, as in the following description of Confusion: " In one hand she gripped a heap
of storms with which at her pleasure she could trouble the
waters."⁶⁰ In connection with his indebtedness to the Bible it
is interesting to remember that he had a hand in two biblical
dramas⁶¹ when that species was dying out.

In this superficial survey, little account has been taken of his
delving into curious lore or of his innumerable allusions to

⁵¹ G., IV, 7–8.
⁵² The Gull's Hornbook, G., II, 211.
⁵³ Patient Grissill, G., V, 213, but Sir John Mandeville was the title of a
play recorded by Henslowe in 1591.
⁵⁴ If It be not Good, P., III, 340; A Strange Horse-race, G., III, 370.
⁵⁵ See below, p. 178.
⁵⁶ Work for Armorers, G., IV, 101.
⁵⁷ G., II, 7.
⁵⁸ G., III, 1–60.
⁵⁹ The Four Birds of Noah's Ark, G., V, 1–101.
⁶⁰ Lanthorn and Candlelight, G., III, 189.
⁶¹ Jephthah with Munday, and a prologue and epilogue for Pontius Pilate.

contemporary plays,[62] ballads,[62] stories, and pamphlets. Of contemporary playwrights he naturally enjoyed Shakespere most, especially "A Midsummer Night's Dream," "Romeo and Juliet," and "Hamlet."[63] He shows his admiration sometimes by imitation or quotation, but perhaps more often by adaptation, as when, to illustrate on a small scale, he modifies a well-known line, spoken by Puck, to describe "God's arm, like a girdle going round about the world."[64] When one considers Dekker's general reading, what one misses, on the whole, is a knowledge of Italian literature, and, in his plays, a dependence upon Italian motive, although it is necessary to remember that his taste seems to have shrunk from the sort of Italian motives most popular.

Books, to him, were certainly a source of solid pleasure: "Art thou sad? where is sweeter music than in reading? Art thou poor? open those closets, and invaluable treasures are poured into thy hands."[65] How Dekker obtained his reading, we do not know. He may have had access to private libraries; such "a companion to scholars" as Nash may have helped him out; he probably had the bookstall habit; it may be that he showed what has been called his "hopeless improvidence" by buying some of his books. From this subject I cannot wholly dissociate his pity for poor scholars, long noted by the critics; for while it may possibly have derived its poignancy from his own experience, it was early exhibited and seems to me, judging from what I surmise as to his methods of writing, more likely to have come from the trials of some one to whom he was attached. In his "Misery of a Prison and a Prisoner," there is a portrait,[66] strongly individualized and drawn with great feeling, of an old man to whose gentle nature loss of

[62] There are over thirty allusions to plays and ballads in *Satiromastix* alone.

[63] See discussion of *The Whore of Babylon, Honest Whore,* and *Match Me in London.* For the whole subject, see E. Koeppel's *Studien über Shakespeare's Wirkung* in *Materialien,* 1905. Some few of the parallelisms seem to me slight. Fleay also has notes on this subject in his article on Dekker.

[64] *A Rod for Runaways,* G., IV, 305.

[65] *Work for Armorers,* G., IV, 101-2.

[66] G., II, 337-343.

freedom was most irksome; he had been a scholar and in his happier moments "could read comfort to himself out of his own library, which was his memory." Another passage testifying to Dekker's sympathy with the poor scholar was written earlier, and though out of place in the mouth of the speaker, forms one of the vivid spots in a lifeless play.

> " The dragons that keep learning's golden tree,
>   As you now have, I fought with, conquered them,
>   Got to the highest bough, eat of the fruit,
>   And gathered of the sevenfold leaves of art
>   What I desired; and yet for all the moons
>   That I have seen wax old and pine for anger
>   I had outwatched them, and for all the candles
>   I wasted out on long and frozen nights
>   To thaw them into day, I filled my head
>   With books, but scarce could fill my mouth with bread."[67]

There is no evidence that Dekker was brought up to do anything in particular. He shows a peculiar sympathy for prentices, indeed, bringing mention of them into his plays in and out of season; one of the most pathetic and specific prayers in "The Dove" is that to be said by a prentice "going to his labour";[68] but it would be unwise to assume that Dekker was ever a prentice himself, for he was born with the artist's eye for detail, and prentices cut a considerable figure in all street demonstrations. Besides, this kind of argument proves too much. We are no sooner convinced that he knew all about the linen-draper's trade, for example, than we discover that he was more familiar with the shoemaker's; and then we are constrained to remember that "The Shoemaker's Holiday" was derived directly from a definite story of shoemakers, and that shoemakers were a part of the stage spectacle before Dekker's time.[69] Moreover, this sort of thing is entirely absent from the prose, except the book of prayers, which is necessarily semi-dramatic in character; the point of view is always that of the man of letters—poet, scholar, commentator on manners, or preacher. Nor was Dekker ever a player; the

---

[67] *The Whore of Babylon,* P., II, 223–224.
[68] Quoted in part below, p. 145.
[69] As in *Locrine.*

passage quoted in the Introduction in which he apologizes for
bringing an actor into the company of poets shows his usual
attitude toward players, an attitude not contradicted by the
affectionate dedication[70] of one of his plays to his "loving and
loved friends," the actors, for it has not the tone of a man who
has ever been one of them. Again, although Dekker shows
unusual acquaintance with law,[71] its phraseology and its
processes, and in serious and humorous metaphors reverts
readily to its language,[72] there is no proof that he was ever
entered at the Inns of Court, and we must needs attribute his
legal accomplishments to his lively interest in human things
and to his intimacy with such of his friends as were students
of law, Middleton and Ford among them, perhaps Marston
too.[73]

It is very possible, however, that at some time during his
youth, Dekker had a brief experience in the wars waging in the
Netherlands, where so many English fought for glory, pay, or

[70] *If It be not Good*, P., III, 261.

[71] Noted by Ward, II, 453.

[72] Such phraseology is so scattered through Dekker's writings that it is
difficult to indicate briefly its abundance. In *News from Hell*, G., II, it is
found not only in the account of "sessions," but also in the use of such
expressions as the favorite "*in forma pauperis*," p. 91 ; "*noverints*," p. 93;
"*fieri facias*," p. 97. *The Gull's Hornbook*, G., II, has technical phrases on
p. 245, p. 248, p. 262. *The Dead Term*, G., IV, offers, besides extended
praise of law, a summary of particular laws, p. 56–58. *The Strange Horse-
race*, G., III, brings forward a banquet of legal documents, p. 371–373.
The Raven's Almanac, G., IV, contains a gibe at Littleton, p. 175, and
Work for Armorers, G., IV, a proclamation full of legal verbiage, p. 145–
149. In *The Bellman of London*, G., III, 117, a legal phrase is explained.
"The Statute of Rogues" in *The Wonderful Year*, G., I, 79, is not important although used metaphorically, but less to be expected in a playwright's
mouth is the "Verdimote Inquest" of *The Seven Deadly Sins*, G., II, 61.
There is satire on "the punies and young fry of the law" in *The Raven's
Almanac*, G., IV, 174–5. In the *Prayer for a Lawyer*, G., V, 53, occurs the
significant reminder, "Equity is the ground upon which law is builded."
Very frequent is the use of sessions or court in a figurative sense. Aside
from the oft-recurring sessions in hell, we have, for example, Elizabeth
summoned to the Star-Chamber of heaven, *The Wonderful Year*, G., I, 86 ;
a heroine who believes that she is dying feels "the spiritual court" breaking up, *Satiromastix*, P., I, 251, and there are many other cases.

[73] R. A. Small, *Stage-Quarrel*, 62.

religion.   This hypothesis would serve to explain, as no other
does, some of his unusual tastes and unusual knowledge.   His
liking for the terms of war probably means nothing, although
such metaphors are astonishingly frequent;[74] but brief pictures
of military life like the Tilbury scenes in the " Whore of Babylon "[75] and the account of the emotions and talk of soldiers
after a great battle,[76] are well executed; and the lame or
wounded soldier has been noticed by every reader of his plays
and is found as frequently in the prose.   Perhaps, too, his
many references to war in the Low Countries, to Low Country
captains and the like, may mean little, for they are found to
some extent in other writers, and, as Dekker puts it in 1609:
" The Low Countries . . . have, in renown, gone beyond kingdoms of higher fame, only for thus repairing and keeping open
those old and ruinated temples of Bellona."[77]   Not significant
either may be his use of the Low Countries as a synonym for
hell,[78] for Nash, his master, used it first, and Dekker, on his
own account, could never resist an invitation to pun.   But
there is also a considerable body of allusions and references full
of specific and concrete detail.   He speaks contemptuously of
a certain class of rogues who " carry the shapes of soldiers
and can talk of the Low Countries though they never were

[74] Work for Armorers, G., IV, is an extended allegory of social conditions couched in terms of war, with a preface addressed to soldiers.   There
is a call to arms in the preface of Lanthorn and Candlelight, G., III.   Going
to law is going to war, The Dead Term, IV, 26–27; and a prison is a camp,
Jests to Make You Merry, G., II, 354–355.   The titles of two lost works
are: The Artillery Garden, and Wars, Wars, Wars.

Brief war metaphors are so frequent in the prose as to constitute a
mannerism: the pen is " a most dangerous piece of artillery," Epis.-Ded.,
Work for Armorers, G., IV, 89–90; " the powder of their wit being wet and
not so apt to take fire," The Dead Term, G., IV, 82; etc.

[75] P., II, 270, 273–4.

[76] The Wonderful Year, G., I, 118.

[77] Work for Armorers, G., IV, 92.

[78] " The seven electors of the Low Infernal Countries," The Seven Deadly
Sins, G., II, 78; " those Low Country commodities of hell," The Bellman of
London, G., III, 116; Charon's boat is " the Flemish hoy of hell," News
from Hell, G., II, 119.   These are specimens; there are many more, to
weariness, especially in the books dealing with hell: News from Hell; the
opening chapters of Lanthorn and Candlelight; A Strange Horse-race.

beyond Dover."[79]   The seventeen "valleys of Belgia" are
"those seventeen Dutch virgins "[80] or the seventeen daughters
"young and fair" of the Netherlannders.[81] Low Country
soldiers were compelled to feed "upon cabbage, upon roots,
and, upon Christmas day, instead of minched pies, had no
better cheer than provant (mouldy Holland cheese and coarse
brown bread)."[82]   Dekker speaks of fellows "that looked like
Flemings, for they were as fat as butter; "[83] of "huge Dutch
aldermen's sleeves ";[84] and remarks of one of his characters,
"they harnessed the Grand Signior's coach, mounted his
cavalry upon curtals, and so sent him most pompously, like a
new-elected Dutch burgomaster, into the city."[85]   Again:
"Their hall that now is larger than some dorps among the
Netherlands was then no bigger than a Dutch butcher's
shop ";[86] and again, "A drollery or Dutch piece of lantskop
may sometimes breed in the beholder's eye as much delectation as the best and most curious masterpiece excellent in that
art."[87] Drake

> "Swears, Fleming-like, by twenty thousand devils."[88]

To this list of quotations, by no means exhaustive,[89] may be

[79] *The Bellman of London*, G., III, 93.
[80] *Induction to The Seven Deadly Sins*, G., II, 9.
[81] *The Whore of Babylon*, P., II, 219.
[82] *Work for Armorers*, G., IV, 117.
[83] *A Strange Horse-race*, G., III, 341.   Also "the four trumpeters of the
world . . . like four dropsy Dutch captains standing sentinels in their
quarters," *News from Hell*, G., II, 97.
[84] *Work for Armorers*, G., IV, 162.
[85] *The Seven Deadly Sins*, G., II, 33.
[86] *The Gull's Hornbook*, G., II, 210.
[87] *Epis.-Ded.* prefixed to *The Seven Deadly Sins*, Cambridge Edition, not
given by Grosart. For a similar passage, see *The Bellman of London*, G.,
III, 87.
[88] *The Whore of Babylon*, P., II, 262. See also the advice given to the
gallant out late at night, to curse and swear "like one that speaks high
Dutch." *The Gull's Hornbook*, G., II, 261.
[89] The following might be added as being somewhat different: "The estimation of them [books] riseth and falleth faster than the exchange of
money in the Low Countries." *To the Reader, Jests to Make You Merry*,
G., II, 271 ; "You will by and by suppose yourself in the Low Countries,

added a reminder that Dekker had a knowledge of the Dutch language, which, except for a few cant phrases, seems to have been an unusual attainment among playwrights. It has even been deemed probable that it was through Dutch that he had access to the German folk story of "Old Fortunatus and his Sons."[90]

In general, although Dekker had lived through the period of the Spanish Armada and the taking of Cadiz, whenever he thought of war he thought of the Netherlands, and mention of the Dutch sprang to his lips more frequently than mention of any other nationality. Traces of unusual cosmopolitanism in his writings[91] would almost seem to demand as a pre-requisite some residence in a foreign land. He does not claim all virtues exclusively for England. He may indeed share in the stale satire of things "Italianate"[92] although in such a way as to reflect upon the imitators rather than upon Italy; but he also ridicules ascribing treachery and violence to Italy,[93] and in "Patient Grissill" that "sweetest country in the world" is defended from the attacks of her traducers.[94] In his prayer to

for as the soldiers there, so these here, talk of nothing but stratagems and points of war." *The Dead Term*, G., IV, 26; the two following are probably commonplaces: "She slips from one company to another like a fat eel between a Dutchman's fingers." *The Roaring Girl*, P., III, 156, and "Alas! there you find worse enemies than those of Breda had in Spinola's camp. A Spaniard is not so hateful to a Dutchman as a Londoner to a countryman." *A Rod for Runaways*, G., IV, 292.

In *The Royal Entertainment*, Dekker describes both the Italian and the Belgian pageants, the latter with far more sympathy. See P., I, 283–295, especially pp. 292–3.

The mention of "Tannekin the Froe" in *Patient Grissill*, G., V, 175, has no particular significance except to show how easily such words ran from Dekker's tongue.

[90] For a discussion of this question, see below, pp. 33–34.

[91] Mr. Rhys thinks that the name—whether Dekker or Decker—suggests Dutch origin. *Introduction* to the Mermaid edition of Dekker's plays, p. xi.

[92] *Old Fortunatus*, P., I, 119.

> "Fantastic compliment stalks up and down,
> Tricked in outlandish feathers; all his words,
> His looks, his oaths, are all ridiculous,
> All apish, childish, and Italianate."

[93] *Gull's Hornbook*, G., II, 215.

[94] G., V, 168.

be used in time of civil war, he takes note of the sorrows of other nations,—of France, "that doth yet mourn in the ashes of those fires, and Germany is even now stifled with the smokes:"[95] Elsewhere[96] he expresses a passionate pity for the same countries; I quote briefly from the apostrophe to France: "O gallant monarchy! what hard fate hadst thou, that when none were left to conquer thee, thou shouldst triumph over thyself. Thou hast wines flowing in thy veins but thou madest thyself drunk with thine own blood." This appreciation[97] did not keep Dekker from making his French characters act and speak absurdly, and the same discrepancy exists in the case of the Irish, for over against his stage Irishmen may be set a little passage of praise[98] unusual at that time.

Whether Dekker spent his youth in study or in fighting or in both, he developed no taste for the Court, and his love for Queen Elizabeth, often and ardently expressed,[99] was never soured by disappointed hopes of preferment. Nor did he hang about the houses of nobles; when he was compelled to seek patronage he did so unwillingly and addressed his epistles-dedicatory more often to magistrates[100] than to any other one class. His known friends were poets, players, a water bailiff

[95] G., V, 57. With Dekker, "Germany" often means the Netherlands, as in the passage next mentioned.
[96] G., II, 9–10.
[97] Noted by Jusserand.

[98]
> "You have a son
> Rebellious, wild, ingrateful, poor, and yet
> Apollo from's own head cuts golden locks
> To have them grow on his: his harp is his,
> The darts he shoots are his: the winged messenger
> That runs on all the errands of the gods
> Teaches him swiftness; he'll outstrip the winds."
> The Whore of Babylon, P., II, 206.

[99] See below, pp. 40–41.
[100] The Wonderful Year to the "water-bailiff of London"; The Seven Deadly Sins to a clerk of the peace; Wars, Wars, Wars to the lord mayor and the two sheriffs of London and Middlesex; English Villainies, 1638, to the justices of the peace in Middlesex; The Bellman of London to "all those that either by office are sworn to punish, or in their own love to virtue, wish to have the disorders of a state amended"; Canaan's Calamity to a "justice of the peace and quorum."

of London,[101] a "gentleman."[101]   Impecunious poet though he was, he set the highest value upon good citizenship, especially upon the necessity of enforcing and obeying the laws of the commonwealth.   Whether directly or indirectly, consciously or unconsciously expressed, his views were those of the growing democratic spirit, a spirit nobly crystallized in his well-known characterization of Christ:

"The first true gentleman that ever breathed."[102]

He was modern, too, in his pity for the animals whose torture furnished amusement to the multitude,[103] and in his feeling, as keen as that of a modern painter, for the romantic charm of city scenes and city streets, as well as for their humorous values.

Since among those who write about Dekker, it has become a species of commonplace to assume that he was somehow disreputable, it should be added that there is no reason for thinking that his youth was a period of sowing wild oats.   Like his own Andelocia, he was probably "not given" that way, and, to me at least, the moral idealism of "Old Fortunatus" counts for something.   Down to 1604 when he was over thirty years old, his plays contain neither characters nor situations that could offend the fastidious, and his vocabulary, for the times, is comparatively free from grossness.   If Captain Tucca is an exception, why "that heretical libertine Horace taught me so to mouth it."[104]   Dekker's worst habits when he comes into view in 1598 were, apparently, a steady attendance at the theatre and a prodigious industry in producing plays.   For one habit of good-fellowship indeed he seems to have had an especial aversion: he always speaks scoffingly of tobacco; his gulls make an Indian chimney of the nose and are curious in their taste for it;[105] his women dislike it;[106] death[107] and the devil[108]

[101] See epistles prefixed to *The Wonderful Year* and *News from Hell.*
[102] *1 Honest Whore*, P., II, 90.
[103] See below, p. 141.
[104] *Epilogus* to *Satiromastix*, P., I, 265.
[105] *The Gull's Hornbook*, G., II, 224, 265.
[106] *Westward Ho*, P., II, 344–345.
[107] *Old Fortunatus*, P., I, 97.
[108] *To the Reader, News from Hell*, G., II, 89.

are "tobacconists," the former "a lean tawny-face tobacconist;" in his own person as Demetrius, he refuses contemptuously the "right pudding" offered by Asinius Bubo.[109] There remain some few tastes and interests that Dekker doubtless acquired in his youth. Although, like Lamb, he preferred London to the country, he was far more sensitive to natural beauty than most of his contemporaries.[110] One whole play or masque, "The Sun's Darling," is devoted to the changing sentiment of the seasons. He had a special liking for birds:[111] for the nightingale, for the lark's "silver leer-a-leer,"[112] for the cuckoo, that "like a single sole fiddler that reels from tavern to tavern, plied it all the day long."[113] Like his friend Webster, he had a sort of fearful joy in the cry of the screech owl,[114] and, before Coleridge, he combined the owl and the ivy-tod.[115] He loved flowers, the daisies, the "sad violet"; and he speaks of the cornfields, the lustrous leaf of the willow,[116] of "white butterflies."[117] and "the waters of the crisped spring."[118] Like Day, another friend, he was fond of bees,[119] too; and he must have done a great deal of star-gazing, for stars or "battlements of stars"[120] are often found in his most eloquent verse.

To the charm of some of the fine arts he was susceptible. He liked to describe buildings; and if no such rooms, so deco-

[109] Satiromastix, P., I, 196.

[110] For a rather detailed description of nature, see the opening pages of The Bellman of London, G., III.

[111] Bird metaphors, not especially effective, are found in The Whore of Babylon, P., II, p. 230, 232, 249, and elsewhere.

[112] The bird song in The Sun's Darling, p. 304.

[113] The Wonderful Year, G., I, 84.

[114] Idem, p. 85, 104; and in many other passages.

[115] Jests to Make You Merry, G., II, 359.

[116] News from Hell, G., II, 153.

[117] The "white butterflies" are Paul's boys. Gull's Hornbook, G., II, 233.

[118] Song in Patient Grissill: "Art thou poor," etc.

[119] "The Muses' birds, the bees, were hived," etc. Satiromastix, P., I, 213. See also speech of Genius Loci in Kings Entertainment, idem, 273, but there are many others.

[120] See Hipolito's speech, 1 Honest Whore, P. II, 59. Again, there are many others.

rated, as those of Torrenti[121] and Sir Alexander Wentgrave[122] ever existed, their suggestion of strange beauty is just as great. He was fond of pictures and often uses figures from painting or drawing when he speaks of his books.[123]

Dekker shared the then general love of music to such an extent that he could hardly speak of it without breaking into a sort of rapture.

" [I] secretly
Commanded music with her silver tongue
To chime soft lullabies into his soul."[124]
" Go; let music
Charm with her excellent voice an awful silence
Through all this building, that her sphery soul
May, on the wings of air, in thousand forms
Invisibly fly, yet be enjoyed."[125]
" Take instruments,
And let the raptures of choice harmony
Thorough the hollow windings of his ear
Carry their sacred sounds."[126]

Doubtless he sang, he who could, with little excuse or none at all, bring out a gay little song for boating, a heartier one for a drinking bout, a love song with May and the nightingale in it, a tender lullaby, or the sweetest song for the poor ever sung. I quote one, not by any means the best, but one that is peculiarly Elizabethan in a kind of breathless vitality.

" My Muse that art so merry,
When wilt thou say th'art weary?
Never, I know it, never!
This flight thou couldst keep ever:
Thy shapes which so do vary
Beyond thy bounds thee carry.
Now plume thy ruffled wings,
He's hoarse who always sings."[127]

[121] The Wonder of a Kingdom, P., IV, 249.
[122] The Roaring Girl, P., III, 141–142.
[123] See Epilogus, The Roaring Girl, P., III; and the brief figure in Lectori, Whore of Babylon, P., II, 189; and there are many others, especially in the prefaces.
[124] Old Fortunatus, P., I, 139.
[125] Westward Ho, P., II, 333.
[126] Old Fortunatus, P., I, 92.
[127] A Strange Horse-race, G., III, 378.

CHAPTER III

THE EARLIEST PLAYS

The first mention of Dekker's name is in Henslowe's "Diary," when, January 8, 1598, he was paid for a book, that is, a play. As during that year he had a hand in fifteen or sixteen other plays and as he was in September named by Meres as among the best in tragedy, he could hardly in January have been a novice in the drama. Moreover, as in February, 1596, a Fortunatus play appears in the "Diary," there is some reason for believing that he was then working for Henslowe, possibly earlier.[1] Unfortunately the "Diary" has almost no record for 1593; there are gaps in 1596, 1597, and 1600, and the names of the authors are not given until 1598; yet, incomplete as it is, it remains our only authority for the titles of Dekker's plays down to 1600 and our chief authority to the end of 1602. Of the various anonymous plays found in the "Diary" before 1598 and tentatively assigned to Dekker, it is necessary to speak here of but two: "Philipo and Hippolito" under the date of July 9, 1594, and "Antony and Valia," Jan. 4, 1595. Plays bearing virtually the same names[2] were registered to print in 1660 under Massinger's name. The only reason for connecting these two plays with Dekker is that Massinger is known to have refashioned his "Virgin Martyr." It seems a slight reason; Warburton's servant has put the question beyond the possibility of a solution.[3]

[1] Greg says pertinently: "We should have to regard it as something of a coincidence that he should have begun to write just at the very moment that Henslowe began to record the names of the authors connected with the company. *Henslowe's Diary*, II, 257.

[2] Philenzo and Hippolita, June 29; and *Antonio and Vallia*, June 29. Greg has corrected Fleay's error in the date of the former. *Diary*, II, 165.

[3] Fleay's identification of *The French Doctor*, October 18, 1594, with *The Jew of Venice*, a lost play by Dekker, not registered to print till 1653, is nothing but a guess. See Greg, *Diary*, II, 170–171, for an intricate note

28

When it comes to assigning an existing play by Dekker to an earlier year than 1598, the matter is somewhat different; yet even then a special difficulty arises from the fact that all of his work for that year, with a single exception, has perished, and that the exception, " Phaeton," or, as it was later christened, " The Sun's Darling," suffered revision from Ford in the only version that has come down to us; there is, accordingly, less basis for comparison than could be desired. In spite of all difficulties, however, there are reasons for believing that two extant plays, " Old Fortunatus " and " The Whore of Babylon," belong, in their original form, to an early date in Dekker's dramatic history. In both cases the evidence is chiefly internal, consisting mainly in their dependence upon influences and stage-conventions that had become archaic at the dates usually assigned to these plays and in their weakness in characterization. The third play discussed in this chapter is generally acknowledged to belong to an early date, and the crudeness of what I shall try to show is Dekker's share points to inexperience.

The first mention of an English Fortunatus play is found in the entry in Henslowe's " Diary," already referred to, dated February 3, 1596: " First Part of Old Fortunatus." Later entries in February, in April, and in May speak simply of " Fortunatus." Nearly four years later, on November 9, 1599, Dekker is named as receiving two pounds for the " whole history of Fortunatus," and by November 30 he had received the full payment of six pounds. The next day he had another pound for " altering " the play, and on December 12, two pounds for " the end of Fortunatus for the Court." It was acted before the Queen on Christmas Day by the Admiral's men and was printed[4] in 1600, with Dekker's name at the end but not on the title-page. It seems to be generally accepted that the alterations and the end for the Court comprise, be-

---

on *The Jew of Venice.* He there discusses the German version, entitled *The Righteous Judgment of a Girl Graduate, or The Jew of Venice.*

Mr. F. W. Moorman's assignment to Dekker of a share in *The Birth of Merlin* (date uncertain) does not seem to me convincing. See *Cam. Hist. Eng. Lit.,* V, 280–281, for his argument.

[4] *The Pleasant Comedie of Old Fortunatus.*

sides the Prologue and the Epilogue at Court, the Virtue and Vice scenes,[5] including all of the play that follows the original conventional close:

> " England shall ne'er be poor if England strive
> Rather by virtue than by wealth to thrive."[6]

Possibly the passage in praise of courts[7] was also added; the phrasing is somewhat similar to that of the courtly compliment in the first prologue.

There would seem to be no reason for denying to Dekker the " First Part." He was almost certainly writing for the theatre as early as 1596, and the later " Fortunatus " shows no trace of any other hand. It is probable also that two parts already existed in 1596. The very use of " first " presupposes a second.[8] Nor is it probable that any one, fascinated as the author evidently was by the story, should stop at the death of the father; nor that four years later, after long experience in a very different kind of work, he could so well have maintained the continuity of character and of tone: in the latter half of the play as in the first, Andelocia is the very copy of his father in boyish love of adventure and thirst for enjoyment and in a sort of unmoral way of looking at things; for in spite of all his efforts Dekker could not completely moralize the old story. It seems unlikely, too, that as late as 1599 Dekker could have conceived the unlovely character of Agripyne, and by that time Shadow would have lost some of his Lylian airs and graces.[9] Let us then assume that Dekker had originally written two parts—or two plays[10]—from which in 1599 he was

[5] For these scenes, see C. H. Herford's *Literary Relations of England and Germany in the Sixteenth Century,* 1886, Cambridge, pp. 211–212, 215–218.

[6] P., I, 170.

[7] P., I, 118–119.

[8] Fleay's assumption that sc. 1–6 constitute the first part and that the " whole " play was produced by the addition of sc. 7–12 is hardly tenable if for no other reason than that the original play must have been long enough to occupy the usual time in acting.

[9] The question of pay need not disturb us, for Dekker was then the brightest star in Henslowe's firmament, and his task was perhaps as difficult as writing a new play.

[10] The first dealing with the history of Fortunatus, the second perhaps with his death and certainly with the history of his sons.

directed by Henslowe, who remembered their early popularity, to fashion a whole play. His procedure may have been something like this: he retained the most striking features in the history of Fortunatus,—the adventure with Fortune, the theft of the flying hat, and his sudden death, and the most striking feature in the history of Andelocia,—his pursuit of Agripyne, and relegated the rest to a chorus that seems modeled on that of "Doctor Faustus" and possibly on that of "Henry V." To me it is nearly certain that he also omitted a portion of the sentimental experiences of some one, Andelocia or Orleans, for as the play now stands, the opening line of the Prologue is meaningless:

"Of love's sweet war our timorous Muse doth sing,"[11]

since "love's sweet war" is assuredly not the theme of the "whole Fortunatus" of 1599. We do not know when this Prologue was written, certainly not for the Court, for a separate and appropriate prologue is provided for that purpose. It may have been composed for the original second part, or there remains the possibility that when the Vice and Virtue episodes were added some love scenes were cut out to make room for them.

But, so far as we know, "Fortunatus" was not a new play in February, 1596. An earlier date, 1595 or possibly 1594, is probably nearer the truth. As Fleay has pointed out, the prose parts are full of Lylian reminiscence.[12] It appears in the characters. Shadow, the witty, the fantastic, the impertinent, the faithful, feeding his hungry master at command upon "a dish of paradoxes," and finally disappearing in the allegory, is no other than a Lylian page. But before he fades out of the play, Dekker humanizes him with his inimitable touch. "I'll

---

[11] P., I, 85.

[12] Fleay indeed is so impressed by the character of the first six scenes that he would put them back to 1590, a needlessly early date, for the influences then at work were still vital in 1594. The phrases "an almond for a parrot" and "crack me this nut" were long current. Dekker uses "an almond parrot" in *Westward Ho*, P., II, 356, and Henslowe records a contemporary play called *Crack Me This Nut*. In his *John Lyly*, p. 485, note 1, Feuillerat calls attention to two specific imitations of Lyly in *Old Fortunatus*.

go hence," cries Shadow, "because you send me: but I'll go
weeping hence for grief that I must turn villain as many do,
and leave you when you are up to the ears in adversity."[13]   In
Shadow Dekker improved upon his model; not so in the case
of Agripyne.   It is true, as critics have observed, that Dekker
is limited by the plot necessity of a pride so excessive as to deserve punishment, but Agripyne is not proud in an agreeable
way; she is greedy, not to say stingy, and we are made to feel
neither her beauty nor that which most enchanted Orleans,
"the rich brightness of her mind."   Dekker's failure to give
her one single trait of a heroine lies, it seems to me, in the fact
that he is trying to depict, after Lyly, a nimble-witted court
lady, who talks in a clever shallow way about lovers and
questions of love;[14] but he lacks the peculiar superficial dainti-
ness of his model and he had not yet learned to substitute
the saving note of humanity that belongs to his later
women.   In most of the prose dialogue Lyly's influence is just
as obvious, not merely in the mention of popinjays, squirrels,
apes, owls, wagtails, or in the abuse of the word "sweet," or
in the frequent talk about destiny, but in the quality of soliloquy and repartee.   There are many comparisons, antitheses,
and rhetorical questions, very frequent and effective use of
parallel phrasing, much punning, though this was Dekker's by
direct inspiration, and there is some alliteration, as in Shadow's
"Then defiance to Fortune and a fig for famine."[15]   There is
Lylian satire on logic, on traveling abroad, and on courtly language.[16]   The satire on logic is the most easily recognizable as
belonging to Lyly's school, but of course the total effect is that
which convinces or fails to convince.

If Lyly most influenced the prose style and the characters of
"Old Fortunatus," the situation and the point of view owe
most to Marlowe, and specificially to "Doctor Faustus."   Herford points out the parallelism in outline and detail, and in particular the circumstance that Fortunatus's choice of riches in-

[13] P., I, 142.

[14] With P., I, 129-133, compare *Sapho and Phao*, I, 4; *Midas*, III, 3;
there is considerable of the same sort of thing in *Love's Metamorphosis*.

[15] P., I, 103.

[16] P., I, 114-116, 126, 139-140.

stead of wisdom assumes the fatality of the compact with the Devil made by Doctor Faustus.[17] There are many "Tamburlaine" echoes also: in situation, as when Fortune "treads" on the kings in order to mount her "chair"; and in the language of both Fortune and the Kings. Bajazet in fact is taken directly over from Marlowe's play.[18]

This frank imitation of Lyly and Marlowe, in both matter and form, unparalleled by anything in Dekker's later drama, is a mark of immaturity; so, too, is the preponderance of the lyrical that makes the piece almost as much a poem as a play. There are some other archaic elements, such as the echo dialogue and possibly the successive "Triumphs" of Fortune, Vice, and Virtue.[19] It seems to me, then, careless criticism that would assign "Old Fortunatus" to a date following that of "The Shoemaker's Holiday" and "Patient Grissill," with their firmly conceived personages and their robust and vital prose.

The play is founded upon the German folk-story of Fortunatus and his sons, but the immediate source has not been discovered. The first known prose version of the story in English belongs to the second half of the seventeenth century,[20] but there may have been an earlier, as Halliwell thinks. The suggestion has been made that Dekker may have read the story

[17] *Literary Relations,* 213–214.

[18] There is no reason for thinking that Dekker ever collaborated with Marlowe or that he added any of the comic scenes of *Doctor Faustus.* This theory should have fallen to the ground when it was discovered that the entry for December, 1597, in Collier's edition of the *Diary,* crediting him with such additions, was a forgery. Fleay, however, has continued to find in these scenes "the style and metre" and the "tone of thought" of Dekker, as well as "minor indications of his handiwork, such as 'baw-waw' and the introduction of fireworks" (Ap. A in Ward's ed. of *Doctor Faustus*). No one else has expressed any confidence in this internal evidence. Ward considers it "of a doubtful kind" (*Eng. Dram. Lit.,* II, 468); and Greg, who is otherwise rather inclined to agree with Fleay, "hardly conclusive" (*Diary,* II, 169). Bullen roundly asserts that there is not "the slightest tittle of evidence to convict Dekker." (*Introd.* to *Works of Marlowe.*)

[19] Pointed out by Herford, pp. 215–216.

[20] For a discussion of English prose versions, see *Literary Relations,* Appendix III.

in a Dutch version, possibly an earlier edition of that dated 1631.[21] A simpler solution rests upon my theory that Dekker was at some time during his youth a sojourner in the Low Countries. Since German books must have found their way over the border, he could there have read the German story itself, for it would have been no hardship for one acquainted with Dutch to worry the meaning out of an attractive tale written in the simplest possible German. From the miscellaneous mass of adventure and intrigue provided by the story, Dekker chose the incidents with taste and dramatic tact. Shadow is his creation and so are the faithful Orleans and the other nobles at the English court. In spite of the profoundly tragic motive put into the story by amplifying the part of Fortune and by making the choice of riches a moral issue that must result in downfall and death, there is, besides the comedy, so much spectacle—Fortune mounting to her throne on the necks of chained and conquered kings, the fairy troops, Vice and Virtue and their trees, the dance of satyrs about the dead Fortunatus, together with considerable song and music—as to make the reader partly understand the otherwise amazing description of the play as " a pleasant comedy."

Since even in his maturest work Dekker showed little skill in structure, it is not surprising to find that " Old Fortunatus" sins more than ordinarily; a part of the confusion no doubt arose from the successive recastings that the play suffered, especially the introduction of Vice and Virtue with their befogging relations to Fortune,[22] and perhaps the relegation of Andelocia's serious wrong-doings to the chorus, for there is nothing in the action that deserves the punishment of death. Some minor difficulties, too, perhaps sprang from a revision that was not merely a process of adding but one of combining, omitting and condensing. The promise of Fortunatus to make a purse for the King of Babylon was probably intended to be a

[21] For this suggestion and for a discussion of Dekker's treatment of his source, see Dr. Hans Scherer's introduction to his critical edition of the play. *Münchener Beiträge,* band 21, 3-14.

[22] Relations that probably did not trouble the audience chiefly interested in Dekker's intention to compliment the Queen by making her superior not only to Fortune but also to the Virtue of the play. Cp. with Peele's compliment in *The Arraignment of Paris.*

boastful lie, for Andelocia tells the same story to Agripyne; but more serious is the promise of Fortune to return to Andelocia the hat and the purse, for he never sees the hat again and he gets the purse, only to lose his life for his pains.

But notwithstanding every criticism that can be brought against "Old Fortunatus," it is the only play of its kind in the English drama: there is in it a fresh childlike joy in the marvellous, something of the young hunger that would devour the universe; and to this is added a splendid scorn for money and all other dross, and the confident belief that wisdom, or virtue, is the only good of all possible goods; there is, besides, gay and graceful comedy, with a fool, clown, page—but no, all names are too gross for the incomparable Shadow; there is the apotheosis of constant love; and above all there is an abundance of poetry, the pure magic of which Dekker never surpassed except in some limpid passages that reach the very springs of human tenderness. Although he had listened to Marlowe, to Peele, and to Spenser, he had indeed in himself "poetry enough for anything." And since this discussion of the play has taken note of little but questions of scholarship, let it close with Orleans' famous worship of Deformity, a speech that the audience was intended to remember in a later scene.

> " Thou art a traitor to that white and red,
>   Which, sitting on her cheeks, being Cupid's throne,
>   Is my heart's sovereign: O, when she is dead,
>   This wonder, beauty, shall be found in none.
>   Now Agripyne's not mine, I vow to be
>   In love with nothing but deformity.
>   O fair Deformity, I muse all eyes
>   Are not enamored of thee: thou did'st never
>   Murder men's hearts, or let them pine like wax,
>   Melting against the sun of thy disdain;[23]
>   Thou art a faithful nurse to chastity;
>   Thy beauty is not like to Agripyne's,
>   For care, and age, and sickness hers deface,
>   But thine's eternal. O Deformity,
>   Thy fairness is not like to Agripyne's,
>   For dead, her beauty will no beauty have,
>   But thy face looks most lovely in the grave."

[23] Swinburne's emendation of "thy destiny." *The Age of Shakespeare,"* p. 66, footnote. Scherer and Rhys omit "thy" and retain "destiny."

Unworthy to be named in the same breath with "Old Fortunatus" is "The Whore of Babylon," the second of the plays
that show signs of early work. To the most casual reader it
must be clear that it was first acted long before it was printed
in 1607. The title[24] perhaps and the preface certainly were
affected by the excitement following the failure of the Gunpowder Plot; and the same cause may have brought about
the revival of the play. As the reasons for assigning it to an
early date are chiefly internal, it will be necessary to speak
briefly of the contents. They are, as the title indicates, partly
controversial, dealing with Catholic plots against Elizabeth's
throne and life as well as with "the greatness, magnanimity,
constancy, clemency, and other the incomparable heroical virtues of our late Queen."[25] Events are not treated in exact
chronological order: "I write as a poet, not as an historian
and . . . these two do not live under one law,"[26] said Dekker
hotly in the preface, replying to critics who complained that he
falsified "the account of time." His obvious intention was to
marshal before the audience all the great public facts of the
Queen's life up to about 1594–1596: her accession to the
throne, treated in dumb show only; the marriage negotiations,
the invasion of the Jesuit missionaries, the plots against her
life, including that of Dr. Lopez, who was executed in the
summer of 1594, the Irish disorders, the aid sent to the Netherlands and to a pretender to the Portuguese throne, the signing
of the death warrant of Mary of Scotland, and, as climax and
conclusion, the defeat of the Spanish Armada. As Dekker did
not feel that he could use real names, especially in the case of
the more exalted personages, he borrowed some of his nomenclature from "The Faerie Queene" and the names Oberon and
Titania from "A Midsummer Night's Dream." In his use of
such "tropical and shadowed colors" he was again following,
though very far off, the lead of Lyly, who had clothed with
allegory his presentation of contemporary history.

While it is hard to imagine that the play ever had much

[24] *The Whore of Babylon. As It was acted by the Princes Servants.*
Vexat Censura Columbas.

[25] *Lectori*, P., II, 189.

[26] *Idem*, 190.

coherence, a corrupt text makes the matter worse.[27] A glance
at the *dramatis personae* shows that some of the original characters have dropped out,[28] and a glance at the text, that at least
one of the old characters has been re-christened.[29] The play
shows other signs of revision. There is an allegorical passage
about the Moon[30] which can have applied in the first instance
only to Mary Stuart, but which goes on, with the "she"
changed to "he," in lines applicable only to the "Luciferan
insolence of the Earl of Essex."[31] The change is easy to
explain: in his enumeration of great events Dekker could
hardly have omitted mention of Mary's death, but he could
not have long dwelt upon it even during the reign of Elizabeth,
hardly at all during that of Mary's son. A second alteration is
found in the elaborate, awkward, and unhappy passage describing King James as a second Phoenix.[32] A third and probably later set of changes is to be found in the mention of "The
Isle of Gulls," written in 1605 or 1606, and in a possible contemporary reference to the presence of women at executions—

[27] The confusion of Kings, in particular the Second and the Third, is
especially annoying, for it has some bearing on the date of the play. On
p. 204, the Third King is Spain; on p. 205, Italy or Rome: what land is
represented by the Third King on p. 206, who says of the Irish nation,
"Yet we do succor him"? One's first instinct might be to answer "Spain,"
for towards the end of the century Spanish soldiers landed in Ireland to
help the rebels. But some twenty years earlier Sir Thomas Stukely, after
he turned traitor, received ships and soldiers from the Pope for the invasion
of Ireland, although the expedition never reached its destination; and in
1580 a small Italian party was cut to pieces on Irish soil by Lord Grey.

[28] Three of the four "ladies attendant."

[29] Ropus (who is Dr. Lopez) becomes Lupus, p. 231; doubtless there
seemed less reason for disguising his name as the date of his execution
receded.

[30] P., II, 246–247.

[31] This is Fleay's interpretation and should stand until his critics offer a
better. A second moon passage confirms the reading as far as Mary is
concerned. P., II, 257, last two lines.

[32] P., II, 234, Fleay thinks, without reason, that Dekker did not write
this passage; in the *King's Entertainment* he again speaks of James as a
second Phoenix rising from the ashes of the first. P., I, 302.

Perhaps "the Albanois" was given that name in order again to compliment the King.

both spoken by Plain-dealing in a scene[33] that reads rather like an interpolation, for Plain-dealing's satire upon London, especially its ordinaries, has nothing whatever to do with the main plot or any branch of it;[34] its purpose may have been to give humor to an uninteresting play.[35]

Fleay identifies "The Whore of Babylon" with "Truth's Supplication to Candlelight," entered in the Diary as a Dekker play in January, 1600; he may be right, for Truth appears in the prologue and in the dumb show, and is actually a very minor personage, rather sweetly characterized as having

> "such pretty and delightful songs
> That you will count your sorest labour light,
> And time well spent only to hear her sing."

But if this identity be granted, we must look, again with Fleay, for a still earlier version.[36] For, in the first place, the general character of "The Whore of Babylon" is, even for 1600, highly archaic: it has a large amount of dumb show;[37] an undisguised morality element in the parts played by Truth, Time, and Plain-dealing; a scholastic argument;[38] signs of early influences exhibited in the borrowings from Spenser and from "A Midsummer Night's Dream," and in the attempted imitation

[33] P., II, 212–215.

[34] Elsewhere Plain-dealing is a simple servant, rather asking for information than giving it, and his talk is related to the plot. See P., II, 241–246.

[35] There were probably changes, certainly a cutting down, in the passage about the Prince or the King of Portugal, p. 220. It seems to have been founded upon a misapprehension of the facts, for King Sebastian, slain at the battle of Alcazar, 1578, left no children. Queen Elizabeth's promise of aid, however, was fulfilled when in 1589 she sent a fleet to help Antonio, nephew of Sebastian, the then pretender to the crown. The real facts of the case, however, were so little understood in England, even at the end of the century, that people received as truth the adventures of a false Sebastian who pretended to have survived the battle, and in 1601 Dekker and Chettle wrote a play, now lost, founded upon those adventures.

[36] The payment of only two pounds for *Truth's Supplication* rather favors this point of view, though of course Henslowe's entries can hardly be regarded as telling the whole truth and nothing but the truth.

[37] P., II, 192, 204, 227, 243, 254.

[38] *Idem*, 239–241.

of Lyly's method of dealing with contemporary history.[39]   In the second place, there is almost unredeemed indistinctness of characterization, the dialogue is frequently uneasy and stilted, and often couched in clumsy phrasing; there is almost no humor and hardly a touch of Dekker's peculiar humanity from beginning to end:—impossible feats, one would say, in 1600, when he had to his credit, besides many lost plays, "Old Fortunatus," "The Sun's Darling," "The Shoemaker's Holiday," and a large share in "Patient Grissill"; impossible, even taking into consideration the intractability of the subject.[40] The most brilliant military event during the last decade of the Queen's life was the taking of Cadiz by Essex.   This would have furnished Dekker with just the sort of material he needed and his theory of chronology proper to a poet would not have prevented his using it almost anywhere in his play.   The absence of any such material may be regarded as significant, and the date of the play in its original form may be set down as falling between the execution of Doctor Lopez in the middle of 1594 and the fall of Cadiz two years later.   With this date agree, so far as I have recognized them, the allusions not yet noticed.[41]

[39] Perhaps also such chorus-like effects as are found on pp. 201, 203, 241, 247, 255.

[40] The somewhat elaborate accounts of the attempts upon the life of the Queen made by Paridel (Parry) and Ropus or Lupus (Lopez) may also, perhaps, be considered as pointing to a date when such events were fresh in the memories of men.   Heywood, in his *If you know not me, you know nobody,* also uses the story of Dr. Parry, but very briefly.   He either borrowed from Dekker or they both used the same source.

[41] There is a reference to the massacre of St. Bartholomew, p. 221; a reminiscence of the *Old Hamlet* in the passage about "the air's invulnerable breast," p. 227, pointed out by Koeppel; and an adaptation, as it seems to me, of a well-known line in *Richard II* in the following passage:

> " Her kingdom wears a girdle wrought of waves
> Set thick with precious stones,"

p. 196.   Perhaps the lines, p. 218, that bring together "maiden shores" and "dolphins" were written with the vague memory of a famous passage from *A Midsummer Night's Dream* in the poet's head.   Koeppel thinks that the line "I stand, colossus-like, striding o'er seas," p. 205, is an echo of Cassius's

This mixture of allegory and controversy, loyalty and patriotism, seems to have been very well liked. While its popularity doubtless sprang chiefly from its spectacular effects, including, besides the dumb show and other such elements already mentioned, music and dancing, the reception of ambassadors and kings, and the production of the "scarlet-colored" beast, it offered a more legitimate appeal in its emphasis upon well-known and well-loved traits of character in the Queen, an emphasis that is interesting both to the student of history and to the student of Dekker. Although he paid a number of perfunctory compliments to James, the lasting object of his admiration was Queen Elizabeth. Aside from the flattery in the Court plays, there are various passages in his prose that, after she had passed beyond the reach of human words, eloquently extol her greatness. The first is in "The Wonderful Year": she was summoned, he writes, to appear in the Star chamber of heaven.

"The summons made her start, but having an invincible spirit, did not amaze her: yet whom would not the certain news of parting from a kingdom amaze? But she knew where to find a richer, and therefore lightlier regarded the loss of this, and thereupon made ready for the heavenly coronation, being (which was most strange) most dutiful to obey that so many years so powerfully commanded."[42]

[42] G., I, 86.

About four years later, in "The Seven Deadly Sins," a compliment to James is preceded by a fervent passage about Elizabeth addressed to London:

"She, that for almost half a hundred of years, of thy Nurse became thy Mother and laid thee in her bosom; whose head was full of cares for thee whilst thou slept upon softer pillows than down. She that wore thee always on her breast as the richest jewel in her kingdom, who had continually her eye upon thee, and her heart with thee: whose chaste hand

---

> "He doth bestride the narrow world
> Like a colossus,"

but aside from the unlikelihood that so obvious a figure should have remained unused before Shakespere, it seems in the Dekker quotation almost inevitable; for Spain is described as "standing" upon the Pillars of Hercules.

clothed thy rulers in scarlet, and thy inhabitants in robes of peace: even she was taken from thee when thou wert most in fear to lose her."[43]

Again, in " The Dead Term," Westminster is made to boast that within her precincts Elizabeth lies buried, "who if she had no monument at all consecrated to memory, yet were her name sufficient to eternize her sacred worth and the wonders of her forty-four years government."[64] This quotation shows good judgment in the citizen; perhaps the judgment was less good that prefixed to the collection of prayers known as " The Eagle " a prayer made by the Queen.[45] The significant thing is not, however, as Swinburne would have us believe, the inferiority of her English to his, but the fact that Dekker felt that he was enhancing the value of his book by quoting the ruler in whose " spacious times " his youth and early manhood had been lived. In spite of the general inadequacy of " The Whore of Babylon " and of Dekker's inability to use Elizabeth's own vigorous language, many of her great qualities are actually suggested: her confidence in the wise ministers she had chosen, her aversion to entering into entangling foreign alliances, her insight into character, her unwillingness to shed blood, and her great personal courage.

The play requires little other comment. It should perhaps be noticed that the controversial element is necessarily rather political than ecclesiastical, that Rome stands less for a false faith than for a national foe that would undermine the independence and the prosperity of England. In this connection it may be observed that the only one of the characters that receives a touch of Dekker's intimate sympathy is the brilliant and ill-starred Jesuit, Edmund Campion, "Campeius " in the play. While in construction this drama is naught, and while the general level of the verse is mediocre, much of the poetry would be efficient if the subject were more interesting, and here and there occur lines of memorable charm, such as the following fragment that has in it all the magic of that which it describes:

[43] G., II, 11.
[44] G., IV, 19.
[45] G., V, 39–40.

" Five summers have scarce drawn their glimmering nights
Through the moon's silver bow . . . "

With Dekker's early work should be classed his share in
the play entitled " The Weakest Goeth to the Wall,"[46] a mixture of pseudo-history, romantic comedy, and realistic comedy,
printed in 1600 without the author's name. Apparently
Edward Phillips was the first to assign the play to Webster
and Dekker; he was followed by Winstanley, but Sir Egerton
Brydges, in an enlarged edition of Phillips' " Theatrum Poetarum" in 1800, remarked that they were mistaken. Fleay
believes that Munday wrote it about 1584;[47] Ward alone of
recent scholars who have expressed an opinion upon the matter
thinks that the humor " bears a certain resemblance to the
handiwork of Dekker."[48]

The most important of the humorous characters in this old
play is " the fag-end of a tailor," " in plain English a botcher,"
named Barnaby Bunch, who goes on his way singing, punning,
rhyming, simple yet shrewd, with an " honorable humor to
learn languages and see fashions," kindhearted for the most
part, but blunt at times, even vituperative upon occasion—
much the most lifelike person in a play that is otherwise well
worth reading. The scenes in which he is prominent must
have been introduced chiefly for their humor, but whether they
belonged to the original play or whether they were added to a
revised version, Bunch has some slight share in the plot as it
has come down to us; in the Flanders town whither a noble
family had fled for refuge, he tries to protect the two women
from their landlord, a bad-hearted Duchman, and tactfully

[46] " The Weakest Goeth to the Wall. As it hath been sundry times plaid
by the right-honourable Earle of Oxenford, Lord great Chamberlaine of
England his Servants." Included by Hazlitt in vol. 4 of his edition of
Webster. London, 1857. All references are to this edition.

[47] As acted by the Earl of Oxford's servants, a company which, he continues, is heard of as in London only between 1584 and 1587. Chr., II,
113–114.

To me the probability that Chettle wrote the greater part of the play
seems strong; the love scenes, for example, have the kind of sentimentality
found in similar scenes in Hoffman; and they are written in the same kind
of verse.

[48] Eng. Dram. Lit., III, 56.

removes him when he would be in the way. Upon Bunch's first appearance[49]—in France—he is equipped, say the stage directions, "with a pair of shears, a hand-basket with a cross-bottom of thread, three or four pair of old stockings, pieces of fustian, cloth, etc." In his opening soliloquy he explains that he has been a London ale-draper. Then more stage directions tell of his hanging stockings on a stick and of his sewing a hose-heel. As he works, he sings a ballad, alternating every line with directions to an otherwise unmentioned Kate to heat properly his pressing iron. In later speeches too he talks about his trade, and he is equally specific about his new work when he becomes sexton at Ardres,[50] promising, for example, "the honest prentices," if they please him, not to "ring the four o'clock bell till it be past five."[51] He has a sort of simplicity, as when he begs his friends who are going up to "high France" to send the plague down to Picardy that he may get money by digging graves, and when a messenger arrives, he asks him if he has not brought some such commodity down to Ardres.[52] He is full of puns good and bad: the name of his host Jacob van Smelt supplies him with many an opportunity, and he shows an interesting knowledge of etymology when he describes himself, at that moment mending stockings, as being "a corrector of extravagant hose feet."[53] Possessed of a rough but genial humanity, he would pay the debts of his noble friends with the score of stivers that he has earned;[54] when the women are left to his protection, he cries, "I'll break my heart to do them good,"[55] and later, in the same scene, "God be wi' ye, sir, I could weep, but my tears will not pleasure ye."[56]

In nearly every respect Barnaby Bunch has a family likeness to Dekker's clowns. They usually have a trade: even the family servant Babulo is a basket-maker;[57] Firk and his com-

---

[49] Act I, sc. 2, pp. 228–233.
[50] Act V, sc. 2, pp. 294–295.
[51] Act IV, sc. 3, p. 283.
[52] Act IV, sc. 3, p. 282, and V, 2, p. 294.
[53] Act I, sc. 2, p. 232.
[54] Act II, sc. 3, p. 251.
[55] *Idem*, p. 252.
[56] Act II, sc. 3, p. 252.
[57] *Patient Grissill.*

rades are shoemakers;[58] Scumbroth a cook;[59] Bilbo has been
an apprentice and when the play opens has servants under
him.[60] They bring their tools or the insignia of their trade
upon the stage; they enumerate them and talk light-heartedly
and punningly about their work. Except for their acquaintance with Latin and some other knowledge unusual in their
class, Dekker's clownish characters are also consistent; they
are strongly individualized and no two are alike, save in a
shrewd simplicity united to an unusual warmheartedness that
seems peculiar to Dekker.

Again, many of Dekker's fun-making characters use a
speech full of repetition, of heaping of synonyms,[61] and of
parallel phrases in twos or threes to express haste or swiftness.[62] Barnaby Bunch often talks after this fashion. His
praise of ale illustrates the first peculiarity; "fresh ale, firm
ale, nappy ale, nippitate ale, irregular, secular ale, courageous,
contagious ale, alcumistical ale;[63] and so does his rough reproach of Jacob: "Now mine host rob-pot, empty cask, beer-
sucker, gudgeon!—smelt, I should say."[64] Illustrations of the
second peculiarity may be seen in such quotations as the following: "Fie! fie! down with my stall, up with my wares,
shift for myself;"[65] "It would clear my sight, comfort my
heart, and stuff my veins;"[66] or, "if ye have any hose to heel,
breeches to mend, or buttons to set on, let me have your
work."[67]

[58] *The Shoemaker's Holiday.*

[59] *If It be not Good.*

[60] *Match Me in London.*

[61] This hardly needs an illustration, but one may be given. In the course
of a single speech Simon Eyre cries out, "It's a mad life to be a lord
mayor; it's a stirring life, a fine life, a velvet life, a careful life. . . . His
Majesty is welcome; he shall have good cheer, delicate cheer, princely
cheer." P., I, 62.

[62] As "On with your masks, up with your sails, and westward ho!"
Westward Ho, P., II, 322; or "No man I wrong, no man I fear, no man I
fee." 2 *Honest Whore,* P., II, 104.

[63] Act I, sc. 2, p. 229.

[64] Act III, sc. 4, p. 263.

[65] Act I, sc. 2, p. 232.

[66] *Idem,* p. 229.

[67] Act I, sc. 3, p. 237.

Next to Barnaby Bunch the most prominent person in the realistic comedy is the Jacob van Smelt already mentioned. For the most part he speaks Dutch, or Dutch mixed with English, very similar to that spoken by the disguised Lacy and the skipper in " The Shoemaker's Holiday" and Hans van Belch in " Westward Ho."

The presence of two such characters in the same scenes creates a strong presumption in favor of Dekker, not diminished by the fact that his name has once been associated with the play in which they occur, and strengthened by a number of details too minute to be mentioned here.[68] I am inclined to think, however, that he was not the original writer of these scenes but that he worked them over with a very thorough hand. In any case they should probably be assigned to a comparatively early date in his history, for the stage spectacle in the first scene is conventional, and the dialogue throughout at times crude and violent. Although his scenes in this old play add little to Dekker's fame, they have an interest apart from their intrinsic value in that they conceivably helped him to see the dramatic possibilities hidden in the tale of a shoemaker who becomes lord mayor.

The three plays discussed in this chapter are so unlike in character and the probability of lost plays is so great that there are grounds only for few and scattered generalizations. The order of writing is possibly that in which they have here been taken up: it seems so to me. " Old Fortunatus " is a drama of youth as surely as " Romeo and Juliet," and the rags of antiquity that hang about the " Babylon " play belong in part to a young attempt to put together all the elements of a taking spectacle; the robust characterization of Barnaby Bunch should come later. While we know little about Dekker's theatrical relations, the history of " Old Fortunatus " seems to indicate a connection with Henslowe as early as 1596, but there is no certainty that he was not at the same time writing or revamping plays elsewhere. Although he was never to repeat the peculiar charm of " Old Fortunatus," some

---

[68] Such a semi-pun, for example, as Bunch's " By my shears, and that's a shaving oath " (Act III, sc. 5, p. 268) is wholly in Dekker's manner.

elements of his later development may be seen in these plays: his liking for the romantic and the idealistic which was not to leave him wholly after it ceased to be popular on the stage, his inclination towards wholesome realism, and towards both the comedy of wit and the comedy that consists in a kindly but humorous interpretation of character. Dialect he continued to use, feebly in the broken English of the supposed French and Irish, with power in mixed English and Dutch. In the group considered as a whole, there are few hints of Dekker's great power to delineate character, none at all of his success in depicting certain types of women. In dramatic technique Dekker had much to learn: structure he never mastered, but no later play is so incoherent as "Old Fortunatus" or so shapeless as "The Whore of Babylon." In lyrical poetry and in Lylian prose, his power was full-grown, but he had yet to put into his verse dramatic appropriateness and into his prose the directness of the people's speech. Enough has been said elsewhere about his permanent tastes, but a word may be added to note the sympathy that could pass from the love of the courtly Orleans to the humble duties of the sexton at Ardres, or from the poverty of the neglected Catholic scholar or the charm of the despised Irish race to a rapture over the achievements of Drake.

CHAPTER IV

With Henslowe, 1598–1600

From January, 1598, to the end of 1602 we have in Henslowe's "Diary" a rich account of Dekker's dramatic activities. Yet it is not complete: the record for 1600 is broken by a gap of a month or thereabouts, and that for 1601 mentions but a single play; it is from other sources that we learn what he was doing that year. Although by the close of 1602 he apparently ceased to be one of Henslowe's regular men, early in 1604 the "Diary" mentions the sale of "1 Honest Whore" to his former manager. These plays written for Henslowe were acted under his management by the Admiral's men at first at the Rose and after some uncertain date in the latter half of 1600 at the newly built Fortune; but from August, 1602, to the end of the year Dekker's plays were acted by Worcester's men at the Rose still under Henslowe's management.

During these five years that industry so praised by more than one contemporary is known to have assisted in the composition of some thirty plays and to have produced eight alone.[1] Still larger would have been the output if Dekker had maintained the pace set by the first two years. During the year that closed with December, 1598, he wrote two plays

---

[1] See Greg's convenient table of Dekker's plays written for Henslowe, *Diary, Part II*, 367–368. His interpretation of difficult entries and his identification of plays that fall within this period have, for the greater part, been followed in this study. He identifies *Bad May Amend* altered to *Worse Afeard than Hurt* with *2 Hannibal and Hermes*, and *Two Shapes*, or *Two Harpies*, with *Caesar's Fall*.

In the enumeration above, I have excluded *Truth's Supplication to Candlelight* as probably identical with *The Whore of Babylon*, and *Old Fortunatus* as written earlier, together with alterations of and additions to plays. *The Introduction to the Civil Wars of France* is included as probably a separate play. On that head, see Greg, *Diary*, II, 197.

47

alone and fourteen in collaboration with others. Every month except February has its record, and as on the first of March he was paid for a play written without aid, that month is accounted for. It may be significant that in all the collaborated plays of the first part of the year he shared the responsibility with two or three others, in the latter part with but one. The year 1599 was not less busy, for though he assisted in the writing of but six plays he wrote four alone, and in addition revised " Old Fortunatus " and prepared it for presentation at Court. 1600 saw the production of four collaborated plays, one written alone, and one 1598 play altered for the Court. Except for these alterations there is no record of any work between September, 1600, and April, 1601. During the year 1602 he was paid for collaborating in five plays and for one comedy, besides some miscellaneous work,—alterations, additions, a prologue and an epilogue.

If Dekker worked hard, he was rewarded, contrary to the usual opinion, by a fair income. Henslowe's ordinary price for a play was £6, which should be multiplied by eight to lift it to terms of modern money. If these figures are borne in mind it will be readily seen that Dekker's receipts during the first year of the period under consideration were in the neighborhood of £340,[2] during the second year somewhat more. So far as we can judge from the evidence, he was among the best paid of Henslowe's writers. We have seen that he received £9 for his work upon " Old Fortunatus " when an old play. For " Page of Plymouth," collaborated with Jonson, £8 were paid, and for " Patient Grissill," collaborated with Chettle and Haughton, possibly the large sum of ten guineas. The " Diary " also records that he was getting ten shillings for a prologue and an epilogue at a time when Chettle and Middleton were receiving half that sum for similar work.

Of the thirty collaborated plays the greater number is composed of chronicle-histories, and the most prolific year in that species is, as we might expect, the first. Ten draw their material from British history, ranging from such an unidenti-

---

[2] He wrote two plays alone, collaborated with one other playwright upon five, with two others upon four, and with three others upon five.

fied subject as "Connan Prince of Cornwall" or such an early one as "Earl Godwin,"[63] to the history of Lady Jane Grey; three deal with the civil wars of France, one with Sebastian, King of Portugal.[4] There is a group of plays on classical subjects, the most interesting title among which is "Troilus and Cressida."[5] Another group of three belongs to the type called the domestic tragedy, especially popular between 1597 and 1603, which had found its most famous early expression in "Arden of Feversham" and was to be rendered in its most unrelieved horror in "The Yorkshire Tragedy."[6] "Jephthah" is a late representative of the biblical play, and Dekker provided a prologue and an epilogue for "Pontius Pilate." Among those unclassified, some like "Christmas Comes but Once a Year," point to comedy. "A Chance Medley" may be a comedy of errors or possibly a tragedy.[7] "Fair Constance of Rome" suggests Chaucer, and "The Golden Ass and Cupid and Psyche" seems to be explicit. Nothing is known of "The Seven Wise Masters."

[3] For a possible source of this play, see Creizenach, *Geschichte des neueren Dramas*, IV, 205–206.

[4] Founded on Munday's translation of a French account of the adventures of Marco Tullio, who pretended to be the long-dead Sebastian. It should be noticed that this is Dekker's second play with a Moor in it; the first was *The Spanish Moor's Tragedy* of the preceding year. Perhaps these two plays explain Jonson's gibe, if he intended any, and Dekker's supposed reply in the following passages from *Satiromastix:* "As for Crispinus, that Crispin-ass and Fannius his play-dresser, who, to make the muses believe their subjects' ears were starv'd and that there was a dearth of poesy, cut an innocent Moor i' th' middle, to serve him in twice; and when he had done, made Paul's work of it . . ." P., I, 212.

On the supposed evidence of this passage, Fleay assigns to Dekker "*Stewtley,*" entered on the *Diary*, Dec. 11, 1596. The extant play, *The Famous History of the Life and Death of Captain Thomas Stukeley* shows no trace of Dekker's style.

[5] For a "plot" of a play on the Trojan War, possibly Dekker's, see Greg, *Henslowe Papers*, pp. 142 and 144.

[6] For such tragedies, see Professor Thorndike, *The Influence of Beaumont and Fletcher on Shakespere*, 99, and Creizenach, *Geschichte*, IV, 237–242.

[7] Greg says that while the phrase had come to mean a series of random actions, it had also a legal sense, meaning a casualty not purely accidental. *Diary*, II, 196.

Dekker's most frequent collaborators in these plays were, at first, Chettle, Drayton, and Wilson, but the name of the last soon disappears. Chettle and Drayton share the honors in sixteen plays each, both names occurring most frequently in connection with the chronicle-histories, a species for which Drayton had a special aptitude, but Chettle had a hand in almost every other variety too except the biblical. Munday was Dekker's sole collaborator in "Jephthah" and aided him in two other plays. Heywood collaborated in two plays, and the undistinguished Smith and a little known Hathaway in one each. "Young Haughton" helped write two plays, one of which still exists. Other and for the most part more interesting collaborators, who will be discussed later, were Jonson, Day, Middleton, and Webster.

Out of this library of collaborated drama but one whole play and the fragments of another have certainly come down to us.[8] If we feel that we could spare the latter, represented by "Sir Thomas Wyatt," very different is the case with "Patient Grissill," for nowhere else has Dekker so convincingly portrayed the loveliness of family life, poor in everything but affection and content, or exhibited more winningly the sweetness of his humor. It is then no comfort to reflect that in the lost plays under discussion Dekker did not work alone. Two of them call for special regret. The first is "Page of Plymouth," written in conjunction with Jonson and paid for in August and September of 1599. The subject is indicated by the title of a contemporary ballad: "The Lamentation of Master Page's wife of Plymouth, who being enforced by her Parents to wed him against her will, did most wickedly consent to his murder for the love of George Strangwidge; for which fact she suffered death at Bar[n]stable in Devonshire. Written with her own hand a little before her death." It was one that would appeal to Dekker's sympathies, for enforced marriage was an evil of society that early and late roused his

[8] The largest destruction of Dekker's plays doubtless occurred when the Fortune was burned. He also suffered from Warburton's carelessness. Possibly some plays were lost when the Cockpit was burned in 1616. See Bullen, *Introd.* to his edition of *The Works of John Day*, 14, note.

special horror. If each poet even approached his best work in this play, if to Dekker's warmhearted and life-like characterization was added the careful art of Jonson, then our loss is indeed great.[9] The second play is "Jephthah," collaborated with Munday, which was recorded in May, 1602, after what was for Dekker a long period of inactivity. The pathos of the story and the charm that the Bible exercised upon him perhaps called out finer qualities of heart and mind than "Page of Plymouth."

When we come to the plays written alone, only two[10] of which survive, our sense of loss is necessarily greater, especially since, as it seems to me, the early work, even that collaborated, shows a singleness of aim and a clarity of moral outlook sometimes blurred in the later plays. The titles of some of the lost plays more or less indicate the subject or the treatment. "Truth's Supplication to Candlelight," whether identical with "The Whore of Babylon" or not, points to allegory; "Bear a Brain, or Better Late than Never"[11] to comedy. Of the "Introduction to the Civil Wars of France" we know nothing, not even what civil wars form the subject. "Orestes' Furies"[12] claims relationship with other classical plays. "Medicine for a Curst Wife" belongs to the series in which patient and impatient wives get punished in pretty equal measure—a subject that Dekker treated, with no sympathy for passive obedience, in "Patient Grissill" and in a sub-plot of "The Honest Whore." Nothing is certainly known of "Fortune's Tennis," but Greg suggests that as it was one of the first plays taken in hand after the company left the Rose, some allusion to the new house may have been intended.[13] The title of the remaining play, "The Triplicity[14] of Cuckolds," has been supposed to

---

[9] See Creizenach, *Geschichte*, IV, 240.

[10] *Phaeton* under its later title *The Sun's Darling*, and *The Shoemaker's Holiday*.

[11] Certainly not to be identified with *Look about You* as Fleay suggests. See Greg, II, 204. However, Greg's identification of this comedy with *The Shoemaker's Holiday* has nothing to support it.

[12] Fleay: *Orestes Furious*.

[13] *Diary*, II, 215.

[14] Triplicity means triangle.

be explicit: if it were an intrigue play, it forms the only specimen of its class in the list of Dekker's plays down to 1604. It
is necessary, however, to remember that titles cannot be wholly
trusted, since they often indicate merely the features expected
to attract an audience rather than the plots in their true proportion. For example, the apparently full title, "The Honest
Whore, with the Humors of the Patient Man and the Longing
Wife," ignores the exquisite love story of Hippolito and Infelice, so purely told and in such lovely verse.

This period of playwriting was preceded by the production
in 1598 of a long religious poem, which is fairly thrilling when
compared with Middleton's "Wisdom of Solomon Paraphrased" produced the year before, but is still so dull that
Swinburne would not lay it upon Dekker's shoulders, especially
as it is signed "T. D.," initials, he remarks, that Thomas
Deloney might claim, and perhaps others. But the episle-dedi-
catory of the edition of 1618, the earliest that has come down
to us, is wholly in Dekker's manner, and as he always retained
the ability to write uninspired verse, there seems to be no
reason to take from him the credit of this popular and oft-
reprinted[15] poem. It was registered to print January 5, 1598,
as "The Destruction of Jerusalem by Titus, son of Vespasian,"
and published as "Canaan's Calamity, Jerusalem's Misery, and
England's Mirror." The most conspicuous incident, related
with astonishing fluency and flatness, is the story of Miriam,
who killed and partly devoured her young son. In this story,
Dekker seems to follow Nash's "Christ's Tears over Jerusalem," a likeness that has been explained by their use of the
same source;[16] even so, Nash's tract perhaps suggested to his
disciple the subject. The only merit that the poem shows is
a considerable degree of narrative power; its six-line stanzas
are devoid of imagination and no second couplet sounds so well
as the following:

> Sanctum Sanctorum, so that place was called,
> Which Titus' wondering mind the most appalled."

At the time that this poem was registered Dekker was at

[15] Fleay mentions editions of 1598, 1604, 1617, 1618, 1625.
[16] McKerrow, *Works of Nash,* IV, 214.

work upon his earliest extant play of the period, "The Sun's
Darling,"[17] identified by Gifford with "Phaeton"[18] entered in
the Diary under his name, January 15, 1598, and in December,
1600, as altered for presentation at Court. At the end of the
first act remain a dozen lines of Dekker's characteristic recognition of the courtly audience,[19] and possibly "the beauty of
the garden's Queen"[20] may have been a compliment to Elizabeth. But the play appeared many years later, at a different
Court, altered by a different hand. When "The Sun's Darling" was licensed by Herbert on March 3, 1624, Dekker had
known Ford for at least three years, for "The Witch of
Edmonton," on which they collaborated, was written in 1621.
There is therefore no external reason why the two poets
should not have worked on the masque together; but it is
practically certain that Ford, with or without the knowledge of
the older man, made the revisions in the fourth and fifth
acts that so modify the character of Dekker's graceful progress
of the seasons, and possibly he altered the first act.[21] To
Dekker belongs the vivid delight in nature that set him apart
from all his contemporaries except Shakespere, together with
the whimsical humor and the songs. The beautiful bird song
in the second act was once ascribed to Lyly on the slight evidence furnished by the fact that in an altered form it was
inserted by Blount in his 1632 edition of six of Lyly's comedies. It has lately been shown that the version in "The Sun's

---

[17] *The Sun's Darling: A Moral Masque: As it hath been often presented
by their Majesties' Servants; at the Cockpit in Drury Lane, with great
Applause.*

The names of the authors, "John Foard" and "Tho. Decker," are
bracketed as "Gent." The date is 1656.

[18] Dyce's revised Gifford's *John Ford* (1869), I, *Introduction*, xxiii.
Gifford's vague "with play of this name" is corrected by Dyce to *Phaeton*.

[19] P., IV, 302. Cf. *Old Fortunatus*, P., I, 84, and 118–119.

[20] P., IV, 332.

[21] See Swinburne's essay on *John Ford*. See also Gifford, *Ford's Works*
(revised by Dyce), III, 169. Ford is responsible for the awkward political
digression and the compliments to Prince Charles, including the speech of
Winter that borrows from the *Epilogue* of *Every Man out of His Humour*.

Darling" with its two stanzas and cuckoo refrain must have been the earlier.[22]

Although the general effect of the play is blurred by Ford's changes, the moral of the allegory is to be found in the words of Raybright:

> " Now if I fail, let man's experience read me;
> 'Twas Humor, joined with Folly, did mislead me."

It is not the moral, however, that impresses one: Dekker could not help putting the moral intent into his work, but when he wrote this masque he was feeling most the freshness and sweetness of the outdoor world—the birds and the flowers, the gentleness of Spring, the languor of Summer, and Autumn's bounty; his mood is lyrical and the expression is lyrical, whether it takes the form of the eight-syllable line, as it occasionally does, or blank verse, or song.

The characters are not mere abstractions. Raybright, petulant and spoiled child of the Sun, is not without flashes of wisdom:

> " He who is high-born never mounts yon battlement
> Of sparkling stars, unless he be in spirit
> As humble as the child of one that sweats
> To eat the dear-earn'd bread of honest thrift."

But he pitifully wastes out his year of probation in ceaseless search after new pleasures. He soon leaves the garden of Spring, with its appealing mistress and her youngest girl, the " rosy-finger'd May." She had offered him two kinds of music much loved by the writer of the masque: poetry and the song of birds.

[22] Greg, *The Authorship of the Songs in Lyly's Plays*, Mod. Lang. Rev., I, no. 1, 43–52. He tentatively identifies " the collector, adaptor, and writer " of some twenty lyrics in Lyly's plays with Dekker, or Dekker and Middleton. Feuillerat agrees with Greg, *Mod. Lang. Rev.*, I, no. 4. Fleay is inclined to think that all the other songs not in Lyly's original text were written by Dekker. Bullen further points out, in his edition of *Middleton*, III, 358, note, that the song, " O for a bowl of fat Canary " at the end of *A Mad World, my Masters,* is also found in *Alexander and Campaspe,* and adds " Perhaps neither Middleton nor Lyly wrote it." The song is a good song of its kind, and Dekker wrote that kind very well indeed.

> " The selfsame Bay tree into which was turn'd
> Peneian Daphne, I have still kept green;
> That tree shall now be thine; about it sit
> All the old poets with fresh laurel crowned,
> Singing in verse the praise of chastity;
> Hither when thou shalt come, they all shall rise,
> Sweet cantos of thy love and mine to sing,
> And invoke none but thee as Delian King; "[23]

and

> " Not a lark that calls
> The morning up shall build on any turf
> But she shall be thy tenant, call thee Lord,
> And for her rent pay thee in change of songs."

After Spring has fainted and died, Raybright remembers her princely mind and her temperance:

> " Thou wouldst not waste
> The weight of a sad violet in excess."

His new mistress, Humor, a beautiful changeable lady, faithful, in her fashion, to Raybright and to nothing else, has also an eloquent tongue:

> " I'll raise, by art, out of base earth, a palace,
> Whither thyself, waving a crystal stream,
> Shall call together the most glorious spirits
> Of all the kings that have been in the world,
> And they shall come only to feast with thee."

Humor's squire Folly is the clown of the play; he is sometimes genuinely amusing and sometimes he dallies with the innuendo that the age permitted; he is not without ingratiating qualities; "Carbonado me, bastinado me, strapado me, hang me, I'll not stir; poor Folly, honest Folly, jocundary Folly, forsake your Lordship!"[24] To add further to the humor, Dekker introduces a characteristic group of foreigners,—a French tailor, an Italian dancer, a Spanish comfit-maker. Among other masque elements are eight songs, a morris dance by the "country gray," other dances, an "echo of cornets," and the repeated apparition of the Sun[25] "above." Next to

---

[23] This is the picture that Dekker later developed in *A Knight's Conjuring*.
[24] Cf. with Barnaby Bunch.
[25] Attired in a "white satin doublet." Greg, *Diary*, I, 83.

the bird song, the best is that of the "country-fellows," with its pleasant and spirited medley of girls and flowers, country sights and sounds, and the joys of hunting and hawking. Certainly, though London-born, Dekker knew and loved the country. Another song—a drinking song—contains the charactertistic lines:

> "Money is trash, and he that will spend it,
> Let him drink merrily, Fortune will send it."[26]

But after all it is the sweetness and spontaneity of the verse that leaves the strongest impression upon the reader. The air grows hot and the Sun calls out:

> "Ho Eolus,
> Unlock the jail and lend a wind or two
> To fan my girl the Summer."

Cries Raybright after a kiss:

> "The rose-lipped dawning
> Is not so melting, so delicious;
> Turn me into a bird that I may sit
> Still singing in such boughs."

Dekker's next extant play is first mentioned on the fifteenth of July, when he was paid three pounds to "buy" a book called "The Gentle Craft."[27] It was acted before the Queen on New Year's day, 1600, and was printed anonymously the same year under the title, "The Shoemaker's Holiday or The Gentle Craft, with the humorous life of Simon Eyre, shoemaker and Lord Mayor of London." It was provided with a prologue for the Queen and an appropriate little dedication to "all good fellows, Professors of the Gentle Craft."[28] "Nothing is purposed but mirth," affirms Dekker; "mirth

---

[26] Both songs are given in Schelling's *Seventeenth Century Lyrics*.

[27] Fleay's extraordinary doubt of Dekker's authorship needs no comment; and the hypothesis that Robert Wilson, the actor, shared the authorship rests upon worthless evidence; for presentation of that theory, see Introduction to *The Shoemakers' Holiday*, edited by Warnke and Proescholdt, Halle, 1886. The list of actors furnished by "Dramaticus" (*Shak. Soc. Papers*, IV, 110) is doubtless, as Fleay says, a forgery.

[28] In this form of dedication, Dekker, and later Rowley, follow their source Deloney: "To all the good yeomen of the gentle craft."

lengtheneth long life, which, with all other blessings I heartily
wish you." The play was thrice reprinted during the author's
lifetime.[29]

The source of "The Shoemaker's Holiday" is Thomas
Deloney's "Gentle Craft,"[30] a lively and humorous collection
of stories about shoemakers, full of details about London and
bourgeois life and very specific in matters of dress, tools, and
customs.[31] From the third tale in the first part Dekker took
his main plot, the story of a shoemaker rising through the
purchase of the cargo of a vessel to wealth and station until
he finally became Lord Mayor of London; with this plot he
combined a romantic love story, borrowing the idea of disguising a noble lover as a shoemaker from Deloney's second
tale; and to these threads he added a tender little drama of his
own, relating the troubles of a young wife when her shoemaker husband is forced to go to the wars. Some minor details he also borrowed from Deloney: the trouble at the church
door when Jane and Hammon are to be married, and, especially, the presence of a Dutchman among Simon Eyre's shoemakers.[32]

But Dekker's combinations and insertions amount to creation. This is especially true of his characterization, for which
he received no hint in his source except in the case of Dame
Margery. Simon Eyre, the hearty, the genial, overflowing
with "mad" uproarious talk,[33] with common sense and with

[29] There seems to be no reason for dating the play earlier than its entry
in the *Diary*. Fleay's date, 1597, has nothing to support it. Deloney's
Gentle Craft, though entered S. R. October 19, 1597, does not seem to
have been printed before 1598.

[30] Edited by A. F. Lange, *Palaestra*, xviii.

[31] See *Cam. Hist. Eng. Lit.*, III, 422, for Deloney's contribution to the
drama by way of stories and ballads. William Rowley's *Shoemaker's a
Gentleman* derives its plot from *The Gentle Craft*.

[32] For specific borrowings, see notes in Lange's edition of *The Gentle
Craft*.

[33] Mr. E. E. Stoll has an article in *Modern Language Notes*, v. 21, called
"The Influence of Jonson on Dekker," in which he puts forward the theory
that Eyre's speech is derived from Juniper's in *The Case is Altered*. It is
far less convincing than his alternative suggestion that the few catch-words
and phrases used in common by the two characters belong to "the hilarious
cant of the day."

kindness, possessed of innocent vanities and an honest heart, is surely a memorable personage in English comedy, one moreover that does not need to be bolstered up with evil talk or evil surroundings. He is the first of Dekker's "old" men, "green" because they have led good lives; "merry" because they are not in need of repentance. Dekker's too is Jane, with the little touch of spirit that he likes to give to his gentlest women, for when "checkt" by Dame Margery, "away she flung," to appear next in her "sempster's" shop, adored far off by the love-lorn Hammon, likewise Dekker's creation, a figure not without pathos—or humor either—as he eyes in vain "her pretty hand," "her happy work," and muses what women see in other men that he "still wants." "The Shoemaker's Holiday" is indeed the first play that exhibits not only Dekker's great powers of characterization but also his insight into motive, his sincere and healthy outlook upon life, resulting in realism if you like, but the sort of realism that selects the normal and the human, not the degraded and the beastly; and he had the rare artistic ability to make the normal and the human as lovable in a play as they are in real life. How firmly the characters are handled, how solidly their feet rest upon the ground, like those of Millet's peasants, and how swift, direct, naïve at times, is their utterance! Sane, sweet, and democratic was the mind that could so view life and so present it; without satire, for it is only with humor that Dame Margery, Sybil, Firk, Eyre himself, are conceived; without illegitimate appeal to the gallery, for Lacy's Dutch, for example, is used with restraint and good effect. In "The Shoemaker's Holiday" we have the most attractive picture of citizen life presented on the Elizabethan stage, and perhaps it is the truest. If for Dekker, the verse lacks imaginative charm, it is efficient verse, and we have, as a substitute for poetic beauty the intoxicating quality of the prose, its abundant vitality, spontaneity and its almost lyrical rhythm, so perfectly suited to the invincible gayety of mood in which the play was planned and carried out. In keeping with the mood too are the hearty little lyrics, a love song and a capital drinking round, the latter beginning suggestively and appropriately:

absolute rubbish

> "Cold's the wind, and wet's the rain,
> Saint Hugh be our good speed:
> Ill is the weather that bringeth no gain,
> Nor helps good hearts in need."

Although the next extant play that shows Dekker's hand cannot as a whole be compared with "The Shoemaker's Holiday," it has a special interest, partly because it is a play of great though interrupted charm and partly because it shows more than one way in which Dekker collaborated. For "Patient Grissill," the three authors apparently received the large sum of ten guineas, beginning with an undated payment to Chettle alone between October 16 and November 1, 1599, and closing with the payment of five shillings to Dekker and Haughton respectively on December 28 and 29.[34] The large payments were made to all three. It was acted in January, 1600, when Henslowe mentions buying "a grey gown" for Grissill; and registered to print on March 28, 1600, but not published until 1603. The main plot of this romantic tragicomedy deals with the familiar legend of Griselda[35] with the addition of two new figures, her brother Laureo and a family servant, Babulo. To this, as a relief, is joined the first sub-plot, a variety of the shrew story, relating the strife for mastery between a Welsh knight and his bride and conqueror, a Welsh widow, cousin of the Marquis. The scene in which Sir Owen tears up his wife's rebato may have had its inspiration in the behavior of Petruchio anent his wifes cap and gown.[36] The second and slighter sub-plot centres about Julia, the sister of the Marquis—remotely if at all suggested by Shakespere's Beatrice[37]—who decides that it is a pleasanter task to lead

[34] The relatively large payment is against a theory put forward by Professor W. Bang, *Dekker-Studien, Englische Studien*, 28, 208–213, to the effect that the main plot represents an old play written by Chettle alone some six years earlier.

[35] For the probable sources, see G. Hübsch's *Introduction* to his critical edition of the play, *Erlanger Beiträge*, band 15. See also F. von Westenholz's *Die Griseldis-Sage* (Heidelberg), 86–116. To John Phillip's *Play of Patient Grissell*, published in the Malone Soc. Reprints, the play in question owes nothing.

[36] Westenholz speaks of a general obligation to *The Taming of the Shrew*, p. 89.

[37] See Westenholz, 104.

apes in hell than to be a wife on earth and there endure hell, a natural conclusion when one considers the conduct of her nearest relation.

There is general agreement that to Chettle belongs the greater part of the story of Grissill, to Haughton that of Julia, and to Dekker the scenes in which Babulo and Laureo figure. There should be no doubt that the whole story of Gwenthyan and Sir Owen was written by Dekker;[38] he had a considerable liking for Welsh, introducing another "British knight" into "Satiromastix" and another into "Northward Ho"; and in each case handling easily the dialect of plausible broken English sprinkled with Keltic words and delighting in the opportunity for punning and other word-play. It is an entertaining farce that is enacted with so much unconscious humor by the solemn "Prittish" pair. Especially well maintained is the attitude of the lady, who, without any sense of the unusual, administers to her husband on a small scale the treatment meted out to Grissill on a large: "As her cousin has tried Grisill, so Gwenthyan has Sir Owen." On his side, Sir Owen closes the strife with equal complacency, reflecting that if he had not been patient, his lady had not been "pridled."

Without any desire to take from Chettle credit for the scenes in which Grissill appears, it should be added that Dekker touched them here and there, especially when she shows flickering signs of sense alien to the monstrous mush of concession long admired by the credulous. When, for example, her children are finally taken from her, she bitterly cries out in Dekkeresque language:

> "I must, Oh God! I must: must is for kings,
> And low obedience for low underlings."[39]

She speaks of herself as loaded with wrongs,[40] and her peculiar

[38] Perhaps there is no doubter except Fleay, who gives the Welsh to Chettle. One incident in the Sir Owen-Gwenthyan plot, that in which the latter refuses to feed her husband's guests, Dekker had found in the French satire that he translated in 1603. He used it again in *1 Honest Whore,* as observed by Professor Bang.

[39] G., V, 194. Nearly the same words are used by Celestine in *Satiromastix,* P., I, 247. This is noted by Professor Bang.

[40] G., V, 179.

virtue wears very thin when she turns to or from the Marquis
with the sarcastic remarks:

> " Your patience I commend that can abide
> To hear a flatterer speak, yet never chide."[41]

Undeniably Dekker's throughout is the most lovable character in the play—Babulo, family servant, basket-maker,
" fool "; fun-making, pun-making; fiercely loyal to Grissill,
" knocking " the Marquis when he tries to kiss her, and when
the same hero twits his wife with the russet gown she used
to wear, crying out, " Grissill was as pretty a Grissill in the
one as in the other "; always delightful whether he sings a
nursery catch to one of his mistress's babies, or plays with
his sword and discourses Lylian language to his boy, his
" courtier in decimo sexto," or urges honest work upon the
discontented Laureo, or bestows upon the Marquis's servant
his real opinion of court life:

> " Good Furio, vanish; we have no appetite, tell your Master. Clowns
> are not for the Court; we'll keep Court ourselves, for what do Courtiers
> but we do the like: you eat good cheer and we eat good bread and cheese:
> you drink wine and we strong beer: at night you are as hungry slaves as you
> were at noon; why, so are we: you go to bed, you can but sleep, why and
> so do we; in the morning you rise about eleven of the clock, why there we
> are your betters, for we are going before you; you wear silks, and we
> sheep skins; innocence carries it away in the world to come; and there-
> fore vanish, good Furio, torment us not, my sweet Furio."[42]

There is a universal appeal in his account of the pains of
getting up early:

> " Old Master, here's a morning able to make us work both tooth and
> nail, (marry, then, we must have victuals). The sun hath played bo-peep
> in the element any time these two hours, as I do some mornings when
> you call: ' What, Babulo,' say you: ' Here, Master,' say I; and then this
> eye opens, yet dun is the mouse, lie still: ' What, Babulo,' says Grissill:
> ' anon,' say I, and then this eye looks up, yet down I snug again: ' What,
> Babulo,' say you again, and then I start up, and see the sun, and then
> sneeze, and then shake mine ears, and then rise, and then get my break-
> fast, and then fall to work, and then wash my hands, and by this time I
> am ready."

[41] G., V, 154.
[42] G., V, 216. Cp. Shadow's dispraise of travel, *Old Fortunatus*, P., I, 126.

But quotations give a small idea of this dear cousin of Shadow, more of the earth indeed, but more lovable. He is an important member of the attractive group before Laureo and the Marquis invade it—humble, hard-working, and singing their song of sweet content and golden slumbers, than which there is no lovelier lyric on the bright pages of Elizabethan song books. Laureo, the poor scholar, is also Dekker's creation,[43] but he is treated with no particular sympathy: Babulo scoffs at his idleness, advises him to leave Latin and fall to basket-making, and shrewdly inquires how the nine Muses are doing—pride, covetousness, envy, and the rest. Like Babulo, he resents the cruelty of the "trial," but at the end, in words that Dekker must have penned, he tamely joins the admiring chorus that surround the Marquis.

To Dekker have also been ascribed the scenes[44] in which the fantastic dandy Emulo has a part, especially that in which he employs a "gallimaufry of language" to describe his duel with Sir Owen. It has long been noticed that he bears a close resemblance to Fastidious Brisk in Jonson's "Every Man out of his Humour,"[45] and it is thought that both men utilized separately an actual event and a well-known character.[46] Dekker, however, was first in the field, and uses the material with greater dramatic effectiveness;[47] and there remains the possibility that Jonson may have borrowed the incidents and characters, and thus given occasion to the unexplained taunt in

[43] The following passage has been thought to resemble Dekker:

"Such are our bankrouts and our fugitives,
Scarce having one good leg or one good limb,
Outrun their creditors and those they wrong." (p. 214.)

See also Laureo's praise of court life, p. 191, which has points of resemblance with that of Fortunatus, P., I, 118.

[44] G., V, 136–141, 164–168.

[45] Gifford's *Jonson* (1904), vol. I, Act IV, sc. 1, pp. 119–120. Cf. also the description and talk of Clove, p. 97, and 99, with Dekker's "brisk spangle-baby," G., V, 132–133. Such ignorant pretensions seem to have been common enough. See *The Gull's Hornbook*, G., II, 265. Asinius Bubo in *Satiromastix* belongs to the same type.

[46] On this subject, see R. A. Small, *Stage-Quarrel*, 42–43. He follows Fleay and Penniman.

[47] See *Dekker-Studien*, 214.

" Satiromastix ": " Demetrius [Dekker] shall write a scene or two in one of thy strong garlic comedies, and thou shalt take the guilt of conscience for it and swear 'tis thine own, old lad, 'tis thine own."[48]

By 1600, when Dekker was perhaps twenty-eight years old, he was thinking, so far as we know, in terms of imaginative idealism, or of tender or merry realism; he saw chiefly not the sordid side of poverty or the wicked potentialities in human nature, but love and loyalty of every kind, that which exists between servant and master as well as that between lover and lass, and the pleasant comradeship among men doing the same sort of work, with their swift readiness to help one another. In all these plays, his wit and humor have their way. Yet to a date shortly following the presentation of " Patient Grissill," Fleay and Swinburne would assign that orgy of blood and evil passion known as " Lust's Dominion," identifying it with " The Spanish Moor's Tragedy," upon which Dekker collaborated with Day and Haughton early in 1600. The play belongs to the early type exemplified by " The Jew of Malta " and " Titus Andronicus."[49] It is not only wholly unlike the known work of Dekker, but it is also for the most part unlike that of his collaborators: Haughton, whose one extant play written alone is " Englishmen for my Money," a sort of comedy of tricks; and Day, whose satirical-romantic gift is almost as far removed from the drama of blood, but who might conceivably have added the curious Oberon scenes. The Queen and Eleazer were conceived by a more " robust " mind than that of Dekker, who never drew either a convincing villain or a bad woman of imposing presence, or told in his plays a story of successful lust. Nor can I see any evidence in characterization or in phrasing that he retouched this drama, least of all the opening scene, which Swinburne so positively claims for him.

[48] P., I, 201.

The theory that Jonson was an unmentioned fourth collaborator on *Patient Grissill* creates more difficulties than it solves. For that theory, see *Dekker-Studien*, 213–214.

[49] Fleay acknowledges " an undercurrent of pre-Shakesperian work." See art. *Haughton*. Neither Ward nor Bullen thinks Dekker had a hand in this play.

CHAPTER V

The only play by Dekker mentioned in the "Diary" for
1601 is "King Sebastian of Portugal," a lost topical play on a
popular subject, collaborated with Chettle and paid for in April
and May. It seems possible that even then or during the
earlier empty months of that year he was engaged upon a
tragedy of much promise intended for Henslowe and the Admiral's men. While it was still unfinished, however, circumstances arose that compelled him to throw it aside and bend all
his energies to a peculiarly exacting form of personal satire.
As the satire by itself was not long enough to constitute a play,
he united it to the part of the tragedy he had already written,[1]
and we have the result in the medley known as "Satiromastix."[2]
As the line between the tragical and satirical portions is sufficiently clear, it will be simpler to discuss them separately.

The subject of the unfinished tragedy was the killing of
William Rufus by Wat Tirrell, but although it therefore falls
loosely within the category of revenge tragedies popular between 1598 and 1602, it was apparently to have been developed
without the aid of their more sensational features. It opens
gracefully enough with two gentlewomen strewing, upon the
stony way to church, flowers "with their yellow-sunk eyes,"
and discoursing in a rather Lylian strain. This is followed
by other preparations for the wedding, amidst which comes to
the front the comic sub-plot concerned with the three suitors—
one of them a Welshman—of Mistress Miniver, an ignorant,

---

[1] Swinburne first put forward the theory that the satire on Jonson was
added to an incomplete tragedy that Dekker had on hand; Small, in his
Stage Quarrel, developed it.

[2] *Satiro-mastix or the Untrussing of the Humorous Poet. As it hath bin
presented publikely by the Right Honorable, the Lord Chamberlaine, his
Servants; and privately by the Children of Paules*, 1602.

naïve widow. Afterwards there is music, dancing to "the soft wind of whispering silks," broken snatches of talk between the King and Celestine, and finally the sinister interview in which the King's repeated "Thou dar'st not, Wat," calls out the bridegroom's foolish oath that is to bring on the catastrophe. After more of the comedy, including the orations in favor of long hair and of baldness, the latter spoken in a garden, and a brief troubled consultation between bride, groom, and father, comes the noble scene in which Celestine gladly drinks the poisoned wine prepared by her father. It is full of tragic feeling and poignant phrasing. As Sir Quintilian presents the cup, he cries:

> " O my son,
> I am her father; every tear I shed
> Is threescore ten year old."

And Terrill:

> " Oh,
> That very name of poison, poisons me;
> Thou Winter of a man, thou walking grave,
> Whose life is like a dying taper, how
> Canst thou define a lover's laboring thoughts?
> What scent hast thou but death? What taste but earth?
> The breath that purls from thee is like the steam
> Of a new open'd vault: I know thy drift,
> Because thou art travelling to the land of graves,
> Thou covetst company, and hither bringst
> A health of poison to pledge death: a poison
> For this sweet spring: this element is mine,
> This is the air I breathe: corrupt it not;
> This heaven is mine, I bought it with my soul
> Of Him that sells a heaven to buy a soul."

But the end of the scene as it now stands is an anticlimax inserted to prepare us for Celestine's return to life, made necessary by the intention of subordinating the tragical scenes to the satirical additions, or, to use Dekker's apologetic words,

> " to wed a comical event
> To pre-supposed tragic argument."

It was Ben Jonson who caused the ruin of this tragedy. About 1600–1601 he was suffering from one of the most malignant attacks of egotism recorded in literature, and he took his own symptoms so seriously as to mislead most critics down to the present century; he did not so mislead his contemporaries. During its earlier stages the quarrel[3] between Jonson and his fellow dramatists had involved Anthony Munday, but by 1600 it had narrowed down to a duel between Jonson and Marston, in which the honors and the acridities were pretty evenly divided. With both men Dekker had been on friendly terms; as late as September, 1599, he was collaborating with the former and others—possibly Marston among them[4]—on "Robert II, King of Scotland," and throughout the period he was intimate with the latter. This intimacy was the chief, perhaps the only reason why about February or March he was dragged into the affair by Jonson in "Cynthia's Revels." In that inhumanly tedious play, he is chiefly ridiculed as Anaides, the humble friend of Hedon or Marston; he is poor, he knows the classics only superficially, yet accuses Crites or Jonson of plagiarizing from them, and is, in general, "a light arrogating puff" rhymingly bracketed with Marston as "impudent and ignorant enough."[5]

To this attack Dekker showed no signs of replying, but Jonson, by his arrogance and his onslaughts upon other poets, had roused the wrath of a more numerous foe, and the Chamberlain's men, according to Jonson's own account,[6] asked Dekker to reply, or, to use his enemy's words, "hired him to abuse Horace [Jonson] and bring him in, in a play." Even then, he showed so little eagerness for battle that he was engaged upon his tragedy, when, probably in June, Jonson concentrated his powers of satire in "The Poetaster," directed primarily towards

[3] In discussing this subject I have drawn largely from R. A. Small's *Stage-Quarrel between Ben Jonson and the So-called Poetasters*, especially pp. 118–132 and 199–200. For another point of view, see J. H. Penniman's *War of the Theaters*, Boston, 1897.

[4] See Small, 90–92.

[5] As Small points out, Dekker himself accepts this interpretation of Anaides and Hedon. See P., I, 195, where Horace quotes "The one a light voluptious reveler," etc.

[6] Jonson's use of the word "hire" has led the docile critic to speak of Dekker as "a hired mercenary," as if Dekker were the only dramatist who wrote in part to make a living.

the glory of Ben Jonson, secondarily against Marston and Marston's friend, and incidentally against players, lawyers, courtiers, citizens and citizens' wives. As he knew that Dekker was going to write a play against him he cleverly endeavored to discredit in advance that expected satire by representing his opponent as worthy of nothing but contempt: "O, sir, his doublet's a little decayed; he is otherwise a very simple honest fellow, sir, one Demetrius, a dresser of plays about the town here,"[7]—a dresser or decker of plays: perhaps at this point Jonson was actuated less by contempt than by the desire to make a pun. However that may be, he puts into the mouth of Demetrius a poem mean in thought and doggerel in form;[8] represents him as spiteful and given to slander,[9] and, as in "Cynthia's Revels," guilty of criticising Jonson's free use of the classics although he does not thoroughly understand them himself;[10] finally, when brought to the bar he is made to take an oath not to slander Jonson or any other superior, and is forced to put on the cap and gown of a fool, to wear them "in every fair and generous assembly," and to think himself only what the cap and gown show him to be.[11] Together with Marston he is also accused of calumniating and envying Jonson, and of "taxing him falsely of self-love, arrogancy, impudence, railing, filching by translation, etc."[12]—charges specifically made to forestall the expected satire.

Whether roused by his own indignation, or, as seems more likely, by the insistency of Marston or the Chamberlain's men, among whom was Shakespere,[13] Dekker apparently set to work upon his reply as soon as "The Poetaster" appeared. As he ridicules Jonson for requiring fifteen weeks for the completion of his play—"What, will he be fifteen weeks about this

[7] *Poet,* III, 1, p. 234. This reference and the following are to Gifford's edition, 1904.

[8] *Idem,* V, 1, pp. 257–258.

[9] *Idem,* III, 1, p. 235.

[10] *Idem,* IV, 1, p. 239; V, 1, p. 257.

[11] *Idem,* V, 1, pp. 255, 258, 261–262.

[12] *Idem,* p. 255.

[13] Shakespere's part in the quarrel mentioned in *II Return from Parnassus* has not been satisfactorily explained; perhaps he did nothing more than join in the invitation to Dekker.

cockatrice's egg too? "[14]—he presumably finished his answer in
a shorter time: about September, thinks Fleay; August or September, writes Small.[15] Pressed for time, or unable or unwilling to make an entire play of the satire he joined it to his
unfinished tragedy. The connection with the main plot is made
by representing Horace or Jonson as writing a nuptial ode for
Celestine and Terrill, and, at the close, by making William
Rufus preside over the trial and punishment of Horace, just
as Caesar Augustus had presided over the trial and punishment
of Crispinus and Demetrius.[16] The satire is more closely connected with the sub-plot, for Captain Tucca becomes a fourth
wooer of Mistress Miniver and finally carries off the prize.
The medley was acted, as the title tells us, at the Globe by the
Chamberlain's men, in private by the Children of Paul's. It
was registered to print November 11, and was published the
next year, with an incomplete list of characters and some
errata[17] styled by Dekker "a comedy of errors."

For the task of putting down Jonson, Dekker had many
qualifications. In his own field of genial comedy he was as
great as Jonson in his field of the comedy of humors, and it
must have been recognized that he was too kindly as well as
too wise to attempt to return scorn for scorn and that he might
therefore be trusted to employ against arrogance the only
effective weapon, which is laughter. Again, Dekker knew
his subject, and while there is no well-defined reason for
thinking that the collaboration with Jonson left any soreness
on either side, there must have been, in the inevitable discus-

[14] *Satiromastix*, P., I, 202.

[15] Small's date depends upon his dating of Jonson's plays: he would assign
Cynthia's Revels to February or March, 1601, because he thinks that Actæon
represents Essex, who was executed February 25, 1601, and because that
date would agree with Jonson's known habit of producing a play a year.
But *The Poetaster* was written in fifteen weeks, for Dekker says so; and
was therefore produced about June.

In the *Introduction* to his edition of *Satiromastix* Dr. Hans Scherer, who
in general follows Small, incorporates some suggestions for a later date
which are not convincing.

[16] To Horace is also given a little oration in honor of baldness originally
intended for some other character.

[17] Found in the notes in Pearson's edition, restored to their proper place
in Dr. Scherer's.

sion and criticism of each other's work when they came to joining scenes and to harmonizing characters, abundant opportunity for temperament to rub against temperament. Jonson, in any case, could have been no easy partner, though it must be added that, as far as the evidence goes, he seems to have collaborated "more" with Dekker than with any one else.[18] Since one expected charge in particular, that of plagiarism and of "filching by translation," rankled so deeply in Jonson's mind and since Dekker actually does emphasize that charge,[19] probably it had some basis in fact, not necessarily in anything written for the stage but in the give-and-take of men engaged in "the same trade of poetry," as Dekker reproachfully puts it. The latter may, for example, have said to his scholarly collaborator, "You get that out of Horace," or he may conceivably have written a scene or two that went under Jonson's name alone. But if that was the case, it is very certain that in those days of loose literary ownership, neither gave the matter a second thought until open war forced petty details into misleading prominence.

In Dekker's dedication, "To the World," prefixed to "Satiromastix," he states his point of view in respect to "that terrible Poetomachia lately commenced between Horace the Second and a band of lean-witted poetasters." "Horace," he explains, "questionless made himself believe that his Burgonian wit might desperately challenge all comers; and that none durst take up the foils against him: It's likely if he had not so believed, he had not been so deceived, for he was answered at his own weapon."[20]

In answering the common enemy at his own weapon, Dekker took over from "The Poetaster" the names that Jonson had used for himself and his two victims—Horace, Crispinus, and

[18] With Chettle too he twice collaborated, but Dekker was his only sole collaborator in any play.

[19] He makes it three times at least: in the passage quoted on p. 63; in the application of the epithet "Lucian" (P., I, 235) to Jonson, thus calling attention to the fact that the latter had borrowed from Lucian the manner of Marston's punishment in *The Poetaster;* in the passage (261–2) in which Jonson is made to swear "not to bombast out a new play with the old linings of jests stolen from the Temple's Revels."

[20] P., I, 181.

Demetrius, and he likewise appropriated the name of Captain Tucca, but transformed him from a noisy coward and time-server into a partisan of the two poetasters, endowed with an extraordinary gift for blustering invective and a wide knowl-edge of ballads and plays—a telling stage figure. Into his mouth Dekker put nearly all the rougher part of the satire and the personal retort. When criticised for copying Jonson's creation, he replied that Jonson had first copied "honest Cap-tain Hannam"; "neither was it much improper to set the same dog upon Horace whom Horace had set to worry others."[21] He then added to the group Asinius Bubo, satellite of Horace, toady and ignoramus, possibly a portrait drawn from life but representing a common type. The correspondence of Asinius and Horace to Faber and Lampatho in "What You Will" by Marston has been attributed to the latter's helping hand, and so have the dash and vigor of the whole Horace plot.[22] There can be no doubt that he had some share in the play, for Cap-tain Tucca's clever little epilogue[23] speaks of "my poetasters" and Jonson in his "Apologetical Dialogue" uses the plural number, but it seems to have been confined to suggestion, for the style is Dekker's.

The reader fresh from Jonson's satires, in which his aston-ishing arrogance claims for himself all the virtues, poetic and manly, must be struck most of all by the modesty and good-nature of Dekker's reply. Level-headed throughout, he keeps himself entirely in the background, and though he allows his pen to pay a brief compliment to Crispinus[24] and naturally makes him the judge over Horace at the end, he does not permit even that friend to become prominent. Twice, how-ever, in his own person, he speaks out his real indignation, the first time as follows:

> " Out of our loves we come,
> And not revenge, but if you strike us still,
> We must defend our reputations:
> Our pens shall like our swords be always sheath'd,

[21] *To the World*, P., I, 182.
[22] Small, 122.
[23] P., I, 265–266.
[24] P., I, 256. "We make him thine," etc.

Unless too much provokt; Horace, if then
They draw blood of you, blame us not, we are men:
Come, let thy Muse bear up a smoother sail,
'Tis the easiest and the basest art to rail."[25]

The second quotation is a reply to Jonson's common accusation
of envy:

"Good Horace, no; my cheeks do blush for thine,
As often as thou speak'st so; where one true
And nobly-vertuous spirit, for thy best part
Loves thee, I wish one ten, even from my heart.
I make account I put up as deep share
In any good man's love which thy worth earns
As thou thyself; we envy not to see
Thy friends with bays to crown thy poesy.
No, here the gall lies, we that know what stuff
Thy very heart is made of; know the stalk
On which thy learning grows, and can give life
To thy (once dying) baseness; yet must we
Dance antics on your paper.

. . . .

This makes us angry, but not envious;
No; were thy warpt soul put in a new mould,
I'd wear thee as a jewel set in gold."[26]

Contrary to the usual opinion, Dekker treats Jonson the
dramatist with great moderation, not only praising his poetry
but granting that his satire had sometimes drawn blood with
justice.[27] In the amusing little scene[28] that opens the play in
which Horace is represented in the agonies of composition and
calling upon the Muses for aid as he fumbles for the right
word and the right rhyme, the resulting ode, in spite of the
absurdity of the total effect, is not a mere parody of Jonson's
drinking song[29] but is possessed of lyrical movement and some
grace of expression. The twice-repeated "O me thy Priest
inspire" has its origin in Jonson's description of himself as

[25] *Idem*, 198–199.
[26] *Idem*, 244–5.
[27]   "He whose pen
Draws both corrupt and clear blood," etc., p. 263.
[28] P., 191.
[29] *Poetaster*, III, 1, 223.

"poet and priest to the Muses.[30]   As the purpose of the poetasters was to satirize the arch-satirist, the punishment meted
out to him is not improper; he is indeed threatened with tossing
in the blanket, for Jonson's own hint[31] to that effect could
hardly be neglected, but the threat is not really carried out,[32]
and Horace's penalty consists in being compelled to look upon
his own picture and that of the true Horace placed side by side,
in having his satyr's coat that he had assumed from pride and
scorn, not "allegiance to bright virtue," pulled over his head,
in feeling his "stinging wit" crowned with "stingling net-
tles"; and in his finally being made to promise good behavior
for the future.

For the rest, the humor of "Satiromastix," and the sting too,
lies in the fact that the play is full of echoes and reverberations
from "Cynthia's Revels" and "The Poetaster"[33]—so full indeed that any critic of Dekker's method in any specific case
should feel the necessity of turning back to Jonson for the
occasion.[34]   There are hits at Jonson's compliments to himself,
his praise of his own poetry and his own valor, his assumption
of shrinking innocence, as when he explains that he had never

[30] *Idem*, V, 1, 255.

[31] *Cynthia's Revels*, III, 2, 165.   Anaides-Dekker says of Crites-Jonson,
"I'll send for him to my lodging and have him blanketed when thou wilt,
man."

[32] This is not the usual opinion, but it should be noticed that when near
the end of the scene the women are called upon for a "verdict" (p. 245)
they all cry, "Blanket," a verdict that would have no point if it had already
been fulfilled; at that moment Sir Vaughan interposes with "Hold, I pray,
hold," and offers his "fine device" of carrying Horace's "terrible person"
to Court—a plan that is actually and immediately carried out.   The "one
lash more" (p. 244) that possibly to Gifford (*Poetaster*, 218, note) suggested the use of the bastinado seems rather to refer to the verbal chastise-
ment of Captain Tucca.

[33] Many of these echoes, replies, and correspondences are noted by Small,
Penniman, H. S. Mallory, in the notes appended to his edition of *Poetaster*
(Yale Studies, 1905), and by Dr. Scherer in the annotated *Satiromastix*.

[34] For example, the apparently weak scene, p. 242, in which Captain
Tucca stabs at Horace, who cries out, "Ah gentlemen, I am slain; oh
slave, art hired to murder me?" may have had a three-fold origin: in
Jonson's boasting of his courage, in his representing Crispinus-Marston as
suffering from fear at the court of Caesar, and in his "We have hired
him, etc."

been known to " wrong or tax a friend," and his assertion that he wrote for learned ears alone. At one end of the scale he is made to complain that his enemies misinterpreted him even while he was dipping his pen in " distilled roses," at the other, to express his hatred of the habit of uttering solecisms,

" To do which I'd as soon speak plasphemy."[35]

To Jonson's attacks upon the personal peculiarities of Marston, Dekker replied in kind, not sparing details of face, figure, dress, manners, and history, or even a hint at his foe's religion —a species of retort for which he felt it necessary to apologize when he printed the play. He does not, however, attack Jonson's moral character, although it would seem from a speech put into the mouth of Crispinus[36] that the latter at least had thus been attacked in Jonson's satires.

In general, when we leave out of consideration the incoherence and incongruity resulting from the union of tragedy and comedy, Dekker's satire must be recognized as essentially better art, for it depends for its effect upon recognized facts about the life and character of Jonson, while the latter made the unpardonable literary blunder of taxing his victims with faults for the most part imaginary, employing so little truth of detail, indeed, as to give little aid to Dekker's biographers and small comfort to the compilers of Who's Who in the whole Poetomachia. It may be added that to a reader not overawed by Jonson's name, " Satiromastix" will offer the greater entertainment, for in addition to the poetry of the tragical part it contains many a picturesque phrase, and many a passage of wit and unexpected humor. What bachelor of either sex, for example, could find today a more descriptive phrase, with wider circles of suggestiveness, than the " single and simple life" of Mistress Miniver?

However goodnatured Dekker's mood had remained through the satire, he showed considerable heat when after the play had been produced various unjust charges were brought

[35] Jonson had spoken of Marston's " lewd solecisms and worded trash." *Poet.*, III, 1, 224.

[36] *Satiromastix*, 197. Crispinus complains that Jonson had folded in riddles the vices of his best friends.

against him. In his partly humorous, partly scornful and
angry preface, he not only asserts that the poetasters merely
defended themselves, but he also swears by his strongest oath,
"the divinest part of true Poesy," that his satire attacked no
one but "our new Horace." He is most annoyed by the criticism that it would have been nobler to have exposed the
"deformity" of Jonson's mind rather than his "fortunes and
condition of life," and replies rather bitterly that he had followed Jonson's own methods and that if the latter had looked
as closely upon himself as upon others, "Horace would not
have left Horace out of "Every Man in's Humour."[37] But
so little did Dekker like his own satire and so little did he
desire to commit it to "the perpetuana of print" that he would
not have published the play had he not been compelled to do so
by the appearance of unauthorized versions: "neither should
this ghost of Tucca have walked up and down Paul's Churchyard, but that he was raised up in print by new exorcisms;"[38]
sincere words, these, for he never reprinted the play or
reverted to the subject, and he never again engaged in the
sort of personal satire that could conceivably hurt its object.
The play brought him additional reputation. Several years
later, Chettle thought "quick anti-Horace" the most suitable
phrase by which to distinguish his friend;[39] and Jonson seems
to hint in the "Apologetical Dialogue" that the "multitude of
voices" had been with his adversary. Yet perhaps there was
pain as well as scorn in Dekker's preface, and it is very probable that "this lamentable merry murdering of innocent
Poetry," as he there termed it, seemed just that to the author
of the unfinished tragedy.

The poetasters, however, had been successful in silencing
Jonson's bitter tongue, for he made no reply except to reiterate
in the "Dialogue" his vague charges and to announce that
since the Comic Muse had proved so ominous, he would turn
to Tragedy. He was reconciled off and on with Marston, and

[37] P., I, 182. In this reply Dekker hardly did his own satire justice.
[38] *Idem*, 183.
[39] The amiable Rowlands in 1610 described Dekker as "an upstart pam-
phlet-maker" and "satirical libeller." Martin Mark-All, 10.

a few years after the war he did not hesitate, together with Chapman and Marston, to write a friendly imitation of the "Westward Ho" of Dekker and Webster.[40] It is true that in 1619, at Hawthornden, he branded his old rival as a rogue, joining with his name those of Day and Sharpham; but it would be absurd to attach any importance to this outbreak of temper, for it occurred in that famous "censure of the English poets," of whom Shakespere "wanted art" and Spenser "pleased him not."

"Satiromastix" ended Dekker's play-writing for 1601, but early in the following year he was writing a prologue and an epilogue for "Pontius Pilate" and "altering Tasso," possibly the anonymous "Tasso's Melancholy"[41] mentioned in the Diary in 1594; in that case alterations were needed, for Tasso had died during the interval. Curiously, the payment of four pounds extends over a period of nearly twelve months. Later he made additions to "Sir John Oldcastle," presumably the lost second part,[42] wrote independently "Medicine for a Curst Wife," and collaborated in "Lady Jane," 1 and 2, and "Christmas Comes but Once a Year." Chettle, Heywood, Smith, and Webster also assisted in the production of "Lady Jane."[43] The original "Lady Jane" is lost, but there seems to be every reason for believing with Dyce[44] that the share of Webster and Dekker is represented in "The Famous History of Sir Thomas Wyatt. With the Coronation of Queen Mary and the Coming in of King Philip. As it was played by the Queen's Majesty's Servants. Written by Thomas Dickers and John Webster, 1607."[45] It was played at the Rose by Wor-

[40] It must be added that he said he had a small share in the play.

[41] Fleay thinks Dekker may have written the original play, but there is no evidence except that given above, which is obviously inconclusive.

[42] But see Greg, *Diary*, II, 206.

[43] Fleay assumes that the same collaborators worked at both parts, plausibly, for, although Dekker's name alone is mentioned in connection with the second part, the record is incomplete, since neither he nor the body of collaborators could have written it for five shillings. See also Greg, *Diary*, II, 232.

[44] *Webster* (1859), xiii.

[45] Fleay says that another name for the play was *The Overthrow of Rebels*, for which properties were bought in November.

cester's men, and after the accession of James by the Queen's servants, who succeeded them. The fact that the play kept the stage attests to some popularity; a second edition was brought out in 1612. It has come down to us in a bad condition; it is very short, and many of the scenes are fragmentary. The story, beginning with the death of Edward and closing with the execution of Jane and Dudley, incorporates the history of Wyatt's rebellion, but there is nothing that corresponds exactly with "the coronation of Queen Mary" and King Philip does not "come in." The source is Holinshed's "Chronicle," and the play follows the scheme of the then old-fashioned chronicle history. It is not likely that Dekker devised the plan, for neither "The Whore of Babylon" nor the historical tragedy of William Rufus was formed on a conventional model.[46] It is more likely that the credit should be given to Chettle, who was the older man, whose name is mentioned first in the Diary, who was especially at home in the chronicle history, and whose work in "Patient Grissill" and "Hoffman" bears the marks of older influences than does that of Dekker.

The collaboration of Dekker and Webster presents a very interesting question that has not yet been wholly solved. It was to be ten years before the latter was to produce an unaided play, but that one is so great that we might reasonably expect some foreshadowing of its qualities in the fragment under discussion, although, of course, we have no means of knowing just the method of collaboration. Fleay's summary division into halves separated by the neutral territory of the tenth scene, which gives the first half to Webster, the second to Dekker, has really the merit of assigning to each most of the scenes generally recognized as marked by some characteristic of his style. It gives to Dekker Wyatt's speeches to his soldiers,[47] full of puns and iteration; the dialogue in prose

[46] Dr. E. E. Stoll in his *John Webster* has discussed the authorship of *Sir Thomas Wyatt;* and Dr. F. E. Pierce has a monograph, called *The Collaboration of Webster and Dekker* (Yale Studies, 1909). Dr. Stoll assigns to Dekker the plot and general conduct of the play (p. 54), and Dr. Pierce agrees with Dr. Stoll. The latter also discusses the treatment of the source.

[47] P., III, 110–114 (sc. 12). The first speech contains the characteristic

between Brett and the clown in which fear of the Spanish is ridiculed,[48] and the pathos of the interviews between Jane and Dudley in the Tower[49] and on the scaffold.[50] It gives to Webster the first scene[51] with the unmistakable phrasing—as it seems to me—of the opening lines, the second scene[52] in which Jane and Dudley talk in a sombre strain of the unhappiness of their state, using Websterian figures and a rhythm unlike Dekker's, and the sixth scene[53] in which Wyatt addresses the Council in a manner impossible to the Wyatt of the Dekker scenes. But Fleay's line cannot be sharply drawn; for to Dekker belongs the clown[54] who speaks a Dutch phrase and shows a characteristic unwillingness to bear off the gold of the dead Homes until he has thrust "the dog in a ditch." His also, I think, is the trial scene,[55] the chief feature of which is the "loving strife" between Jane and Dudley which melts all the court but Winchester. To Webster must be given the tenth scene,[56] in which Wyatt vehemently protests against the Spanish match in the same sort of language and swearing the same oaths that he had employed in the sixth scene.[57] Of the remaining scenes, the only one that demands comment is the fourth,[58] where the patriotic unwillingness of Northumberland to fight against his countrymen rather favors Dekker.

line: "Masters, friends, soldiers, and therefore gentlemen," which, incidentally, seems like a parody on Shakespere.

[48] *Idem*, 114–116 (sc. 13).

[49] *Idem*, 109–110 (sc. 11).

[50] *Idem*, 126–130 (sc. 17).

[51] *Idem*, 83–85.

[52] P., III, 85–88.

[53] *Idem*, 92–95.

[54] P., III, 95–96 (sc. 7), and 100–103 (sc. 9).

[55] *Idem*, 120–124 (sc. 16).

[56] *Idem*, 104–108.

[57] So far, with the exception of sc. 1 and sc. 16, this in the main agrees with Dr. Pierce's conclusions. His total assignment to Webster, based upon Webster's preference for a latinized and sonorous diction, consists of scenes 2, 5, 6, 10, 14, 16. He adds that some of these scenes were certainly retouched by Dekker "and all of them may have been" (p. 159). See ch. 9 of his book for his discussion of the play. The suggestion about Wyatt's speeches, I owe to Mr. Greg, *Diary*, II, 233.

[58] P., III, 89–91.

While "Sir Thomas Wyatt" does not add much to the fame of either author, Webster's part is not wholly colorless, and Dekker's, aside from the characterization, contains some humor and some poetry worth remembering. Steady theatre-goers must have been delighted with such a Shakesperian quotation as is put in the mouth of Brett: "I say again that Wyatt, for rising thus in arms, with the Kentish men dangling thus at his tail, is worthy to be hanged—like a jewel in the kingdom's ear."[59] Of the poetry two quotations must suffice: the first is Wyatt's soliloquy in the Tower, the second is spoken by Dudley and explains itself.

> "The sad aspect this prison doth afford
> Jumps with the measure that my heart doth keep,
> And this enclosure here of naught but stone
> Yields far more comfort than the stony hearts
> Of them that wrong'd their country and their friend.
> Here is no perjured counsellors to swear
> A sacred oath, and then forswear the same,
> No innovators here doth harbor keep.
> A stedfast silence doth possess the place:
> In this the Tower is noble, being base."

> "Look, Norfolk, Arundel, Winchester!
> Do malefactors look thus when they die?
> A ruddy lip, a clear-reflecting eye,
> Cheeks purer than the maiden orient pearl
> That sprinkles bashfulness thorough the clouds:—
> Her innocence has given her this look."

What do we know about Dekker the man during the five years which he spent writing chiefly for Henslowe? Nothing indeed about his manner of living—whether in a home[60] or in lodgings—but some few details about his poverty, on the

[59] P., III, 115. Koeppel notes the quotation.

[60] It is not known whether Dekker was ever married, but it is customary to add that some of the following entries may refer to his family: Dorcas, daughter of "Thomas Dycker, gent.," was christened at St. Giles in 1594: and Anne, daughter of Thomas Decker, yeoman," at the same place in 1602. The register of St. Giles also records the burial of Elizabeth, daughter of "Thomas Dekker" in 1598; and a son of Thomas Dekker was buried at St. Botolph's, Bishopsgate, the same year.

one hand, and about his friendships, on the other. Of impecuniosity and shabby clothes Jonson had accused him, and he had accepted the reproach, intimating at the same time that the misfortune was shared by his accuser.[61] It was certainly shared by Marston, whom Jonson further represented as exposed to arrest for a small debt. He might truthfully have represented Dekker as undergoing the same experience, for twice during the early days of this period he was in prison, though for a short time only in each case. On both occasions Henslowe advanced the money to get him out. The first imprisonment was terminated only a few days after he was paid for "Phaeton," on February 4, 1598, when he was released from the Counter in the Poultry by the payment of two pounds.[62] The second imprisonment occurred about a year later, and ended some ten days after he had been paid for "The First Introduction of the Civil Wars of France," on January 30, 1599, when his manager advanced three and a half pounds "to discharge him from the arrest of the Chamberlain's men."[63] It is not known how he became liable to the rivals of his own company, but as he was on the best of terms with them two years later, the matter cannot have been serious. The Diary also tells us that on other occasions he borrowed money of his manager, whose business included many dealings of that sort: on May 2, 1599,[64] when together with Chettle he had a loan of one pound to free the latter from prison; again, on August 1, 1599,[65] another pound; and on May 5, 1602,[66] five pounds, a debt that he halved with Munday. His total indebtedness during those five years, then, amounted to less than ten pounds; the usual limit for payment was thirty days. Neither these debts nor these brief imprisonments should be taken too seriously, for in those days imprisonment for small debts seems to have been a common occurrence: the staid and respectable Chettle, for example, was likewise twice

[61] P., I, 201.
[62] Greg, *Diary*, 83.
[63] *Idem*, 101, 161.
[64] *Idem*, 107.
[65] *Introd.* to *Diary*, xlix.
[66] *Diary*, 178.

released from incarceration by Henslowe and he was a more frequent borrower from his manager than was Dekker; nor, in view of some prevailing ideas about the latter, should it be allowed to escape our memory that it was Chettle who received aid from Dekker, not Dekker from Chettle. There is no reason to think that the poet himself was much troubled by his misfortunes. Some seven or eight years later he first tried his hand at a prison interior;[67] that picture represents not only the white-haired man to whose despair no solace but sleep is granted, but also a young gallant, who upon his entrance into the Counter roars and rages and calls for pen and ink in order to write " invectives, satires, libels, rhymes " against sergeants-at-law, and who is suddenly converted by some kindness of theirs into a eulogist of those " painfullest members of the commonwealth." This gallant is no portrait of Dekker, for he is " one whose outside only showed he was a gentleman, for within the sumptuous tomb of him was nothing but carcass "; but it is not at all unlikely that the author's own release from prison was accompanied by the emotions of the gallant who wrote so like a poet.

His poverty deserves a word more, especially as the critics have been inclined to agree that it was a wretched sort of existence that he led during these Henslowe years. The evidence has been fully stated. Unfortunately it was not the business of the Diary or the object of Jonson's satire to record the more prosperous intervals in Dekker's life, but we have seen that he was among the best paid of the playwrights who worked for the Admiral's company, and that his income must have been fairly comfortable. The critics have been misled, I think, by the undoubted pain and poverty of a much later period in Dekker's life, of which he has left an account that cannot be misunderstood. Down to 1612 I have not found in his most personal utterances any complaint that he was badly paid or really suffering from poverty, or that he had any cause for misery that did not belong to the common lot of man. But for money, as for titled patrons and courtly favor, there is no sign that he greatly cared. He seems to have started out in

[67] In *Jests to Make You Merry*, etc.

life with the Stevensonian philosophy that the only misfortune is to be a dull fool, for early in 1598 he wrote:

" 'Tis a stout happiness to wear good clothes
Yet live and die a fool—mew ! "[68]

And such sentiments as are voiced in Lodovico's words are not uncommon:

" Why should we grieve at want? Say the world made thee
Her minion, that thy head lay in her lap,
And that she danc'd thee on her wanton knee,
She could but give thee a whole world: that's all,
And that all's nothing; the world's greatest part
Cannot fill up one corner of thy heart.

. . . .

Were twenty kingdoms thine, thou'dst live in care:
Thou could'st not sleep the better, nor live longer,
Nor merrier be, nor healthfuller, nor stronger."[69]

Perhaps a writer endowed with such rare insight into human nature realized that he needed some external compulsion to keep him faithful to the work for which he was born, and that his beauty-loving nature would not have been nourished by a fat and easy life; for in his account of the conflict between Money and Poverty, in which he gaily asserts that he has always fought on the side of the latter, he puts into the mouth of his leader the following words: " Do not I inspire Poets with those sacred raptures that bind men, how dull and brutish soever, to listen to their powerful charms, and so to become regular? Do not I sharpen their invention, and put life into their verse?"[70]

But Dekker was " hackwriter and slave." The " slave " may be dismissed, but when one considers his rapid and abundant output, " hackwriter" has a descriptive value. Yet if his subject was sometimes or frequently dictated to him, it would seem that he treated it as he pleased; and probably his unaided

[68] *The Sun's Darling*, P., IV, 297.
[69] *2 Honest Whore*, P., II, 136. See also *Old Fortunatus*, P., I, 99, "I am not enamored of this painted idol," etc.
[70] *Work for Armorers*, G., IV, 152.

plays owed nothing to the suggestion of his manager, or if a manager suggested that there was a good play in Deloney's "Gentle Craft," or directed him to put humanity into a brutal legend, that would only prove that he had an excellent manager. At least he did not complain; he was apparently unconscious that he needed pity. It is worth while remembering at this point that Dekker's position was not unusual. Almost the whole company of poets inspired by Marlowe came up to London and the theatres for the purpose of earning their living as well as of delivering their souls of great literature. Most of them, for a time at least, were engaged in hackwriting and doubtless glad to get the work. This was the case with Chapman, Drayton, Webster, possibly Middleton, and with Heywood, whose career in many ways suggests a comparison with Dekker's but who added the resources of an actor to those of a writer.

Perhaps this part of Dekker's life may be counted singularly fortunate, for, after all deductions have been made, the fact remains that he was doing the work he most enjoyed and he was seeing it appreciated—three, at least, of his plays by the most critical and brilliant audience in England; if he was forced into a literary quarrel he had the satisfaction of waging a victorious fight conducted chiefly for a friend; and he had the felicity of congenial comradeship in his own "trade of poetry." A list of his collaborators includes every important dramatist of the time except Shakespere and Chapman. The former he probably knew, and there are indications that he was acquainted with the latter, who was writing for Henslowe during the later nineties, and who, by the way, owed that financier of poets ten pounds—all at one heroic moment. Near the end of this period may have begun his acquaintance with Ford, a future collaborator, who was then reading at the Middle Temple, and who assuredly did not neglect the theatres; perhaps he did not fail, either, to seek out the famous playwright who had just put down Jonson. Dekker's collaboration with Middleton and Day began during this period: with the former it did not cease until 1610, and the connection, undoubtedly congenial on the personal and social side, was fraught with

important consequences; the continued friendship of the latter
found expression in commendatory verses prefixed to a 1609
edition of "Lanthorn and Candlelight" and in his renewed
collaboration with Dekker when the latter was released from
his long imprisonment.

The intimacy with Webster deserves a word more. They
began to work together in May, 1602, on "Caesar's Fall," a
much collaborated play; this was followed by "Lady Jane,"
and "Christmas Comes but Once a Year"—three types in all.
In 1602 both made commendatory verses for Munday's
"Palmerin of England," and in 1604 for Harrison's "Arches
of Triumph." In 1604–05 they again collaborated, this time
on two intrigue plays, "Westward Ho" and "Northward
Ho," in which the collaboration is of such a nature as to
puzzle "the doctors." In 1612, Dekker wrote to the actors
of the Red Bull, to whom he dedicated his "If It be not
Good":

"I wish a fair and fortunate day to your next new play for the maker's
sake and your own, because such brave triumphs of Poesy and elaborate
industry, which my worthy friend's muse hath there set forth deserve a
theatre full of very Muses themselves to be spectators. To that fair day I
wish a full, free, and knowing audience.[71] And to that full audience, one
honest doorkeeper." [72]

The play thus affectionately commended was Webster's
"White Devil," in the dedication of which Dekker is
praised together with Shakespere and Heywood for "right
happy and copious industry." A friendship unusually
strong on each side so far as we can judge from meagre
biographical records, a collaboration unusually difficult to
separate into its component parts, doubtless had their origin
in something as fundamental as character. However these
poets may offend our taste at times, we feel in both a founda-
tional rectitude and an incapability of self-deception that go
far in making friendship permanent. And, although this is a
matter of less importance, they had in common many in-

[71] Misprinted "auditor" in the text.
[72] P., III, 262. For the identification of this play with *The White Devil*,
see Stoll, *John Webster*, 21–22.

tellectual tastes, preoccupation with life after death, for example—troubled, " in a mist," in Webster's plays, serene and confessedly Christian in Dekker's works; and along with this, an interest in the outward accompaniments of death, unusual even for Elizabethans, obvious in the case of Webster and manifested by Dekker in two plague books and not infrequent allusions in prose and verse.

Among other friends of this period was Henry Chettle, who, after Elizabeth's death, wrote in "England's Mourning Garment," the following suggestive stanza:

> " Quick anti-Horace, though I place thee here,
> Together with young Moelibee,[73] thy friend:
> And Hero's last Musaeus, all three dear,
> All such whose virtues highly I commend,
> Prove not ingrate to her that many a time
> Hath stoopt her Majesty to grace your rhyme."

In another case, Dekker is the witness. In 1602 he wrote for the third part of " Palmerin of England " a graceful little ode addressed to his " good friend, Master Anthony Munday ":

> " If pure translation reach as high a glory
> As best invention (to deny't were sin),
> Then thou, dear friend, in publishing this story
> Hath graced thyself and thy quaint Palmerin;
> Thou much by him, he most by thee shall win.
>
> For though in courtly French he sweetly spake,
> In fluent Tuscan, grave Castilian,
> A harder labor thou dost undertake
> Thus to create him a fine Englishman,
> Whose language now dare more than any can.
> Nor thou nor Palmerin in choice do err,
> Thou of thy scholar, he his schoolmaster."[74]

We could wish indeed that we might know just what besides his work and his friendships actually did " fill up " the heart of " Tom " Dekker, as Heywood calls him, between his twenty-sixth and his thirty-first year. Not chiefly the ordinary

[73] Marston.

[74] In 1603 Dekker also wrote verses for Munday's translation of *The Maiden of Confolens.* I have not seen them.

and the tavern, I think, though they knew his presence, as they also knew that of Falstaff's creator and of every other dramatist interested in life's comedy; in fact, had he been the most starched Puritan possible of a playwright, the tavern must have been familiar territory. Henslowe tells us[75] that it was at the Sun in New Fish Street that "The Famous Wars of Henry I and the Prince of Wales" was read and five shillings worth of "good cheer" consumed, and it was at "The Tavern" that "Jephthah" was read, assisted by wine to the amount of two shillings.

In closing this long but scattered and imperfect discussion of Dekker's life and work from 1598 to the end of 1602, what shall be said, in summary, of the character and fortunes of the man? Although we must take into consideration his two brief imprisonments, his comparative poverty, and the criticism connected with the Marston-Jonson quarrel, the answer, I think, is clear: honest, acknowledges his enemy; virtuous, asserts his friend; industrious, fairly thunders the record of the Diary; wholesomely happy, proclaims the general tenor of his plays, emphasizing as they do the delights of "honest mirth," the joy of labor, the beauty of the changing seasons, and the charm of human goodness, whether in its humbler aspect of kindliness towards others or, more rarely, its loftier form of facing death with dignity or preferring it to dishonor.

[75] *Diary*, I, 85, 160.

CHAPTER VI.

THE INFLUENCE OF MIDDLETON.

1603 was a memorable year for England. In the midst of the "felicity" of the spring, as Dekker writes, Queen Elizabeth died, and during the summer following, London was swept by the plague, in which, as he expressed it twenty-two years later, her subjects followed "in a dead march a twelve-month long," to the number of 35,578 in London and the Liberties only.[1] In "The Wonderful Year" Dekker wrote an account of both events, and of the panic that followed the Queen's death when "upon Thursday it was treason to cry, God save King James, king of England, and upon Friday high treason not to cry so." As a plague year necessarily entailed a lessening of activity on the part of those who lived by the drama, it is not surprising to find no record of any play for 1603, although of course Dekker may have been engaged in writing the masterpiece that was to appear upon the stage the following year. However this may have been, during the interval Dekker tried his hand at non-dramatic prose. His first book, "The Bachelor's Banquet," a translation of a French satire of the fifteenth century, was published in 1603, and was so well liked as to demand another edition in 1604. The second, "The Wonderful Year, 1603," bears the date 1603 upon its title-page, but it could not have been written until 1604, for it quotes some laudatory verses "heretofore in private presented to the King."[2] The verses are provided with a prologue in which the poet complains, in a rather Pope-like manner, of the fate of his poetry:

> "For such, am I prest forth in shops and stalls,
> Pasted in Paul's, and on the lawyers' walls,
> For every basilisk-eyed critic's bait,
> To kill my verse, or poison my conceit:
> Or some smokt gallant, who at wit repines,

[1] G., IV, 281.
[2] James did not reach London until 1604.

86

> To dry tobacco with my wholesome lines,
> And in one paper sacrifice more brain
> Than all his ignorant skull could e'er contain:
> But merit dreads no martyrdom nor stroke;
> My lines shall live when he shall be all smoke."

Dekker did not at this time avail himself of the custom that permitted an appeal to a patron's purse. Neither preface nor epistle-dedicatory was attached to "The Bachelor's Banquet," and he expressly disclaims any mercenary intention in the affectionate letter prefixed to "The Wonderful Year," addressed to his "well-respected friend, Mr. Cuthbert Thuresby, Water-Bailiff of London,"—a letter that I quote in full.

"Books are but poor gifts, yet Kings receive them: upon which I presume you will not turn this out of doors. You can not for shame but bid it welcome, because it brings to you a great quantity of my love: which, if it be worth little (and no marvel if love be sold underfoot when the God of Love himself goes naked), yet I hope you will not say you have a hard bargain, sithence you may take as much of it as you please for nothing. I have clapt the cognizance of your name on these scribbled papers, it is their livery. So that now they are yours: being free from any vile imputation save only that they thrust themselves into your acquaintance. But general errors have general pardons: for the title of other men's names is the common heraldry which all those lay claim to, whose crest is a pen and inkhorn. If you read, you may happily laugh; 'tis my desire you should, because mirth is both physical and wholesome against the plague: with which sickness, to tell truth, this book is, though not sorely, yet somewhat infected. I pray, drive it not out of your company for all that; for, assure your soul, I am so jealous of your health, that if you did but once imagine there were gall in mine ink, I would cast away the standish and forswear meddling with any more Muses."

On the fifteenth of March, 1604, a pageant was presented to the royal family upon the occasion of their entry into London.[3] The poets chosen to devise the greater part of the pageant were Dekker and Jonson, who thus met once more as equals though not as collaborators. Each was proud of the honor and each

[3] *The Magnificent Entertainment: Given to King James, Queene Anne his wife, and Henry Frederick the Prince, upon the day of his Maiesties Tryumphant Passage (from the Tower) through his Honorable Citie (and Chamber) of London, being the 15 of March. 1603. As well by the English as by the Strangers: With the speeches and Songes, delivered in the severall Pageants.*

published his work.[4] Jonson confined himself to his own work; Dekker gave an account of the whole, including the shows of the Italians and the Belgians or Dutch, and a condensed description of Jonson's share without mentioning his name. It is something of a task to read such a pageant through, as it must have been to listen to the orations and some of the poems, but Dekker mercifully explains at the end of his account: "Reader, you must understand that a regard being had that his Majesty should not be wearied with tedious speeches, a great part of those which are in this book set down, were left unspoken." In general, Dekker's account of the whole pageant is not unlike that of a modern reporter; there is brief account of the occasion, an enumeration of committees and workmen, special praise for the devices of the "Strangers," and for the "excellent action" and "well-tuned voice" of Alleyn, who was a speaker in Jonson's first pageant, and some interludes of description. His devices include one in which figure St. George and St. Andrew, who had "a long time looked upon each other with countenances rather of mere strangers than of such near neighbors," and the Genius of the Place, whom he represents as feminine, "contrary to the opinion of all the doctors." This pageant was laid aside because the King entered the city at a different point from that intended. Dekker's other pageants, the fourth, fifth, and sixth, present a variety of mythological, pastoral and allegorical elements, among them the "bright-haired Graces," "for that epithet is properly bestowed upon them by Homer in his Hymn to Apollo," Vertumnus, "the master gardener and husband to Pomona, and Astraea, the "principal and worthiest," of whom the poet adds: "Having told you that her name was Justice, I hope you will not put me to describe what properties she held in her hands, sithence every painted cloth can inform you." There are speeches in prose and verse, and three lyrics, two clothed in elaborate stanzaic form, the more melodious ringing the changes on the refrain:

> "Troynovant is now no more a city:
> O great pity! is't not pity?"

[4] Dekker's version was registered to print April 2, some two weeks later than Jonson's part.

which was sung by two Paul's boys "in sweet and ravishing voices." There is not much real poetry besides. In the part not presented, the Genius Loci speaks the well-known lines:

> "And when soft-handed Peace so sweetly thrives
> That bees in soldiers' helmets build their hives";

and Fame describes her hundred tongues in a lovely phrase,—

> "mute
> As in an untoucht bell or stringless lute."

Unlike Jonson's account, Dekker's contains little Latin; in fact, he ridicules using "the borrowed weapons of all the old Masters of the noble science of Poesy," specifically of Latin poetry, and continues: "The Multitude is now to be our audience, whose heads would miserably run a-wool-gathering if we do but offer to break them with hard words." For the rest, although he does not forget Elizabeth—"A Phoenix lived and died in the sun's breast"—he permits himself, regrettably but naturally under the circumstances, to speak of "this treasure of a kingdom—a Man Ruler." Dekker thought so well of this pageant, or was so sure of a sale, that three impressions were issued, one for Edinburgh, two for London; and he bestowed an amount of pains upon the editing that one wishes he had given to his plays, going so far as to apologize for some of the errors that "wander up and down in these sheets, under the printer's warrant."

In the passage in which he apologizes for shortening the account of Jonson's first pageant, he adds that "an excellent hand" is "at this instant curiously describing all the seven, and bestowing on them their fair prospective limbs." That hand belonged to Stephen Harrison, mentioned by name at the end of the "Entertainment" as joiner and sole inventor of the architecture. His book, "The Arches of Triumph," contains seven full-page illustrations of the arches and nine leaves of descriptive text.[5] To this volume are prefixed odes to Harrison by Webster and Dekker. The verses of the latter, addressed to his "friend," are as follows:

[5] Presumably by Webster and Dekker, says the article on Harrison in the *Dict. Nat. Biog.* I have not seen the book, which is very rare. The date is 1604.

"Babel that strove to wear
A crown of clouds, and up did rear
  Her forehead high
With an ambitious lust to kiss the sky,
  Is now or dust or not at all.
   Proud Nimrod's wall
  And all his antique monuments,
  Left to the world as precedents,
Cannot now shew, to tell where they did stand,
So much in length as half the builder's hand.

   The Mausoleum tomb;
The sixteen curious gates in Rome
   Which times prefer,
Both past and present; Nero's theater
  That in one day was all gilt o'er;
   And to these more:
  Those columns and those pyramids that won
  Wonder by height, the coloss of the sun,
Th' Egyptian obelisk, are all forgotten;
Only their names grow great: themselves be rotten.

   Dear Friend! what honors then
Bestow'st thou on thy countrymen,
   Crowning with praise
By these thy labors, as with wreaths of bays,
  This royal city: where now stand,
   Built by thy hand,
  Her arches in new state; so made
  That their fresh beauties ne'er shall fade:
Thou of our English Triumphs rear'st the fame
'Bove those of old; but above all thy name."

In the "Entertainment" Dekker gives to Middleton credit for
a mediocre verse-oration of sixty lines. This was not the first
occasion on which they had worked together, for in 1602 they
had collaborated with others on "Caesar's Fall." Later, according to an entry in the "Diary," Middleton aided Dekker in
"1 Honest Whore," and the partnership was renewed in 1610
when they wrote together "The Roaring Girl." Between these
dates fall "Westward Ho" and "Northward Ho," in which
Webster collaborated with Dekker. As these four plays,
together with the second part of "The Honest Whore," form
a group possessed of characteristics not elsewhere found in

Dekker's writings, it is necessary to disregard chronology for the time; and since these common characteristics involve a marked change in choice of subject and situation, in selection of characters, in dialogue, and, to some extent, in moral tone, it seems necessary, at the risk of repetition, to hark back for a moment to Dekker's early work.

It was distinguished, as we have seen, on the one side, by a strong romantic tendency, whether exhibited in his treatment of folk-lore, allegory, or history, and by an inclination to moralize his subject; and on the other, by a tendency, almost as marked, to dwell genially and with a wealth of local color upon the habits of the humble and the gentler emotions of those whose lives are sweetened by labor. Dekker, then, was already in part a realist, but, whether influenced by temperament, stage-demands, or both, dealing with cheerful, healthy matters in a sane moral temper. There is humor in all but one of these early plays, sometimes boyish and extravagant to the point of lyricism, sometimes relying on the aid of dialect, sometimes taking the form of a shrewd-simple wit, but raised above that conventional type by the extraordinary likeableness of the fool or servant who voices it. But for the purpose in hand, which would distinguish between the plays written or acted before 1603, and a group of plays written soon after, it is equally significant that certain elements are not to be found in these early plays, the more so as it has been too generally assumed that these features form an integral part of Dekker's genius. There is neither intrigue nor vice, not even a bad woman; there is no confusion of right and wrong, and almost no coarseness; "Satiromastix" is the worst offender, but for that play Jonson had set the pace, and in its execution Marston stood at Dekker's elbow. Except in this play there is very little satire even of the goodnatured sort. It should also be emphasized that these plays show no special acquaintance with the tavern, the prison, or low life in general, not so much as Shakespere had shown by the same date.

But in the group now to be considered—"The Honest Whore," "Westward Ho," and "Northward Ho"—certain new features are conspicuous: in all three, immoral men and men and women who make a living by vice have a considerable part; in all three there are scenes in houses of ill-fame; in two, courtesans are married to bad men, against the will of the latter; and in all three there is offensive dialogue. In the first of these plays, the subject, the conversion of a courtesan, is treated with such originality, such truth to human nature, and in the total effect with such high seriousness, such vigor of characterization and such noble poetry that the play is considered by many Dekker's masterpiece. In certain scenes and in one character, "Westward Ho" retains the seriousness of "The Honest Whore," but the rest of the play is intrigue, and "Northward Ho" is on a still lower moral level. In the former, especially, there seem to be confused ideas of right and wrong, a fogginess of atmosphere that I do not find in any other plays in which Dekker had a part, except in the intrigue portions of "The Roaring Girl," certainly written by Middleton. It is probable that Webster, who dealt with lust and whose one unaided comedy, "The Devil's Law Case," has an abhorrent plot, is partly responsible for the plan and tone of these comedies. But a partial explanation of the choice of subjects and the manner of treating them is to be found in the change that had been coming over the spirit of comedy. Chapman is perhaps the earliest offender: if the moral point of view is blurred in his great tragedies, it simply does not exist in such a comedy as "The Blind Beggar of Alexandria," printed in 1598. In "A Humorous Day's Mirth," 1597, one wife deceives her husband and two husbands their wives; in "A May Day," acted about 1601, the point of view is cynical and the dialogue and situations are offensive. The cynical point of view is found also in Jonson, especially in his treatment of women, and very certainly grossness is not absent from his plays. Possibly Shakespere made popular the citizen intrigue play in "The Merry Wives of Windsor," and in "Measure for Measure," acted as early as 1603, he seems to have followed the fashion of bringing upon the stage repellent characters, situations, and dialogue.

It was Middleton, however, who carried the comedy of mud to the greatest length, although most of his plays come after the period now being considered. He was of about the same age as Dekker, and shared his interest in the spectacle, the comedy of life; in manners and customs; in details of street life and shop life. As a student of law he very likely knew a great deal about London crime and vice. Excluding " Old Law," which underwent alteration, his earliest extant play is " Blurt, Master Constable,"[6] printed in 1602, in which he began, so far as we know, his satirical studies in the depraved morals and manners of his time, for the most part segregated from the decent:—studies that he continued with tireless industry and inconceivable vivacity for some eleven years, and he did nothing else during those years.[7] By thus concentrating his great gifts upon the evil and the unclean, he lost the power of creating a character, especially a woman, at the same time good, sane, and effective. The mother in " A Fair Quarrel " is " good " but she is monstrous. That other mother, so lovable at first, in " Women beware Women," is as useless upon the stage of life as most of Thackeray's " good " women, and she soon disappears; Middleton could not keep a good woman, even of the flabby variety, alive for more than a scene or two.

Dekker had not, apparently, been influenced by the earlier plays of the intrigue or realistic type, using " realistic " in its customary and misleading sense. Perhaps the demand for that sort of thing was not yet sufficiently strong; perhaps thus far his highly lyrical and morally idealistic temperament had been able to resist what was so alien to its very being. But in him there were two natures, that of the poet and that of the journalist; the latter first came into view in the prose of 1603 and 1604. The success of these works, together with the same external pressure to which Shakespere yielded, prepared him, I think, to receive the influence of Middleton.

The first extant play upon which they collaborated is " 1 Honest Whore," entered in Henslowe's " Diary "[8] in 1604,

[6] This play, in part a story of romantic love, contains a scene so morally impossible that it has puzzled the critics. The charitable view is that a scene may have dropped out. See Bullen's *Middleton*, vol. 1, p. 49; also his *Introd.*, XXII.

[7] Pointed out by Professor Thorndike. *The Influence of Beaumont and Fletcher on Shakespere*, pp. 102–3.

[8] Greg: before March 14. Fleay: about April.

probably in the spring, as by Dekker and Middleton. It was registered to print November 9 and was published the same year.[9] It may have been acted first after the fall of Ostend, September 8, 1604, for Hippolito's servant says to him, "Indeed, that's harder to come by than ever was Ostend,"[10] but such a reference to current events may have been put into the play at any time. As the two parts of the play form Dekker's most ambitious and sustained effort, and as they contain not only the broken lines of poetry that seems so spontaneously dramatic but also long verse speeches that appear carefully planned, like the debate between Hippolito and Bellafront, it is not unlikely that they took considerable time in the making. The two parts of the play have been spoken of together. It is the natural assumption that the second closely followed the first, especially since the second pre-supposes a knowledge of the first. Nor is it likely that Dekker should have waited a long time before availing himself of the popularity of the first, evidenced by the fact that a second edition was brought out in 1605. That the second part was entered on the Stationers' Register only on April 29, 1608, proves no more than does the fact that it was not published until 1630.[11] There are other reasons for an early date for the second part: the continuity of character, a certain parallelism of scenes, notably the Bedlam and the Bridewell scenes which close respectively the two parts, and the circumstance that both plays contain allusions to "Othello"[12] and to the fall of Ostend.[13] Fleay, to whom I owe the suggestion for the date of the second part and who

[9] *The Honest Whore, with the Humours of the Patient Man and the Longing Wife.*

[10] "Sheet E of the singularly correct and interesting edition of 1605 has the head-line of *The Converted Courtizan* throughout." *Memoir*, P., I, XXII, footnote.

[10] P., II, 55.

[11] *The Second Part of the Honest Whore, with the Humors of the Patient Man, the Impatient Wife: the Honest Whore persuaded by strong Arguments to turne Curtizan again: her brave refuting those Arguments. And lastly, the Comicall Passages of an Italian Bridewell, where the Scaene ends.*

[12] P., II, 4 and 114.

[13] P., II, 55 and 142.

mentions the allusions just referred to, adds that "Measure for Measure," 1603-4, and "2 Honest Whore"[14] both employ a contemporaneous statute "closing the suburb houses." He likewise adds that the 1600 soldiers "who went abroad scarce a year since" must refer to the 800 vagabonds seized in 1603 and sent aboard the Dutch fleet.[15]

Although Henslowe mentions Middleton as one of the authors of "The Honest Whore," his name does not appear upon the title-page of the edition of 1604 or that of 1605, and critics have found it hard to distinguish Middleton's part, some even doubting whether he had any share in it beyond "a few suggestions on the general conduct and groundwork of the play."[16]

In reading Middleton's comedies—straight through the list—one must be struck by the fact that certain situations, found also in "The Honest Whore," occur not once but over and over again. Courtesans are favorite characters, and a common device[17] is the marrying of one of them to a male character prominent in the story and just as far removed from a state of innocence; this is usually accomplished by means of a trick and the intent is humorous. In "A Trick to Catch the Old One," where almost all the characters are disreputable, the woman betrayed by Witgood is treated somewhat sympathetically in the first scene in which she appears; the "hero" employs her to further his own mercenary ends before he settles down to a "respectable" marriage, when she is wedded to an old man who believes her to be a rich widow. There is much the same sort of thing in "A Mad World, my Masters." In "A Chaste Maid in Cheapside," the situation reappears on a smaller scale. In "Michaelmas Term," it is varied when Andrew Little is forced to marry his own victim, the Country Wench. It is further to be noted that in all these cases, the woman promises henceforth to lead a regular life, although there is no evidence of conversion except possibly in "A Trick to Catch the Old One." One dramatist must have shown the other the way, and that one was surely Middleton. In the first

---

[14] P., II, 158.
[15] P., II, 167.
[16] P., I, *Memoir*, XXIII.
[17] Bullen speaks of this in his *Middleton*, I, *Introd.*, XXXIV.

place, he preceded Dekker in bringing such situations into a play. In "Blurt, Master Constable," Imperia, the courtesan, commands a far larger share of attention than Violetta, the legitimate heroine. The scene[18] in which Imperia talks with her attendants and afterwards admits her would-be suitors is pretty closely imitated by Dekker, though with less coarseness, in the scene[19] in which Bellafront is waited on by her servant Roger and receives Matheo and the other gallants. The scenes are similar and the general tone is similar.[20] In the second place, Middleton could have felt, to put it mildly, no repugnance for the society of the debased, for it was his chief interest for over ten years: Dekker, on the other hand, did not revert to such subjects either in his plays or in his voluminous prose, except in an incidental way. It must also be added that Middleton, though incapable of Dekker's humanity or poetry, had a more strenuous and persistent genius; he could follow up one success with a whole series of the same kind, he created a school, he was more of a leader than Dekker, who did not work one vein only and whose versatility has been so disconcerting to those who would neatly pigeon-hole his works.

But if Dekker felt the influences in the air and that of Middleton in particular, if he received from the same source direct suggestions as to the management of certain scenes, the individuality that had thus far marked his work did not fail him. In the unpromising material furnished by the story that Chapman had already treated with cynicism and that Middleton was later to repeat so often and so cheaply, Dekker's heart of compassion and his insight into human motives saw an opportunity; and the result is a play in which the chief interest is the transformation of a bad life into a good one, a conversion indeed, not the painless operation crowned with immediate material

[18] Bullen's *Middleton*, I, 33–36.

[19] P., II, 25–33.

[20] Bullen points out that there is a similarity between the scene in *The Honest Whore*, mentioned above, and that in *Michaelmas Term*, Act III, sc. 1, in which the Country Wench dresses to receive company. *Middleton*, I, *Introd.*, XXVI.

Fleay says that "aloof off" is a Middletonian phrase, but Dekker uses it in his preface to *News from Hell*, G., II, 90.

reward so common in the drama, but a slow process involving
the horror of past vileness, the anguish of rejected love, and
continued hunger, blows, and abuse,—a conversion, it may be
added, not at all unusual in the observation of present-day
social workers, however rare it may seem to cloistered critics.
True to nature is the device that makes Bellafront's love for
one who is good the means of her redemption, and equally true
is the mood in which Hippolito meets her, a mood heightened
by the supposed death of Infelice. Very characteristic of
Dekker is the great gentleness of his reply when Bellafront
urges, as his friends had done, that Infelice is dead and is therefore no longer any part of his life:

> " My vows to her fled after her to heaven.
> Were thine eyes clear as mine, thou might'st behold her
> Watching upon yon battlements of stars
> How I observe them. . . .
>   . . . Let it suffice,
> I ha' set thee in the path: is't not a sign
> I love thee when with one so most, most dear
> I'll have thee fellows? All are fellows there."

It is a pity that this spirit could not have dominated the rest
of Hippolito's life, but it must be acknowledged that his change
of rôle from saviour to tempter is dramatically conceived and
carried out, and that, as he does not become a blackguard, his
final emergence from the affair " untoucht" is convincing.
The formal argument between the two is faithful to dramatic
convention rather than to human nature, but it contains the
poignant contrast between innocence and shame so moving and
so natural on Bellafront's lips. Natural too is her attitude
towards her father, at once proud and humble, not permitting
Hippolito to blame him even by implication and answering
scornfully her husband's ill-natured attacks. It is true that
Bellafront is not an heroic or tragic character. She is eager
to satisfy a conventional morality by marrying the man who
betrayed her when a child, and, although she cannot be happy
with the gamester Matheo, she makes the best of a bad situation. But to put real vitality into such a character—not very
unusual in its general make-up—is perhaps a greater achieve-

ment than to portray a tragic heroine who should find only in her own death or that of another a sufficient reparation or revenge.

Closely connected with the story of Bellafront is that of Infelice. Her maiden loveliness is suggested with exquisite reserve in the opening scene, the very best illustration of Dekker's clear and vivid exposition, and in the scene in which she gradually wakens from her deathlike trance; and it appears again when Hippolito closes the doors against everything but his "ceremonious sorrow" and muses upon her picture.

> " My Infelice's face, her brow, her eye,
> The dimple on her cheek; and such sweet skill
> Hath from the cunning workman's pencil flown,
> These lips look fresh and lively as her own,
> Seeming to move and speak. 'Las! now I see
> The reason why fond women love to buy
> Adulterate complexion: here 'tis read,
> False colors last after the true be dead.
> Of all the roses grafted on her cheeks,
> Of all the graces dancing in her eyes,
> Of all the music set upon her tongue,
> Of all that was past woman's excellence
> In her white bosom, look! a painted board
> Circumscribes all."

Seventeen years later, as time goes in a play, the bright pure colors of Infelice's charm and Hippolito's devotion to her are neither so bright nor so pure. The gentleness suggested in the first part she still partly retains, especially in the scene in which Orlando puts into her hands proofs of her husband's would-be infidelity; but she does not deliquesce into a patient Grissill, and it is with indignant frankness that she shows Hippolito that unfaithfulness in the husband is the same as unfaithfulness in the wife and that it must end in the same way.

Of Orlando Friscobaldo, Hazlitt has spoken the final word. He ranks among the great characters of English comedy. Although his usual speech is whimsical, fantastic, and "mad," it sometimes becomes as simple and direct as a child's and its not infrequent roughness conceals a wise head and a heart of passionate tenderness. This is Dekker's second picture of happy old age. It is not negatively so: "I fill this hand, and empty this." And although it is a merry old age, it is near heaven: "I take heed how far I walk, because I know yonder's my home. I would not die like a rich man, to carry nothing away save a winding sheet: but like a good man, to leave Orlando behind me." And again: "When the bell shall toll for me, if I prove a swan, and go singing to my nest, why so!" His wife, though dead, has not departed: "She 's an old dweller in those high countries, yet not from me; here, she's here."

Matheo, although highly objectionable as a domestic character, is a creation almost as original and just as consistently carried out. He was born without a soul and never develops a conscience, yet he is endowed with a sort of irresponsible gaiety that makes one understand why he was able to retain the friendship of the respectable. He does a good turn for a comrade at one moment, to betray him the next. He is a liar as shameless as Falstaff, yet he carelessly confesses the truth when it is sure to lead to punishment; and he puts up with the prospect of a disgraceful death as readily as he accepts what he chooses to consider a disgraceful marriage. In the final scene of reconciliation Dekker does not disturb the integrity of his character by permitting him to "repent," allowing him merely to drop a little remark that evidences his desire to be on good terms with his rich and generous father-in-law.

"The Humors of the Patient Man and the Longing Wife" is hardly at all connected with the other plots. It was undoubtedly added for comic effect, and the situations in the first part are sufficiently amusing; but as Dekker really set a very high value upon the virtue of patience, Candido at times assumes genuine dignity of bearing and speech, which reaches its height in the well-known lines:

> "Patience, my lord! why, 'tis the soul of peace:
> Of all the virtues 'tis near'st kin to heaven.
> It makes men look like gods: the best of men
> That e'er wore earth about him, was a sufferer,
> A soft, meek, patient, humble, tranquil spirit,
> The first true gentleman that ever breathed."

In the second part, however, his "patience" in submitting to insult in the house of Matheo, is, to the modern point of view, more degrading than his yielding to his first wife's whims, for it amounts to cowardice. In this part, the ingenious Viola is replaced by a wife who "detests" ruling, a surprise that must have been effective to an audience mindful of her predecessor.

Though Dekker held the pen, it seems likely that the idea of the Candido plot sprang from the brain of Middleton, the more so as the former was not at all given to depicting humors and the latter was. Middleton, moreover, created two characters very much like Candido in their willingness to put up with almost anything, although their patience has not the moral incentive supplied by Dekker. The first is Quieto in "The Phoenix," who hears unmoved that an "abominable next neighbor" has taken his best carpet, and who is willing to give him the table too rather than go to law about the matter.[20a] The second is Water-Camlet in "Anything for a Quiet Life." Like Candido, he has a shop and submits to bullying customers; like Candido he has a quick-tongued wife and an honest apprentice named George. He figures in a scene[20b] in which gallants bargain and buy, very similar to a scene in "The Honest Whore";[21] and in each case, before the gallants enter, the shrewish wife is conspicuous. As the scene in "The Honest Whore" just referred to, together with a similar scene in which Viola's brother is the gallant,[22] have no parallel in Dekker's other work, they have been plausibly assigned to Middleton by Bullen.[23]

Both parts of the play are marred by some coarseness; yet it must be confessed that when Dekker makes a change in Bellafront's speech accompany a change in her heart, he is near to nature, and perhaps, however he may offend our taste, not very far from art. The closing scenes in each part, one

[20a] Bullen's *Middleton,* vol. I, p. 185 (Act IV, sc. 1). See also Bullen's remarks on Quieto, vol. I, *Introd.,* XXVIII.

[20b] Bullen's *Middleton,* vol. V, p. 268–279 (Act II, sc. 2).

[21] P., II, 17–24.

[22] P., II, 39–48.

[23] *Middleton,* I, *Introd.,* XXVI; together with "a few comic scenes" in Part II.

in a mad-house, the other in a house of correction, are an appeal
to the gallery, but to the present-day reader both are terrible
rather than comic; and perhaps they were to Dekker, too, for
this point of view is not forgotten but is put fittingly into the
mouth of Infelice:

> " Methinks this place,
> Should make even Lais honest."[24]

As far as "The Honest Whore" is concerned, we cannot
regret the influence exercised upon Dekker by contemporary
stage demands and by Middleton. The same thing cannot be
said of "Westward Ho"[25] and "Northward Ho,"[26] which,
though collaborated with Webster, exhibit Middletonian characteristics. They were published in 1607, but were written
somewhat earlier. "Westward Ho" was registered to print
March 2, 1605, as "presented by the Children of "Paul's,"
but it was probably acted towards the end of 1604. There
are two references to cold weather[27] towards the end of the
play and two to the length of the siege of Ostend. Of the
latter the first[28] is not important in itself, but the second,
taken with the first allusion and with one[29] that is very similar
in " I Honest Whore" seems to be significant. It runs as follows: "The book of the siege of Ostend, writ by one that
dropt in the action, will never sell so well as a report of the

[24] Of the Shakesperian reminiscences in this play, the most interesting is
to be found in the reflective character and in the speech of Hippolito,
which rather show the reaction of *Hamlet* upon Dekker's mind than anything so conscious as imitation. We hardly need to turn to *Romeo and
Juliet* for the situation of the lovers, but Father Anselmo plays a part
similar to that of Friar Lawrence. Characteristic of Dekker as it seems to
me, are the two allusions to *Othello,* which speak respectively of the
cruelty and the "blackness" of the Moor. For these and other reminiscences, see Koeppel and Fleay.

[25] *West-ward Hoe. As it hath beene divers times Acted by the Children
of Paules. Written by Tho: Decker, and John Webster.*

[26] *North-ward Hoe. Sundry times Acted by the Children of Paules. By
Thomas Decker and John Webster.*

[27] " I doubt we shall have a frost this night," (P., II, 340), and the other
in Clare's speech (p. 356).

[28] " How long will you hold out, think you? not so long as Ostend?"
(P., II, 284).

[29] " Indeed that's harder to come by than ever was Ostend." (P. II, 55).

siege between this grave, this wicked elder and thyself."[30]   On
September 20, 1604, there was actually entered on the Stationer's Register a book entitled "A remarkable and true history of the siege of Ostend on either side until this present."[31]
If Dekker meant this book, it was probably after its publication
though not so long after as to hinder his using the future
tense; but the whimsical "by one that dropt in the action,"
makes the reference doubtful. As "Westward Ho" was followed up by the "Eastward Ho" of Chapman, Marston and
Jonson, in an effort to trade upon the popularity of the
former,[32] it is not likely that a long interval separated them.
But "Eastward Ho" was registered to print September 4,
1605, and may have been acted some months before. In the
absence of anything more convincing, November or December,
1604, would seem to fit the circumstances better than a much
earlier or later date; possibly it was acted December 21, for
one of the characters asks, "Will you make the townsmen
think that Londoners never come hither but upon St. Thomas's
night?"[33]

The date of "Northward Ho" is more uncertain. It was
not registered until August 6, 1607. But as it was a reply
to "Eastward Ho,"[34] and as its main object was to ridicule
Chapman, who may have had the largest share in writing that
play, it would naturally follow it rapidly; delay in such a case
would have been contrary to Dekker's temperament; we know
that he could write prose with unusual rapidity,[35] and there is
little else in "Northward Ho." This assumption of swift
reply is contradicted by nothing in or out of the play,[36] which

[30] P., II, 339.

[31] Professor Thorndike points out that such a book was published in 1604.
Beaumont and Fletcher, 71, footnote.

[32] See *Prologue, Eastward Ho.*

[33] P., II, 353.

[34] The relations between these three plays and the circumstance that
Northward Ho satirizes Chapman were first made clear by Fleay. Stoll
continues the discussion. *Webster,* 15–16, 65–70.

[35] *The Seven Deadly Sins* in seven days.

[36] Day's *Isle of Gulls* mentions the three plays in the induction but it is
not known whether it was first acted in 1605 or 1606. Stoll's plea for
1606 is not convincing.

may therefore be roughly dated 1605, possibly the earlier half of that year.[37]

In spite of no uncertain signs of popularity, these plays did not greatly commend themselves to at least one of the authors, for Dekker's name is misspelled upon the title-pages and the plays were not reprinted during his lifetime—facts that acquire importance when we remember that he took a great deal of pains with the 1605 edition of "The Honest Whore," and wrote a preface for that stage-show," "The Whore of Babylon," while the prose published between 1606 and 1609 is for the most part well edited. Whoever sent these plays to the press did not take the slight trouble of levelling "Moll" and "Clare," names by which Mistress Tenterhook[38] is variously known. For the first of the two plays, moreover, Dekker—or Dekker and Webster—felt the need of a sort of apology. The former had a habit of apologizing for work that he believed to be inferior; for the satirical portions of "Satiromastix," for instance, for "The Roaring Girl," and for some of his later prose and non-dramatic verse. The passage in "Westward Ho" runs as follows: "Have amongst you, city dames! You that are indeed the fittest and most proper persons for a comedy, nor let the world lay any imputation upon my disguise, for Court, City, and Country are merely as masks one to the other, envied of some, laught at of others, and so to my comical business."[39] Maybery, also, in "Northward Ho," insists upon a "comical" interpretation of his revenge: "A comedy, a Canterbury tale, smells not half so sweet as the comedy I have for thee, old poet: thou shalt write upon't, poet."[40] In connection with this point of view it should be borne in mind that in 1603 Dekker had made an excursion into satire upon women in "The Bachelor's Banquet," from

[37] Fleay's date, c. February, 1605, has, so far as I know, nothing to substantiate it.

[38] Fleay is wrong in saying that both names were given to Mistress Justiniano, who is "Moll" indeed, but who is not named till near the end of Act IV. Mistress Tenterhook becomes Clare in Act II, sc. 3, and resumes the name in Act V. Elsewhere she is "Moll."

[39] P., II, 288.

[40] P., III, 52.

which indeed he borrowed some of the situations in these
comedies: in the first chapter, a wife reminds her husband that
she might have made a better marriage, as does Justiniano's
wife in "Westward Ho";[41] in the second chapter, there is an
account of the ways in which an intriguing wife may leave
home unsuspected, including the device of visiting a sick child
in the country, employed in "Westward Ho";[42] in chapter
six, a lover watches his mistress at church just as the Earl
watches Mistress Justiniano.[43]

"Westward Ho" is in the main an intrigue play bearing
some resemblance in its general plan to "The Merry Wives of
Windsor"[44] but much lower in moral tone: the three idle
women married to London citizens lead their lovers on to an
exposure of their villainy, and incidentally the immorality of
the husbands comes out. At the end there is a monstrous
condoning of the past all around. But the play is partly redeemed by the episode of Mistress Justiniano and the Earl,
treated with true tragic feeling and in poetry that sometimes
rises to a high level. The best scene in the play is that in
which the former, hounded on and deserted by her Italian husband, consents to an interview with the Earl. One look at his
face shows her the true horror of the situation, and to his
flood of eloquence the unsophisticated girl can only answer,
"I wonder lust can hang at such white hairs"; and as he continues to talk, reiterate with natural dramatic strategy, "I will
think upon't. I will think upon't." Worthy of mention too
is the Earl's soliloquy in which he poignantly presents the
allurement of pleasure and the worst sting of evil-doing.
Characteristic of Dekker, I think, is the recognition of the
haughty joy of asceticism:

> "Why even those that starve in voluntary wants,
> And to advance the mind, keep the flesh poor,
> The world enjoying them, they not the world,
> Would they do this but that they're proud to suck
> A sweetness from such sourness?"

[41] P., II, 287. Noticed by Pierce, *Collaboration of Webster and Dekker*,
p. 37.

[42] P., II, 312. Noticed by Pierce, 53 and 111.

[43] P., II, 304.

[44] For Stoll's view of this resemblance, see his *Webster*, 76–78.

"Northward Ho" has no redeeming feature of poetry, beauty or deep feeling, but the humor is more genial than that of "Westward Ho"; and the satire upon Chapman is entirely goodnatured. It consists in putting him as Bellamont into ridiculous situations and bantering him upon his white hair, his learning, classical and otherwise, his preference in his dramas for French subjects, and his making his audience "all fools" in his play of that name. It is probable that Dekker, who was acquainted with Chapman's comedies and very likely with the poet himself, saw no impropriety in this satire which has so stirred the wrath of some critics. It may be added for their comfort that to "Bellamont" is given virtually all the good sense and wisdom, such as it is, in the play: he is the confidant of the jealous Maybery and of his jealous wife, and he satisfies both that their jealousy is unfounded; his reverend appearance converts Doll Hornet from her evil life, and, finally, it was not he who had to pay the expense of that journey northward.

While these plays throw incidental light upon some manners and customs of the time, and while they illustrate Dekker's facile and direct prose, they would be of small importance in his literary history if it were not that they constitute a departure from his usual work. Except in a few passages in "Westward Ho," not one of his great traits as an artist appears: there is not a single character that one can remember, —no gentle woman or idealizing lover, no hearty master or loyal servant, not even a plausible ne'er-do-well or boisterous exponent of goodness. There is neither tenderness nor indignation and but little insight into the human heart. In that medium of intrigue Dekker's genius folded its wings and permitted his unlucky cleverness to have its way. In both plays he freely plagiarizes from himself, both in character and in situation,[45] and in every case he degrades his original; even so minor a character as Sir Giles Glowworm, as pointed out by Fleay,[46] is a debased Captain Tucca, who has no business in

---

[45] See Mr. Stoll's *Webster*, 72–76, for a long list of parallelisms. It seems to me that Mr. Stoll's ardor for parallels has led him astray in the interpretation of some facts and some characters.

[46] *Chr.*, art. *Webster*.

the play except to furnish a low sort of humor in the scene with Birdlime. The dialogue contains innuendo and coarseness of the common kind, though not the grossness of Jonson, Middleton, and Marston, which no care can enable the reader to avoid. More serious is the easy Middletonian treatment of the whole subject of morality: the final reconciling of persons who have every reason for hating each other, and a sort of fog that keeps the reader from finding out how good— or how bad—the people really are. While it would be easy to take too seriously these rapidly written and half-farcical plays, the fact remains that the playwright who in 1600 had felt honest pride in the clean mirth of " The Shoemaker's Holiday," was sinning against light. Of course, in what has been called "theatrical journalism," Dekker, as indicated earlier in the chapter, was not alone. His collaborator Webster was never free from it except in the chilliest of all his plays, and during approximately the time in which the two intrigue comedies came out, were written or acted Marston's " Malcontent," " The Dutch Courtezan," and " The Fawn "—plays so miasmatic at times as to compel a stiff walk among the hills to restore the reader's normal enjoyment of life and literature. "Eastward Ho," to which the adjective "sympathetic" is often applied, seems to me pretty bad, including as it does the ugly motive of making a husband betray his own wife, and closing with a procession of unreal conversions, which has at the head a prodigal preaching in prison with all the ardor and convincing force of Pecksniff.

The vexed question of Webster's part in these plays has hardly been settled.[47] To me it seems clear, though once again "the doctors think otherwise," that he had a considerable share in the plots. The two men were friends and collaborators of several years' standing and they undoubtedly discussed the story. Dekker doubtless needed aid, for he nowhere exhibits skill in the invention of plots, either taking the outline of his fable from a definite source or employing a series of simple normal events hardly elaborate enough to deserve the name of

[47] Fleay, Swinburne and Sidney Lee have briefly expressed themselves upon this subject; E. E. Stoll at greater length in his *John Webster;* and F. E. Pierce in *The Collaboration of Webster and Dekker.*

plot. I should therefore be inclined to assign to Webster the more unusual, subtle or abnormal elements: the device of the diamond in "Westward Ho" and that of the ring in "Northward Ho," perhaps also Greeneshield's betrayal of his wife, although that may have been borrowed from "Eastward Ho."[48] Justiniano's disguise as "a hideous hag" shows an un-Dekkeresque taste for the horrible. Again, the fierce jealousy of Justiniano in one play and of Maybery in the other is wholly unlike Dekker,[49] whose one jealous husband, Cordolente,[50] is a piece of helpless and despairing inefficiency. Again, it would be curious to find in a play of London life by Dekker two Italians and a servant with an Italian name.[51]

The two plays do not present just the same problem. "Westward Ho" reads less like the collaboration of the two men upon one piece than like the building up of their collaborated part about an independent fragment previously composed; as if Dekker, repeating in part the history of "Satiromastix," had begun a serious play in which the Earl was to occupy the chief place, but in the midst of it, either getting stalled or in immediate need of money, had turned the material over to Webster, who created Justiniano, and as Fleay suggests, wrote the greater part of the first three acts[52] and a portion of the fourth, at that point handing the play back to Dekker for completion. The Earl scenes are not well dovetailed into the intrigue drama: it is strange, for example, to find Mistress Justiniano speaking of her home as "her own Paradise" at the very time when her husband has sold the roof over her head and turned her adrift. And again, although Justiniano is made to say that his wife is going to give proof of her innocence, we are entirely unprepared to find her, after the terrible awakening of the first interview with the Earl,

[48] But not by Dekker.
[49] Mr. Pierce speaks of this.
[50] In *Match Me in London*.
[51] The Earl, Justiniano, and Boniface.
[52] Fleay seems to give the poetry to Webster, but every other critic has recognized it as Dekker's; his division has the merit of taking note of the seasons and the weather, which, in this play, are conspicuous enough for the reader to remember independently of Fleay's remarks.

submitting herself to a second and even to his kisses;[53] we do not, in fact, believe it. The whole scene reads like hasty and sensational joiner's work.

"Northward Ho," on the contrary, was evidently a continuous performance, and is without unusual features as a piece of collaboration. To Fleay's ascription to Dekker of the satire on Chapman and of the Doll scenes no objection can be made; and it is not unreasonable to believe, with him, that the rest of the play belongs to Webster, for in both motive and situation it rather resembles the work of the younger than the older man. In both plays, however, it seems not improbable that the more experienced playwright went rapidly over the whole, altering here and adding there.[54]

Since it has been necessary to dwell upon these plays, let the discussion close with a boating song that one could wish removed from its place at the end of "Westward Ho." It was sung, we remember, by the young voices of Paul's boys.

> "Oars, oars, oars, oars!
> To London hey, to London hey!
> Hoist up sails and let's away,
> For the safest bay
> For us to land is London shores.
>
> Oars, oars, oars, oars!
> Quickly shall we get to land
> If you, if you, if you,
> Lend us but half a hand.
> O lend us half a hand!"[55]

[53] P., II, 335–336.

[54] See Mr. Pierce's book for a different point of view. Like Stoll, whose material he uses, he gives Dekker credit for the plot and "everything of real literary value—whether serious or comic" (p. 132), and he sees "his hand" or at least his "influence" in every single scene (p. 131). His various tests, the most important of which is a mathematical comparison of Dekker's preference for short swift words with Webster's liking for a more sonorous and latinized diction, substantially agree in giving to the latter "a considerable part and probably by far the greater part," in *Westward Ho,* of Act I, sc. 1, Act III, sc. 3, and probably Act I, sc. 2, and Act III, sc. 2; and, in *Northward Ho,* Act I, sc. 1, Act II, sc. 2, and the first half of Act V. As far as it goes, this assignment agrees with that of Fleay, but it does not go very far.

[55] Another song mentioned on p. 335 is not preserved.

Dekker's direct collaboration with Middleton did not close with "The Honest Whore," but there was a gap of many years before the writing of their next play, "The Roaring Girl." Although involving a break in the chronological order usually observed in this study, it seems best to speak of the play in this chapter, both on account of the collaboration and on account of the intrigue sub-plot sometimes wrongly attributed to Dekker.[56] Besides, unless there are lost plays—and there is no trace of any—"The Roaring Girl" followed next after "Northward Ho"; between 1606 and 1610 he was writing prose. It was printed in 1611[57] and the title-page tells us that it had lately been acted at the Fortune by the Prince's players, the same company that, about 1607, were playing the revised "Whore of Babylon." The title-page also bears the rather significant and perhaps apologetic motto: "My case is altered, I must work for my living." The prologue tells us that the play had been expected long,[58] and the epilogue that some of the audience may look

> "For all those base tricks publish'd in a book,
> Foul as his brains they flow'd from, of cut-purse[s],
> Of nips and foists, nasty obscene discourses,
> As full of lies as empty of worth or wit,
> For any honest ear or eye unfit."[59]

The only book concerning Moll Cut-purse known to have been written before 1611 is John Day's "Mad Pranks of Merry Moll of the Bankside," registered to print August 7, 1610, but not known to have been published. It is impossible to tell whether it was a source of the play in question, or the bad book referred to in the epilogue, or neither. Near its close the epilogue promises another play on the same subject:

[56] As by Mr. Stoll and Mr. Pierce.
[57] *The Roaring Girle, or Moll Cut-Purse. As it hath lately beene Acted on the Fortune-stage by the Prince his Players. Written by T. Middleton and T. Dekkar.*
[58] P., III, 131.
[59] P., III, 233–234. Middleton's address "To the Comic Play-Readers" would seem to refer to the same book. This address, not found in Pearson, is printed in Bullen's edition of *The Roaring Girl* in *Middleton's Works*, IV, 7–8.

" The Roaring Girl herself some few days hence
Shall on this stage give larger recompense."[60]

It is clear that by 1610, when Day's book was registered, the
general character of the heroine must have been well known;
and to this date the play may pretty confidently be assigned.[61]
It could not have been written much earlier, for Mary Frith,
the heroine, was not born before the middle or later eighties
of the sixteenth century; nor is it likely that it was written in
the year of publication, for by February, 1612, Chamberlain
describes Mary as doing penance at Paul's Cross, very penitent
but maudlin drunk,—a condition of affairs that probably did
not begin at just that date and that would have interfered seriously with the sympathetic interpretation of her character that
Dekker and Middleton thought suitable for the stage.[62] The
argument for 1610 would apply nearly as well to 1609, were
it not for two important circumstances: first, there was a
severe outbreak of the plague during 1609, that, in the case of
a doubtful play, "makes 1610 rather than 1609 a probable
date ";[63] second, during 1609 Dekker wrote four prose works,
one of them being of such a character as to forbid our classing
it among his rapidly written compositions. It would seem that
in 1610 Middleton and Dekker planned to collaborate on a play
that should utilize the public interest in an unusual character,
giving to the subject a kindly interpretation and incorporating
in it a slight romantic comedy of Dekker's creation and an
intrigue sub-plot of Middleton's. Dekker also planned to employ on the stage some of the material on the lives and language
of rogues that he had already used in his " Bellman " books.[64]

[60] Field's *Amends for Ladies,* 1611, fulfills the requirements of this description so far as a part of the title is concerned: " With the Merry Pranks
of Moll Cut-Purse "; but the play, not published till 1618, now contains but
one slight scene with Moll in it. So Fleay.

[61] Fleay's date, 1604, has nothing to recommend it.

[62] See Bullen's *Introduction* to *The Roaring Girl,* 3–6, for the facts given
in the paragraph above, and for some other data derived from a prose work
published in 1662, entitled *The Life and Death of Mrs. Mary Frith, Commonly called Mal Cutpurse. Exactly collected and now Published for the
delight and recreation of all Merry disposed persons.*

[63] Professor Thorndike, *Beaumont and Fletcher,* 30.

[64] For the exhibition of thieving cant in the play, see P., III, 216–222.
For the *Bellman* books, see below, ch. 7.

At this point appeared a book on Moll, whether by Day or another, that perhaps roused a double indignation, first as "vile and full of lies," and second, as forestalling, to some extent, their own play. The title shows that "The Roaring Girl" was printed soon after it was acted; this, indeed, must have been necessary for the reputation of the authors, since another play on the same subject was shortly to appear.

Bullen, whose material I have freely used, leaves little to be desired in his division of labor between Dekker and Middleton.[65] The distribution of the three plots has been indicated; no one who has happened to read these two playwrights at about the same time will quarrel with the judgment that gives Middleton credit for the intrigue plot, but as this has been done, I will quote from Bullen:

"The very names of the characters—Laxton, Goshawk, Greenwit, Gallipot, etc.,—are evidences in his favor. This style of nomenclature, which Middleton commonly adopted in his comedies, was not affected by Dekker. Then the characters are just such as we find in other plays of Middleton. Mistress Gallipot may be compared with Mistress Purge in 'The Family of Love' or with Falso's Daughter in 'The Phoenix'; and Mistress Openwork, the jealous scold, is a repetition of Mistress Glister in 'The Family of Love.' The dialogue is conducted with Middleton's usual smartness and rapidity. . . . The feigning of the pre-contract in the second scene is a repetition of the device in 'A Trick to Catch the Old One'; the conduct of Laxton and Gallipot is precisely the same as that of Witgood and Hoard."[66]

One might add the purely negative argument that if the intrigue plot is not given to Middleton, there will be little left for him except the scene at Sir Alexander's;[67] this, I agree with Bullen, should be assigned to him, but chiefly because it would hardly seem that Dekker could have written a love scene without some touch of tenderness on one side or the

[65] *Middleton, I, Introd.,* XXXV–XXXVII. He gives to Dekker, Act I (P., III, 137–150), Act II, sc. 2 (P., 163–169), and Act V (P., III, 211–232). Though he gives the greater part of Act III (P., III, 169–194) to Middleton, he is doubtful about the meeting of the lovers (P., 194–200), but "inclines" to Middleton; the next scene (p. 200–211) is Middleton's but the rhymes at the end are Dekker's.

[66] *Introd.* to *Middleton's Works,* I, XXXV–XXXVII. See also Arthur Symons, *Cam. Hist. Eng. Lit.,* VI, 74–75.

[67] P., III, 104–200.

other, or some kindly natural words between the two girls so situated.

As usual with Dekker, the opening scenes make clear the situation, and to the lover of poetry they are the most attractive in the play. Characteristic is the one engaging feature in the mercenary old father, the pleasure he takes in the adornment of his parlor and galleries:

> " The furniture that doth adorn this room
> Cost many a fair gray groat ere it came here,
> But good things are most cheap when they're most dear.
> Nay, when you look into my galleries,
> How bravely they are trimm'd up, you all shall swear
> You're highly pleas'd to see what's set down there:
> Stories of men and women, mixt together,
> Fair ones with foul, like sunshine in wet weather.
> Within one square a thousand heads are laid
> So close, that all of heads the room seems made;
> As many faces there, fill'd with blithe looks,
> Shew like the promising titles of new books,
> Writ merrily, the readers being their own eyes,
> Which seem to move and to give plaudities:
> And here and there, whilst with obsequious ears
> Throng'd heaps do listen, a cut-purse thrusts and leers
> With hawk's eyes for his prey: I need not shew him;
> By a hanging villanous look, yourselves may know him,
> The face is drawn so rarely. Then, sir, below,
> The very floor, as 't were, waves to and fro,
> And like a floating island seems to move
> Upon a sea bound in with shores above."

Characteristic of Dekker, too, are the "antic" verbal tricks of the Lylian servant Neatfoote; and, in the same scene, the idea of betrothed love as a knot tied by heaven.[68] Another familiar idea that comes to the front is the hatred of forced marriage, found in his prose and two of his plays,[69] and here put into the mouth of Sebastian. In Sir Alexander we have an old man, a favorite character with Dekker, but not of the type he liked best to portray, so little inspiring indeed that after the first scene his creator could not succeed in making him speak verse that rises above mediocrity. All criticism of the

[68] In *Satiromastix*, P., I, 249–250, this idea is twice expressed.
[69] *The Witch of Edmonton* and *The Wonder of a Kingdom*.

poetry, however, Dekker or Middleton forestalled in the prologue:

> " Only we entreat you think our scene
> Cannot speak high, the subject being but mean;
> A Roaring Girl, whose notes till now ne'er were,
> Shall fill with laughter our vast theatre.
> That's all which I dare promise.

But the chief interest of the play centers in Moll, of whom Middleton finely said in his address to the Reader: " Worse things, I must needs confess, the world has taxed her for than has been written of her; but 'tis the excellency of a writer to leave things better than he finds 'em."[70] Dekker makes her a big, athletic, courageous woman, honest in all senses of the word, endowed with the hawk's eye and the alert mind of a born detective, rather contemptuous of both men and women, preferring the comradeship of men, but resolved to remain " the head of herself." To her the jest of the whole story lies in Sir Alexander's misconception of her character:

> " He was in fear his son would marry me,
> But never dreamt that I would ne'er agree."

But she is glad to give help and pity to " poor ring-doves," and it affords her keen delight to save riotous but foolish Jack Dapper from the Counter, the " university " to which his father had plotted to send him. In times that must have been very bad for unprotected women, she maintains herself by her wit and spirit: " Base is that mind that kneels unto her body"; and she gives a thorough drubbing to the cowards who had thought ill of her and had made a practice of slandering women. It is a pity that Dekker thought it necessary to put so much " realistic " language into her mouth, but in spite of this circumstance, in many ways she strikes a modern note: she is a live human being first and afterwards a woman, possessed of unconventional tastes and of physical strength sufficient to protect herself from insult, but not therefore depraved. In the play, she is found in all sorts of society, from that of the professional cheat whom she exposes, to that of Mary Fitz-

[70] Bullen's *Middleton*, IV, 8.

Allard and Sir Alexander, but she remains throughout a consistent character, never the extraordinary medley we find in "The Fair Maid of the West," good as are some portions of that lively yarn.

At the close of this period of six years we must remind ourselves that Dekker was no longer writing for Henslowe alone, although choice or circumstances were still taking him most often to the Fortune. The long Henslowe connection, lasting from 1598 to the end of 1602, had been broken by but one play that we know of, "Satiromastix," written for the Chamberlain's men. If Dekker produced any plays in 1603, they have not come down to us. During the spring of 1604 he sold "I Honest Whore" to Henslowe, and it was accordingly played at the Fortune by the Prince's servants, who succeeded the Admiral's men; presumably the second part took the same path as the first. Then, probably in 1604 and 1605, came "Westward Ho" and "Northward Ho," both written for Paul's boys and acted by them. The period of prose that followed these plays was interrupted, so far as we know, only by the revival of "The Whore of Babylon" in 1607 by the Prince's men at the Fortune; and there, after another interval of prose, was produced under the same direction "The Roaring Girl."

CHAPTER VII

THE PERIOD OF PROSE

In 1603, we remember, Dekker first began to write prose, achieving at once the brilliant success of "The Bachelor's Banquet," which he followed up in 1604 by "The Wonderful Year." A man entirely dependent upon pen and inkhorn might well be forgiven for working this newly discovered vein, but he continued to produce plays through 1604 and 1605. The following year he turned again to prose, which he wrote uninterruptedly for four years. During this period theatrical conditions were changing somewhat: about 1607 or 1608 the children's companies were breaking up; and popular tastes seemed best pleased, on one side, by the comedy of the Middletonian or Jonsonian order, on another by the romances of Beaumont and Fletcher, so overwhelmingly successful that Shakespere followed the trail they blazed. It would seem that Dekker did not care to continue the sort of comedy attempted in "Westward Ho" and "Northward Ho," and it was only later that he felt the influence of the romances. But possibly his ceasing to write plays arose solely from the fact that prose paid better. However this may be, he seems inclined, both at the beginning and at the close of his prose period, to think that playwrights had a pretty hard lot. In 1607 he wrote of poets, by which he means playwrights: "I know the Lady Pecunia and you come very hardly together, and therefore trouble not you: upon this ancient theater[1] you present your tragical scenes, for here you shall be sure to be clapt";[2] and in 1609 when the plague was raging worse than usual, he complained:

"Playhouses stand like taverns that have cast out their masters, the doors locked up, the flags, like their bushes, taken down; or rather like houses lately infected, from whence the affrighted dwellers are fled, in hope to live better in the country. The players themselves did never work till now;

[1] The debtor's prison.
[2] *Jests to Make You Merry*, G., II, 353.

115

there Comedies are all turned to Tragedies, there Tragedies to Nocturnals, and the best of them all are weary of playing in those Nocturnal Tragedies. Think you to delight yourselves by keeping company with our poets? Proh dolor! their Muses are more sullen than old monkeys, now that money is not stirring; they never plead cheerfully but in their term times when the two-penny clients and penny stinkards swarm together to hear the Stager-ites. . . . O pitiful Poetry, what a lamentable prenticeship hast thou served and, which is the greatest spite, canst not yet be made free."[3]

Of Dekker's life between 1606 and 1610 little is known except what can be learned from his writings. It is likely that the friendship for Middleton, Webster, and Day, which, in all three cases, looked "before and after," was still a source of pleasure; and there were others, among them the unknown "M. R." and "E. G." who wrote commendatory verses for "Lanthorn and Candlelight." Dekker continued poor; lightly and as a matter of course he affirms that in the war between Money and Poverty he served on the side of the latter.[4] It appears, too, that as the years went by, he did not grow richer for appeal to a patron, a procedure that he despised in 1604, was more and more resorted to, though always in a way that shows how deeply he resented its "baseness." But we may be sure that Dekker was not in desperate straits between 1606 and 1610, for when such a time really arrived, both his personal speech and the tone of his writing indicate the true state of affairs. Besides what he received from his prose, presumably he had something from the four plays printed in 1607. The usual price of plays seems to have been, according to Bullen, sixpence a copy, but that does not clear up the more interesting question of Dekker's receipts. We do not know just what calls he had upon his purse, but at least, with no resource but his pen,[5] he managed to keep out of the debtor's prison and to maintain a generally happy spirit. He continued to be "in-dustrious"; for if some of his books were written with extra-ordinary rapidity, like "The Seven Deadly Sins," it is equally certain that others, such as the exposure books, were the result

[3] *Work for Armorers*, G., IV, 96–97.

[4] *Epis.-Ded., Work for Armorers*, G., IV, 89.

[5] There is the possibility that he did some of the odd jobs for which a literary man is fitted, such as preparing manuscript for the press, but there is no evidence that he did so.

of prolonged labor, and the artist's heart and hand must have worked slowly at his book of prayers.

Although Dekker's epistles-dedicatory and other prefaces tell very few facts, they are saturated with personality and reflect his permanent attitude towards some aspects of life as well as his mood at the time of writing. Fortunately his epistles do not always fulfil his own requirement for such a composition,—"an epistle just the length of a hench-man's grace before dinner, which is long enough for any book in conscience, unless the writer be unreasonable."[6] But unfortunately from the view-point of this study, Dekker had no great liking for the personal dedication. This is shown in several ways. Although it is believed that he supervised the printing of his most important plays, including "Old Fortunatus," "The Shoemaker's Holiday," "Satiromastix," and both parts of "The Honest Whore," as well as "The Whore of Babylon," he dedicated but one to a patron; and that dedication was written late in his life.[7] Three of his pageants are dedicated, naturally enough, to the mayors of London in whose honor they were written. Six of the prose works are without the epistle-dedicatory. The one prefixed to "The Wonderful Year," was, as we have seen, addressed to a friend, who might have as much of the author's love as he desired "for nothing"; and the book, asserted Dekker, was "free from any vile imputation" except that it was bold enough to demand acquaintance. In the dedication of "Canaan's Calamity," he avoids the appearance of addressing a patron for pecuniary reward by explaining that his book is "an unfeigned token of our good affection" for favors "shewed in the depth of extremity to some poor friends of mine, remaining in your pleasant lordship of High-cleere." He likewise dedicates "A Knight's Conjuring" to one who had shown him a personal kindness. But for the most part a tone of apology runs through his epistles,[8] usually for the fashion he is following, often for the quality of his work, and once, at

[6] *Lanthorn and Candlelight*, G., III, 240–241.
[7] In 1631 for *Match Me in London*.
[8] See especially the *Epis.-Ded.* of *News from Hell*, G., II, 87–88. Also the dedication of *The Dead Term*, G., IV, 7–8, and of *Canaan's Calamity*, G., I, 5.

least, for going to the press so often. I quote one typical passage:

"It may happily seem strange unto you that such an army of idle words should march into the open field of the world under the ensign of your name: you being not therewith made acquainted till now; you may judge it in me an error; I myself confess it a boldness. But such an ancient and strong charter hath custom confirmed to this printing age of ours, by giving men authority to make choice of what patrons they like, that some writers do almost nothing contrary to the custom, and some by virtue of that privilege dare do anything. I am neither of that first order, nor of this last. The one is too fondly ceremonious, the other too impudently audacious. I walk in the midst, so well as I can, between both: with some fruits that have grown out of my brain, have I been so far from being in love that I thought them not worthy to be tasted by any particular friend, and therefore have they been exposed only to those that would entertain them: neither did I think the fairest that ever was mine so worthy that it was to be looked upon with the eye of universal censure."[9]

There is comparatively little flattery in these dedications; sometimes indeed Dekker is simply blunt, as when he offers his contest between Money and Poverty to Thomas Hewet in the following terms: "Let it not appear strange that from the Regiment of Knights Military I make choice of you to be a chief in the best of these armies, you being no professed warrior. But I myself serve on the one side, and the world marks you out to be an able commander in the other."[10] It is very significant that Dekker's one epistle positively overflowing with enthusiasm and humility is addressed to another poet; incidentally it shows his insight into the true values of life. I quote the greater part of the dedication of "The Dead Term" to "the very Worthy, Learned, Judicious, and Noble Gentleman, Sir John Harington, Knight":

"Sir, the love which your immortal Ariosto tells to the world that you really bear to divine (but now poor and contemned) Poesie, hath a long time made me an honorer of those bright ascending virtues in you, which those holy and pure flames of her have kindled in your bosom. Happy you are by birth, happy by your bringing up, but most happy in that the Muses were your nurses, to whom you have been so tender that they make you an elder son and heir of their goodliest possessions. So that your love to them hath drawn from others an honorable love and regard of you."[11]

[9] *Lanthorn and Candlelight*, G., III, 177–178.
[10] *Work for Armorers*, G., IV, 89.
[11] G., IV, 7.

Similar, though less enthusiastic, is the letter to the dramatist Lodowick Carlell in 1631.[12] If these two epistles show one of Dekker's chief passions, that prefixed to "The Dove," the first part of his book of prayers, shows another,—his ardor for moral beauty:

"Sir, I present unto your view a book of prayers; not that you need my weak instructions for you are known to be a good proficient in God's school and have more of this heavenly language in you by heart than I can teach you by precept. . . . Four birds of Noah's Ark have taken four several flights. The Dove, which is the first, flies to your hand; not by chance, but upon good choice, as knowing you to be a dove yourself. The badge which a dove wears is innocence: and by wearing that Christian armor you defended yourself, and returned safe out of the Lion's den with Daniel, when it was thought you should have been devoured. God hath since heaped graces on your head, and by the hands of his Anointed hath rewarded you with deserved honors in the self-same place into which you were thrown to be swallowed up by destruction. Receive therefore, I beseech you, a Dove, sithence her harmless and spotless wings have carried you over such great danger to so great happiness."[13]

However modest Dekker was in the presence of really great merit like that of the translator of Ariosto, he sometimes followed the practice of his contemporaries by promising immortality to the patron whose name he employed. The following passage from the epistle prefixed to "The Seven Deadly Sins" I quote, partly to illustrate this rather unusual expression of confidence in himself, and partly to use material not readily accessible :[14]

"I am sorry, dear Sir, that in a time so abundant with wit, I should send unto you no better fruit than the sins of a city: but they are not common, for they were never gathered till this year, and therefore I send them for the rarity: yet now I remember myself, they are not the sins of a city, but only the picture of them. And a drollery, or Dutch piece of lantskop, may sometimes breed in the beholder's eye as much delectation as the best and most curious master-piece excellent in that art. Books being sent abroad after they are begotten into the world, as this of mine is, are in the nature of orphans; but being received into a guardianship, (as I make no doubt but that this shall), they come into the happy state of adopted

---

[12] P., IV, 133.
[13] G., V, 5–6.
[14] This dedication, not found in Grosart's edition, is given in the Cambridge edition. It is addressed to Henry Fermor, Esquire, Clerk of the Peace to the County of Middlesex.

children. That office must now be yours, and you need not be ashamed of it, for kings have been glad to do them honor, that ha⁻ː bestowed such a never-dying honor upon them. The benefit you shall receive is this, that you see the building up of a tomb, in your lifetime, wherein you are sure so to lie as that you cannot be forgotten; and you read that very epitaph that shall stand over you, which by no envy can be defaced, nor by any time worn out."

Dekker's general prefaces are often informal little essays upon subjects that he felt strongly about at the time of writing, and so he naturally gave freer rein to his wit and fantasy. In the address " To the World " prefixed to " Satiromastix," we have seen him justly angry and scornful; something of the same mood is seen in his later prefaces when he scoffs at the ignorant critic and the ignorant reader, though usually in a gay and lively manner. Many of the prefaces are addressed to appropriate classes. The first of these is the modest and serious little speech to the " Professors of the Gentle Craft of what degree soever ";[15] another is addressed to " Soldiers,"[16]—" a name more full of ancient honor, or of more honorable worth I cannot speak "; the first of the popular exposure pamphlets[17] is dedicated to magistrates and good citizens; the second exposure book[18] adjures his " own Nation " to come to the defence of " Law, Justice, Order, Ceremony, Religion, Peace, and that honorable title of Goodness "; a plague book written in 1625 has a preface " To the Reader that flies, the Reader that stays, the Reader lying in a haycock, the hard-hearted Country-Reader, and the broken-hearted City-Reader."[19] The preface of "The Raven's Almanack" is a long satire upon the dissipated habits of courtiers, gallants, law students, and those "that are the mere Sons of Citizens, who never heard any music but the sound of Bow-bell." One of the happiest in conception is the dedication of " The Gull's Horn Book " to " all Gulls in general," which I quote in full:

" Whom can I choose, my most worthy Mecaen-asses, to be patrons to this

[15] *The Shoemaker's Holiday.*
[16] *Work for Armorers*, G., IV, 91.
[17] *The Bellman of London.*
[18] *Lanthorn and Candlelight.*
[19] *A Rod for Runaways.*

labor of mine fitter than yourselves? Your hands are ever open, your purses never shut. So that you stand not in the common rank of dry-fisted Patrons, who give nothing, for you give all. Scholars, therefore, are as much beholden to you as vinters, players and punks are. Those three trades gain by you more than usurers do by thirty in the hundred: you spend the wines of the one, you make suppers for the other, and change your gold into white money with the third. Who is more liberal than you? who but only citizens are more free? Blame me not therefore, if I pick you out from the bunch of book-takers, to consecrate these fruits of my brain (which shall never die) only to you. I know that most of you, O admirable Gulls, can neither write nor read. A Hornbook have I invented, because I would have you well-schooled. Paul's is your walk; but this your guide: if it lead you right, thank me: if astray, men will bear with your errors because you are gulls."

But why write an address to the reader, asks Dekker, and replies:

" Oh good Sir, there's as sound law to make you give good words to the Reader as to a constable when he carries his watch about him to tell how the night goes, though perhaps the one oftentimes may be served in for a goose and the other very fitly furnish the same mess. Yet to maintain the scurvy fashion and to keep custom in reparations, he must be honeyed and come over with *Gentle Reader, Courteous Reader,* and *Learned Reader,* though he have no more Gentility in him than Adam had, that was but a gardener, no more Civility than a Tartar, and no more Learning than the most errant stinkard, that, except his own name, could never find anything in the hornbook.

" How notoriously therefore do good wits dishonor not only their calling, but even their creation, that worship glow-worms instead of the sun because of a little false glistering? In the name of Phoebus, what madness leads them unto it? For he that dares hazard a pressing to death, that's to say, to be a man in Print, must make account that he shall stand, like the old weathercock over Paul's steeple, to be beaten with all storms. Neither the stinking tobacco-breath of a Satin-gull, the aconited sting of a narrow-eyed critic, the faces of a fantastic stage-monkey, nor the *Indeed-la* of a Puritanical citizen must often shake him. No, but desperately resolve, like a French post, to ride through thick and thin: endure to see his lines torn pitifully on the rack: suffer his Muse to take the bastoon, yea the very stab, and himself, like a new stake, to be the mark for every haggler, and therefore, setting up all these rests, why should he regard what fool's bolt is shot at him? Besides, if that which he presents upon the stage of the world be good, why should he basely cry out, with that old poetical madcap in his *Amphitruo, Jovis summi causa, clare plaudite:* I beg a plaudite for God sake. If bad, who but an Ass would entreat, as players do in a cogging epilogue at the end of a filthy comedy, that, be it never such wicked stuff, they would forbear to hiss, or to damn it perpetually to lie on a stationer's stall. For he that can so cozen himself as to pocket up praise in that silly sort makes his brain fat with his own folly."[20]

It is characteristic of Dekker that in the midst of a lively description of poor poets—"most pitiful, pure fresh-water soldiers," "thin-headed fellows that live upon the scraps of invention, and travel with such vagrant souls and so like ghosts, in white sheets of paper, that the Statute of Rogues may worthily be sued upon them because their wits have no abiding place and yet wander without a passport"—he explains: "Bear witness all you whose wits make you able to be witnesses in this cause, that here I meddle not with your good poets."[21] These poor poets, Dekker says in the same address, become critics, ignorant ones at that:

"O you book-sellers, that are factors to the Liberal Sciences, over whose stalls these drones do daily fly humming, let Homer, Hesiod, Euripides, and some other mad Greeks, with a band of the Latins, lie like musket-shot in their way when these Goths and Getes set upon you in your paper fortifications; it is the only cannon upon whose mouth they dare not venture: none but the English will take their parts, therefore fear them not, for such a strong breath have these cheese-eaters that if they do but blow upon a book, they imagine straight 'tis blasted: *Quod supra nos; nihil ad nos,* they say: that which is above our capacity shall not pass under our commendation."

More than once, Dekker complains of the difficulty of suiting his publishers or the tastes of his capricious readers. In the preface to "Jests to Make You Merry," written in 1607, the tone is gay rather than otherwise:

"Books are a strange commodity; the estimation of them riseth and falleth faster than the exchange of money in the Low Countries, which alters more often than the Englishman doth the fashion of his apparel. . . . There's no one stationer stall can fit all customers with books to their diet, nor can all men that write, if all that can but speak should write, fit some stationers. Go to one and offer a copy; if it be merry, the man likes no light stuff: if sad, it will not sell. Another meddles with nothing but what fits the time. I would have his shop stufft with nothing but proclamations, because he lies i' the wind only for the change of weather."[22]

[20] General preface, *The Wonderful Year.*
[21] G., I, 79–80.
[22] G., II, 271–272.

He maintains that he is not one of those writers who "find no sweetness but in drawing blood. Of those sharp-toothed dogs you shall find me none. I hold no whip in my hand but a soft feather, and there drops rather water than gall out of my quill. If you taste it and find it pleasing, I am glad; if not, I cannot be much sorry, because the cook knew not your diet, so that his error was his ignorance, and ignorance is a venial sin, to be pardoned." Many years later, when poverty was really closing down upon Dekker, he writes with a rare note of bitterness: "A thousand palates must be pleased with a thousand sauces: and one hundred lines must content five hundred dispositions. . . . He is tied to a stake like a bear to be baited, that comes into Paul's Churchyard to be read."[23]

Dekker's prose works may be roughly classified as follows: books dealing with London life, including two plague-books, "The Gull's Horn-Book," "The Seven Deadly Sins of London," and "The Dead Term . . . Written in manner of a Dialogue between the two cities London and Westminster"; two books exposing current methods of cheating and thieving; two medleys, both having some features in common with the exposure books; a translation; a controversial work of mixed verse and prose; a mock almanac; a non-dramatic morality, and a prayer-book. There is not one of these pamphlets that does not throw light upon the morals or manners of the Elizabethan or Jacobean era, and the larger number seem to have been written with obvious enjoyment. All but the second part of "Jests to Make You Merry" are well edited, and most of them bear Dekker's name, correctly spelled, upon the title-page; two notable exceptions are "The Wonderful Year," which, however, Dekker claims elsewhere,[24] and "The Bachelor's Banquet," which is likewise unsigned.[25]

The first of these prose works is "The Bachelor's Banquet," described by the sub-title as "A Banquet for Bachelors: Wherein is prepared sundry dainty dishes to furnish their

[23] G., III, 311.

[24] *The Seven Deadly Sins,* II, 12.

[25] *The Double P. P.* was also published anonymously, but a presentation copy with Dekker's autograph is said to exist. See *Mem. Introd.* by Grosart, V, XXII.

Table, curiously drest and seriously served in. Pleasantly discoursing the variable humors of Women, their quickness of wits and unsearchable deceits." Upon this book, with its humor, its irony, its wealth of vivid detail, its highly dramatic dialogue, its studied naïveté grimly lighted at times by a flash of tragic feeling, Swinburne exhausts his vocabulary of praise. The praise is deserved, but the critic was apparently unaware that " The Bachelor's Banquet " is a translation of " Les Quinze Joyes de Mariage," a brilliant and finished prose piece of the fifteenth century,[27] summing up in itself the accumulated mediæval satire upon women. Dekker's translation indeed merits mention among Elizabethan translations. It is a singularly vital work, expressed in the purest, most idiomatic English and retaining most of the excellencies of the original, as Swinburne bears witness. He often follows the French closely, almost word for word, but does not hesitate to expand, or, more rarely, to omit[27a] or to insert some reflections of his own. In the total effect, it must be confessed that after passing through that kindly and whimsical mind, the irony of the misogynist loses something of its edge and the style something of its incisiveness. The sub-title indicates, too, a sort of gay exuberance that is very far from the original. This exercise in translation was perhaps a happy circumstance for Dekker's prose style, for as time went on he seems more and more to have striven after precision of phrase, and not infrequently he attained it. On the other hand, it may be possible to trace the influence of this woman-hater's pamphlet in the passages of satire on women, brief and of little variety, scattered through both prose and plays and greatly at variance with his dramatic representation of women.

Dekker's next prose work is " The Wonderful Year. 1603. Wherein is shewed the picture of London lying sick of the Plague. At the end of all (like a merry Epilogue to a dull Play) certain Tales are cut out in sundry fashions, of purpose to shorten the lives of long winter's nights that lie watching in the dark for us." Except for a sort of introduction con-

[27] Attributed to Antoine de la Sale.
[27a] The only important omission is of the introductory chapter.

cerning the death of Elizabeth and the accession of James, the volume corresponds to the title—a vivid and terrible picture of plague-stricken London, for the most part avoiding the disgusting, but full of such minute details as the rise in the price of rosemary from twelve pence an armful to six shillings a handful. About half the book consists of a collection of stories, of such moving and varied interest that they might still serve to shorten such nights as watch for us in the dark. Dekker dwells upon the hardheartedness of the country people, the "Hobbinols," who would not give a cup of water to the fleeing Londoner or bury him when dead; upon the cowardice of the doctors who "hid their synodical heads as well as the proudest, and whose medicines had not so much strength to hold life and soul together as a pot of Pinder's ale and a nutmeg"; and over and over, upon the suddenness with which the "sickness" smote its victim, from the bride struck down during the marriage service to the churchwarden who mockingly kept the churchyard for himself when others needed to use it, and who three days later required that lodging. Characteristic is the story of the Dutchman who fled to Holland, where death, "to shew him that there were other Low Country besides his own," seized his child, "a little frekin"; and still more so, the incident of the sick scholar who desired a decent burying from the friend who had loved him "not because he was poor, yet he was poor, but because he was a scholar."[28]

Comedy shoulders Tragedy. After telling the pathetic story —a sort of generalized story—of the death of the only son of a rich and haughty father, who must with his own hands bury the body, not in a consecrated spot, but in his own orchard or the proud walks of his garden, Dekker's "spirit grows faint with rowing in the Stygian ferry; it can no longer endure the transportation of souls in this doleful manner," and he promises the reader "some prosperous shore." He is slow in reaching it: "I am amazed to remember what dead marches were made of three thousand trooping together; husbands, wives and children being led as ordinarily to one grave as if they had gone

[28] Possibly well known, for Dekker adds "whose name I could for need bestow upon you but that I know you have no need of it."

to one bed"; and he could write down a catalogue of poor
wretches that died without any other succor than the "common
benefit of earth and air." But he reiterates his intention of
relieving his story of death and sorrow:

"We will therefore play the soldiers, who at the end of any notable
battle, with a kind of sad delight, rehearse the memorable acts of their
friends that lie mangled before them: some shewing how bravely they
gave the onset: some, how politickly they retired: others, how manfully
they gave and received wounds: a fourth steps forth and glories how
valiantly he lost an arm: all of them making, by this means, the remembrance even of tragical and mischievous events very delectable."

Of the "comical and ridiculous stuff" that he promises, the
best is the story of the musical, valiant tinker, whose kettle-
drum sounded so sweetly that it drew after it whole swarms
of bees, and who, after burying the body of a plague-killed
citizen, went swaggering through the town with "Have ye any
more Londoners to bury? hey down-a-down dery, have ye any
more Londoners to bury?" The most ghastly of the tales is
that of the drunkard who reeled into a pit half filled with
bodies, imagining that he was in his own house, and that all
his fellows were there, "as they were indeed," and slept soundly
until waked by the sexton who cast upon the sleeper "some
dead men's bones and a skull or two that lay scattered here and
there." One pathetic story, evidently of common occurrence,
Dekker merely outlines:

"Neither will I speak a word of a poor boy, servant to a chandler
dwelling thereabouts, who being struck to the heart by sickness was first
carried away by water to be left anywhere, but landing being denied by an
army of brown-bill men that kept the shore, back again was he brought,
and left in an out-cellar; where, lying groveling and groaning on his face—
amongst fagots but not one of them set on fire to comfort him—there continued all night, and died miserably for want of succor."

Brief quotations hardly give an idea of the style, now simple
and direct, but more often swift, urgent and passionately full.
Let me quote once more:

"What an unmatchable torment were it for a man to be barred up every
night in a vast silent charnel house? hung, to make it more hideous, with
lamps dimly and slowly burning, in hollow and glimmering corners: where

all the pavement should, instead of green rushes, be strewed with blasted rosemary, withered hyacinths, fatal cypress and yew, thickly mingled with heaps of dead men's bones; the bare ribs of a father that begat him lying there; here the chapless hollow skull of a mother that bore him: round about him a thousand corses, some standing bolt upright in their knotted winding sheets: others half mouldered in rotten coffins, that should suddenly yawn wide open, filling his nostrils with noisome stench, and his eyes with the sight of nothing but crawling worms. And to keep such a poor wretch waking, he should hear no noise but of toads croaking, screech-owls howling, mandrakes shrieking: were not this an infernal prison? would not the strongest-hearted man, beset with such a ghastly horror, look wild? and run mad? and die? And even such a formidable shape did the diseased City appear in: For he that durst, in the dead hours of gloomy midnight, have been so valiant as to have walked through the still and melancholy streets, what think you should have been his music? Surely the loud groans of raving sick men; the struggling pangs of souls departing: in every house grief striking up an alarum: servants crying out for masters: wives for husbands; parents for children, children for their mothers: here he should have met some frantically running to knock up sextons; there, others fearfully sweating with coffins, to steal forth dead bodies, lest the fatal handwriting of death should seal up their doors. And to make this dismal consort more full, round about him bells heavily tolling in one place and ringing out in another. The dreadfulness of such an hour is unutterable: let us go further."

1606 was a full year. The first[29] production was "The Double P. P. A Papist in Arms. Bearing Ten several Shields. Encountered by the Protestant. At Ten several Weapons. A Jesuit Marching before them,"—a title that, properly interpreted, gives pretty accurately the table of contents. They consist of a riddle on the "Double P. P.," who, it seems, is the Pope; an extended portrait of the Jesuit, first in verse, then in prose; ten portraits of different varieties of the Papist, designated by terms drawn from heraldry; a riddle on the Single P. or Protestantism; a series of portraits of the "Protestant Army," including among others, the nobility, the clergy, the universities, and the merchants; and finally "The Battaile and Retrayte." Of the portraits, written in rhyme royal, that of "Nautes or the Sea-man" is the best, closing with the characteristic line:

"If thou wouldst know thy maker, search the seas."

[29] S. R., Dec. 9, 1605.

Although the verse is either too fluent or too rugged, the piece has considerable force and heartiness and a degree of pleasant quaintness. It was doubtless written to take advantage of the outburst of patriotism that followed the Gunpowder Plot.

At about the same time appeared " News from Hell; Brought by the Devil's Carrier,"[30] with the running title, " The Devil's Answer to Pierce Penniless." Fifteen years before, in his " Pierce Penniless, his Supplication to the Devil," Nash had sent a Knight of the Post to Hell entreating for the liberation of money. The pamphlet proved to be so popular that he planned to write an account of the return of his messenger, but he never did so. Two others took up the task before Dekker: Middleton, whose " Black Book," published in 1604, contains a sort of sequel to Nash's story, much of it in deplorable taste; and an anonymous writer[31] of whose book, Dekker wrote in the preface of his own: " But it may be, the first answer that he sent by the Post was in the morning, for he strives to speak soberly, gravely, and like a Puritan." Whatever other motives urged him on to the writing of this reply, affection for his friend and a desire to give that friend's book a creditable sequel must have had some weight. The well-known invocation to Nash was followed up by a reasonable degree of success in imitating his style.

" News from Hell " tells, with much spirit and gaiety and with considerable genial satire upon the sins and foibles of the day, the story of the adventures of the Knight of the Post to whom Nash had entrusted his errand; first, among the wicked on earth in order to see fashions and get table-talk, then upon his arrival at Acheron, which looks and smells like Moor-ditch, " when the water is three-quarters drained out." There follows an account of sessions in Hell, when the style grows more serious as it pictures the condemned and Conscience their accuser, " poor in attire, diseased in his flesh, wretched in his face, heavy in his gait, and hoarse in his voice." Securing

[30] Fleay thinks that *News from Hell* is identical with *The Return of the Knight of the Post from Hell with the Devil's answer to Piers Penniless' supplication*, S. R., Jan. 15, 1606, and *The Devil's let loose*, S. R., Jan. 25. Both entries were cancelled Feb. 17 by order of the court.
[31] See Rimbault's *Introd., A Knight's Conjuring*, XIII.

with great difficulty access to the Lord of Hell, the messenger gets an unsatisfactory reply and would return to earth but is interrupted by the horrible figure of a usurer. After a haggling settlement of charges between Mercury and Charon, the reader comes to the last incident, nobly told:

"On the other side of the river stood a company crying out lustily, 'a boat, hey, a boat, hey!' And who should they be but a gallant troop of English spirits, all mangled, looking like so many old Romans, that for overcoming Death in their manly resolutions were sent away out of the field, crowned with the military honor of arms. The foremost of them was a personage of so composed a presence that Nature and Fortune had done him wrong if they had not made him a soldier.[32] In his countenance there was a kind of indignation fighting with a kind of exalted joy, which, by his very gesture, were apparently decipherable, for he was jocund that his soul went out of him in so glorious a triumph; but disdainfully angry that she wrought her enlargement through no more dangers: yet were there bleeding witnesses enow on his breast, which testified he did not yield till he was conquered, and was not conquered till there was left nothing of a man in him to be overcome."

The hero, "scorning to be his own Chronicle" to the questioning Charon, leaves the office to one of his followers, and Charon dismisses the company "to those happy places which were allotted out to none but Martialists." In the meantime the Knight of the Post has gone to Nash, now in the Elysian gardens, and been received "with as few words as he [Nash] was wont to carry pence in his purse." The story closes with a brief picture of the "*insulae fortunatae*," in which "the very benches whereon they sit are buds of violets, their pillows are hearts-ease, their sheets, the silken leaves of willow."

As usual, there is many a contemporary picture, one of the best being that of those surly "key-turners," those "big fellows that stand like giants at lords' gates," with "cheeks strutting out like two foot-balls, being blown up with powder beef and brewis"; many a happy phrase, like the description of Orpheus as "most clear-throated singing man"; many a pun like this: "Poetry, like honesty and old soldiers, goes upon lame feet unless there be music in her."

[32] This hero was William Eps, as Dekker explains in a marginal note in *A Knight's Conjuring.*

The book is good reading today. Then it was so popular that the following year Dekker issued another edition under the title of "A Knight's Conjuring, Done in Earnest, Discovered in Jest."[33] It is provided with a new dedication and a new and picturesque opening which takes less for granted than did that of "News from Hell"; it is divided into chapters with verse-titles; the paragraphs are supplied with marginal topic-sentences,[34] and, above all, there is a noteworthy expansion of the brief description of the abode of the blest. The eulogy of Nash is omitted, perhaps because he becomes so conspicuous a figure in the conclusion. The best known part of the added chapter has already been quoted, but since this study would gladly emphasize anything that reveals Dekker's tastes and ideas, let me quote further from his general description of Elysium.

"The walls that encompass these goodly habitations are white as the forehead of heaven; they glister like polisht ivory, but the stuff is finer: high they are like the pillars that uphold the court of Jove; and strong they are as towers built by enchantment; there is but one gate to it all, and that's of refined silver: so narrow it is that but one at once can enter: round about, wears it a girdle of waters that are sweet, redolent and crystalline: the leaves of the vine are not so precious, the nectar of the Gods nothing so delicious.

"Walk into the groves, you shall hear all sorts of birds melodiously singing: you shall see swains deftly piping, and virgins chastely dancing. Shepherds there live as merrily as kings, and kings are glad to be companions with shepherds. The widow there complains of no wrong: the orphan sheds no tears, for covetousness cannot carry it away with his gold, nor cruelty with the sway of greatness; the poor client needs fee no lawyer to plead for him, for there's no jury to condemn him, nor judges to astonish him. . . . "

"Neither is this a common inn to all travellers," continues Dekker, half humorously. No landlords dwell there, no fencers, vintners, farmers, and not a tailor "unless he creep through the eye of his needle"; few gentlemen ushers, and of

[33] Edited by E. F. Rimbault for the Percy Society, vol. 5; not given in Grosart, except the prefaces.

[34] On the margin Dekker calls attention to the fact that the dispute between Charon and Mercury is borrowed from Lucian, thus forestalling modern scholarship by some three hundred years. See *Cam. Hist. Eng. Lit.*, IV, 404.

women "scarce one amongst five hundred has her pew there."
All infants are welcome, and "holy singers whose divine
anthems have bound souls by their charms." Elsewhere we
have learned that most poets are there, except "some pitiful
fellows, ballad-makers." Scholars are admitted to this society,
"but the number of them all is not half so many as are in one
of the colleges of an university," for they either "kindle fire-
brands in the sanctified places by their contention; or kill the
hearts of others by their coldness."

Again:

"One field there is amongst all the rest set round about with willows;
it is call'd the field of mourning, and in this, upon banks of flowers that
wither away even with the scorching sighs of those that sit upon them, are
a band of malcontents; they look for all the world like the mad-folks in
Bedlam, and desire like them, to be alone; and these are forlorn lovers:
such as pined away to nothing for nothing: such as for the love of a
wanton wench have gone crying to their graves. . . . all the joy that these
poor fools feed upon is to sit singing lamentable ballads to some doleful
tunes: for though they have changed their old lives, they cannot forget
their young loves; they spend their time in making of myrtle garlands and
shed so much water out of their eyes that it hath made a pretty little
river, which lies so soaking continually at the roots of the willow trees
that half the leaves of them are almost washed into a whiteness."

"There is another piece of ground, where are encamped none but soldiers: and of those, not all sorts of soldiers neither, but only such as have
died nobly in the wars: and yet of those but a certain number too: that is
to say, such that in execution were never bloody: in their country's revenge,
severe but not cruel: such as held death in one hand and mercy in the
other: such as never ravisht maidens, never did abuse no widows, never
gloried in the massacre of babes: were never drunk of purpose before the
battle began because they would spare none; nor after the battle did never
quarrel about pledging the health of his whore. Of this garrison, there are
but a few in pay, and therefore they live without mutiny."

This added chapter was written nearly forty years before
Milton's "Areopagitica." Like the greater part of "The Gull's
Hornbook," it is curiously modern even to the matter of para-
graphing; the thought is unencumbered by the sentence structure, and the phrasing, for the most part, is direct and precise.

To 1606 also belongs "The Seven Deadly Sins of London:[35]
Drawn in seven several Coaches, Through the seven several

[35] S. R., Oct. 6, 1606.

Gates of the City; Bringing the Plague with them." It bears
upon its title-page "*Opus septem Dierum,*" and it has all the
rapidity of thought and style and all the perfervid emotion of a
composition written down as soon as conceived. The induction
is full of passionate love for London and for Elizabeth and
eloquent pity for "the seventeen Dutch Virgins of Belgia,"
and France, the "gallant Monarchy," that "was full of princes
and saw them all lie mangled at her feet"; "full of people and
saw in one night a hundred thousand massacred in her streets."
In his indictment of London, Dekker tells us that the plague
has not yet ceased: "that Desolation, which now for three
years together, hath hovered around about thee, will at last
enter, and turn thy gardens of pleasure into churchyards; thy
fields that served thee for walks into Golgotha; and thy high-
built houses into heaps of dead men's skulls." The book has
the form of a seven-fold pageant. Very significant of
Dekker's point of view are the deadly sins, the "actors" in
"this old Enterlude of Iniquity" which "seven may easily
play . . . but not without a Devil." Politic Bankruptism and
Shaving refer to various ways of cheating men out of their
money: the meaning of the first is clear; Shaving includes
usury, the tricks of the law played upon clients, widows and
children, and many others forms of extortion, not omitting
the cruel custom by which prison-keepers might in a short
time make "the charges of the house" three times the debts
of the prisoner. Another "actor," Candlelight, includes all
the sins most easily committed at night. Apishness is imitation; for the presence of such a slight and short-lived sin in
that grave company, Dekker rather apologizes, the more so
as it is chiefly practised by rich fools and by women, who are
men's she-apes, especially in the matter of fashion. The
names of Lying, Sloth, and Cruelty speak for themselves.

Against Cruelty, the indictment is, as one might expect,
the severest and the most vivid. "Cruelty! the very sound of
it shews that it is no English word: it is a Fury sent out of
hell, not to inhabit within such beautiful walls, but amongst
Turks and Tartars." "Cruelty challenges no room," cries
Dekker, in London's "thirteen strong houses of sorrow, where

the prinsoner hath his heart wasting away sometimes a whole prenticeship of years in cares. They are most of them built of freestone but none are free within them: cold are their embracements: unwholesome is their cheer: despairful their lodgings: uncomfortable the societies: miserable their inhabitants: O what a deal of wretchedness can make shift to lie in a little room! if those thirteen houses were built all together, how rich would grief be, having such large enclosures." But, again continues Dekker, Cruelty is not responsible for the whipping-post, the stock, the cart, the scaffold, for Justice must receive no wrong. But the real cruelty lies in the forced marriage of children, especially of a young girl to an old man, of which a vivid and terrible picture is given; near the close of this discussion occurs the comment: "Hence comes it, that murders are often contrived and as often acted; our country is woeful in fresh examples." Dekker next inveighs against cruel creditors who, by locking up their debtors, rob them of all means of paying their debts. There is a passage about cruel masters who, after ill-treating their prentices for seven years, "send them into the world to beg," that is, to find no chance to practice their trade; "as if trades that were ordained to be communities had lost their first privileges and were now turned to monopolies." Two othert forms of cruelty that always roused Dekker's indignation are assailed: the failure to provide London with suitable burying places, and the failure to establish a hospital and grave-space for those who died in the "fields." Entirely modern is the warning, though couched in a poet's language, that if those former pits, "those caves of horror and ghastliness," be opened up for new victims, the very persons who neglected to provide graves will be poisoned by "the contagious damps."

In the section on Politic Bankruptism, there is a curious illustration of Dekker's swift conversion of the abstract into the concrete, for he soon forgets, as does the reader, the deadly sin in his picture of the sinner, "poor rich man," "ill-painted fool," whose wife and children are left to go to ruin after his death.

In October, 1607, was registered the medley entitled "Jests

to make you Merry: With the Conjuring up of Cock Watt, the
Walking Spirit of Newgate, to tell tales. Unto which is
Added, the misery of a Prison and a Prisoner. And a Paradox in praise of Serjeants. Written by T. D. and George
Wilkins." It was printed the same year. To the jest-book is
prefixed a puzzle in the form of a preface, for it uses the
first person, has Dekker's peculiarities and is signed T. D. and
G. W. Of the sixty jests, I should be glad to assign the
greater portion to Wilkins, for Dekker is very seldom dull, and
if he tells a story that could not be told today, it may usually
be seen to have had some point. The sixteenth jest is told
with such swiftness and gusto that it may be his; perhaps he
remembered Middleton's play, though "Blurt, Master Constable," seems to have been a not uncommon expression. The
second part of the book, Cock Wat's discoveries, is really the
first of Dekker's writings, afterwards so popular, that deal
with cheats and thieves and the way they work their game.
The ingenious contrivance of making Cock Wat, the spirit of
Newgate, tell what he knows of the prisoners and their crimes,
also enables Dekker to draw the affecting picture of the old
man who mourns the loss of liberty, and that of the riotous
young man who writes the paradox in praise of sergeants.
The book is full of information of curious sorts, and it cannot
be neglected by one interested in the personality of the author.

The next pamphlet was "The Dead Term or Westminster's
Complaint for long Vacations and short Terms. Written in
manner of a Dialogue between the two Cities London and
Westminster,"[36] 1608. This pamphlet reads like a rather perfunctory piece of work; the humor, small in quantity, is less
spontaneous, the preaching less fervent, than in the prose
already discussed. It begins with a long speech by Westminster, complaining chiefly that the vacations are bad for her
main business, which is Law, and begging that there may be
one continuous term instead. There is considerable history, a
description of the Thames possibly suggested by Spenser's
marriage of the Thames and the Medway, an account of the
sad state of Charing Cross, an enumeration of the sins of the

[36] S. R., Nov. 3, 1607.

city, and, incidentally, a eulogy of the law and "a paradox in praise of a Pen." To every point London replies categorically. Over against Charing Cross is set St. Paul's steeple and its complaint, the best part of which is concerned with the walks in Paul's. In history, London mercilessly relates her whole career. But towards the end, Dekker gets so bored himself that he is constrained to tell a tragic-humorous tale of the plague, including, as a marginal note points out, a description of Sturbridge Fair.

In 1608 the exposure of rogues begun in "Jests to Make You Merry" was continued in "The Bellman of London: Bringing to Light the most Notorious Villanies that are now Practised in the Kingdom. Profitable for Gentlemen, Lawyers, Merchants, Citizens, Farmers, Masters of households, and all sorts of servants, to mark; and delightful for all men to read. *Lege, Perlege, Relege.*" The title-page is provided with a woodcut of the bellman accompanied by his dog. This book was so successful that it was twice reprinted in 1608 and it was followed up the same year by "Lanthorn and Candlelight, or the Bellman's second Night's-walk. In which He brings to light a Brood of more strange Villanies than ever were till this year discovered." To the second edition "newly corrected and amended,"[37] 1609, Dekker prefixed a warning to the reader, singularly contemptuous from his kindly pen:

"There is an Usurper that of late hath taken upon him the name of the Bellman, but being not able to maintain that title, he doth now call himself the Bellman's brother: his ambition is, rather out of vain glory than the true courage of an experienced soldier, to have the leading of the van, but it shall be honor good enough for him, if not too good, to come up with the rear. You shall know him by his habiliments, for, by the furniture he wears, he will be taken for a Beadle of Bridewell. It is thought he is rather a neuter than a friend to the cause: and therefore the Bellman doth here openly protest that he comes into the field as no fellows in arms with him."

This Beadle of Bridewell is Samuel Rowlands, too clever a pamphleteer and versifier, one would think, to need to trade

[37] The first edition was entered S. R., Oct. 25, but I have seen none earlier than that reprinted by Grosart.

upon the popularity of other writers. This was not the first offence; in 1602 he had published a tract under the misleading title, "Greene's Ghost Haunting Cony-Catchers," and possibly he borrowed still more from Nash. Whatever called forth Dekker's disclaimer of any literary affiliation has perished, but Rowlands promptly took to himself the disparaging remarks quoted above and in a pamphlet called "Martin Mark-all, Beadle of Bridewell, his defense and answer to the Bellman of London," published in 1610, tried to turn the tables upon the original Bellman by a somewhat querulous and incoherent complaint that he himself was better acquainted with canting or thieves' dielect than Dekker, and that the latter had used the material collected by Harman in his "Caveat for Cursitors."[38]

Both complaints were founded on truth. No reader of Rowlands doubts that he had a more intimate acquaintance with the sordid details of low life than Dekker. Moreover, Dekker bears witness against his own proficiency when he urges that the dialect is "so crabbed that seven years' study is little enough to reach to the bottom of it, and to make it run off glib from the tongue."[39]

Dekker's obligations to Harman require a word more. "Caveat for Cursitors" was preceded by Awdeley's "Fraternity of Vagabonds,"[40] and so was not the first on the subject. It is composed of definitions of rascals and of their specific modes of cheating or stealing, with a large admixture

[38] "In the meantime, because the Bellman entreateth any that is more rich in canting to lend him better or more with variety, he will repay his love double. I have thought good not only to shew his error in some places in setting down old words used forty years ago, before he was born, for words that are used in these days (although he is bold to call me an usurper, for so he doth in his last round and not able to maintain the title) but have enlarged his dictionary (or Master Harman's) with such words as I think he never heard of (and yet in use too) but not out of vain glory, as his ambition is, but indeed as an experienced soldier that hath dearly paid for it; and therefore it shall be honor good enough for him (if not too good) to come up with the rear (I do but shoot your own arrow back again) and not to have the leading of the van as he meant to do, although small credit in the end will redound to either." *Works of Rowlands.* Hunterian Club (1880), II, 36.

[39] *Bellman of London,* G., III, 156.

[40] Licensed 1560–1, printed the same year and in 1566.

of stories, most of them very far from edifying. If Dekker used Harman—he quite as likely used " The Groundwork of Cony-Catching" which is based upon Harman's tract—he showed modesty and discretion, for he omitted all the stories supplied in both of his books a picturesque framework, greatly amplified most of the definitions and added others. He was no more conscious of dishonesty than when he selected the incidents from Deloney's "Gentle Craft" for a play. Here were a number of rogue-books lying around, agreeing only in the grammar and dictionary of canting, and Dekker conceived the idea of bringing out a new rogue-book, which should discard all the personal matter of the old ones, and should be put into a new framework and suitably embellished and brought down to date; in other words, he was using common property in a fresh way.

The first twenty pages of " The Bellman of London" read like the beginning of a romance. The elements are: a visit into the country, a lovely spot in the greenwood, vocal with the song of birds and paved with yellow flowers and red and white daisies; smoke rising from a mysterious building, which the adventurer naturally seeks out, a huge hall furnished for a banquet, a hidden gallery from which the rogues' feast may be observed, and an old hostess, whose tongue, loosed by drink, tells tales out of school. But the old woman's explanations of villainy grow rather wearisome, and so do those of the Bellman that form the latter part of the book, although they sometimes have an historical interest, and when Dekker drops into narrative, as he often does, he is never dull. But he grows tired of the company he is keeping:

" How long shall I sail upon these godless waters? Is it not time to get to shore? . . . What a battle have I undertaken? and with what an ignoble enemy? to contend with whom is an act inglorious, and to conquer whom, but that they are open and professed foes to the Republic, to honesty, to civility, and to all humanity, were as much dishonor as by them to be overcome."

However, Dekker was "industrious"—"To my industrious friend," writes E. G. in verses prefixed to "Lanthorn and Candlelight." Like its predecessor, this pamphlet was published anonymously as a discovery of the Bellman of London, a circumstance of which Rowlands complained when he wrote, " The spiteful poet would not set to his name," but in the second edition, 1609, reprinted by Grosart, Dekker's name is signed to the epistle. This letter is more than usually apologetic :

" Give me leave to lead you by the hand into a Wilderness, where are none but Monsters, whose cruelty you need not fear, because I teach the way to tame them : ugly they are in shape and devilish in conditions, yet to behold them afar off may delight you, and to know their qualities, if ever you should come near them, may save you from much danger."

Dekker would hardly be Dekker if he did not contrive to lighten up his subject. The first chapter of "Lanthorn and Candlelight" contains an entertaining account of the origin of canting, or "peddlers' French," or thieves' dialect, in the confusion of tongues at the tower of Babel. This is followed by a brief canting dictionary with some specimens in prose and verse. Chapter two takes us to Hell, which Dekker visits with less lightness of spirit than in " News from Hell." The Devil, astonished by the ravages made by the Bellman upon his own kingdom of hell on earth, sends a messenger to bolster up his failing business. The rest of the book is a continuation of the exposure of rogues. By far the most interesting to the student of literature is the section on Hawking. This explains in detail how patrons of letters were cheated by pseudo-pamphleteers, who had either patched up something in the semblance of a book or stolen a forgotten publication, and had then got printed for it as many epistles-dedicatory as they hoped to get patrons for that single book.[41] Of all the many modes of cheating, this roused Dekker's greatest anger :

" O sacred Learning ! why dost thou suffer thy seven-leaved tree to be plucked by barbarous and most unhallowed hands? Why is thy beautiful maiden-body polluted like a strumpet's and prostituted to beastly and slavish Ignorance? . . . You thieves of Wit, cheaters of Art, traitors of schools of Learning; murderers of Scholars. More worthy you are to undergo the Roman *furca* like slaves and to be branded i' th' forehead deeper than they that forge testaments to undo orphans: such do but rob children of goods that may be lost; but *you* rob scholars of their fame which is dearer than life."

[41] Dekker speaks of this custom in *2 Honest Whore*, P., II, 101.

Many of the other sections are interesting in subject and in style; among them, those on "Gull-Groping or How Gentlemen are cheated at Ordinaries," and "Ferreting or the Manner of undoing Gentlemen by taking up of commodities." Dekker does not hesitate to discuss suburb-houses, and if he is not modern enough to put the blame upon the patrons, he at least is modern in casting contempt upon landlords who take such money.

At this point, although it is out of the chronological order, mention must be made of "A Strange Horse-Race,"[42] which, as Grosart says, is "of kin" with the Bellman books. It was published in 1613 and was, as we shall see hereafter, avowedly written for money only. Although the most curious, it is the weakest of the series, as Dekker well knew, for in both prefaces he apologizes profusely. Nevertheless, he re-affirms, though rather weakly, his moral intent: "In this, as in all other my former *Nocturnis lucubrationibus,* I have strove to feed the mind as well as the body," and "the main plot of my building is a moral labyrinth." The contents are a medley, as indeed the full title indicates: "A Strange Horse-Race, at the end of which comes in the Catch-Pole's Banquet; Which done, the Devel, falling sick, makes his last will and Testament this present year, 1613." The races are of all sorts, from the chariot race of the Romans and fanciful races of nature, to races between such semi-morality figures as Prodigality and "Hansthrift"; Niggardliness and Hospitality, the latter a pleasantly drawn character; or that between a drunken English knight and a Spaniard who is "a temperate and very little feeder and no drinker, as all Spaniards are." Among the rogues the Bankrout, as in "The Seven Deadly Sins," holds a bad preeminence. At the end of the book is found the jaunty little song, "My Muse that art so merry."

Towards the beginning of 1609, or as Dekker puts it, "dated the 1. Ides of the first month of this first great Platonical and terrible year, 1609," was published "The Raven's Almanac, Foretelling of a Plague, Famine, and Civil War That shall happen this present year 1609, not only within this Kingdom

---

[42] See *Cam. Hist. Eng. Lit.,* IV, 407, for a discussion of this pamphlet.

of Great Britain, but also in France, Germany, Spain, and
other parts of Christendom. With certain Remedies, Rules,
and Receipts how to prevent, or at least to abate the edge of
these universal Calamities."[43]   It would seem that Dekker did
not edit this medley, for his name does not appear on the title-
page and is misspelled at the end of the dedication.   Perhaps
the self-named " new English Astrologer " was a little ashamed
of his performance.   Both in the amusing dedication to gulls
of various sorts, and also in the body of the pamphlet, he ridicules the astrologers who prophesy what is sure to happen,
using the language of the professional almanac-maker a little
mixed with the phraseology of the bestiary and much mixed
with puns.   Now and then he lightly throws overboard the
whole paraphernalia of the astrologer, as when he remarks of
December the twelfth: "When the said Sun shall be at his
greatest South Declination from the Equinoctial line, and so
forth, with much more such stuff than any mere Englishman
can understand."   Considerably more than half the almanac is
made up of stories, all well told.   One is a licentious story,
the scene an island belonging to Spain and the source certainly
foreign.   A second tells the story of a usurer who dies miserably, overreached by the man he had most cheated.   Another
tells the story of a merry cobbler, " who for joy that he mended
men's broken and corrupted soles, did continually sing, so that
his shop seemed a very bird-cage, and he, sitting there in his
foul linen and greasy apron, shewed like a blackbird."   But
the wife had a tongue as well as he, and the story tells how a
beating reduced her to silence.   But Dekker could not leave
the matter there; accordingly in the fourth story he tells at
greater length and with much more sympathy " how a woman
may be safe from a cruel husband."   This tale contains " a
song sung by an old woman in a meadow."

> Of all the plagues which make poor wights
>   Unhappy and accurst,
> I think a wicked husband is,
>   Next to the Devil, the worst.
> But will young women come to me,
>   I'll show them how they shall,

[43] S. R., July 7, 1608.

With pretty sleights and privy tricks,
Straight rid them from such thrall.

The husband frowns, and then his fist
Lights on her tender cheek,
And if she do reply a word,
A staff is not to seek.
But will," etc.

A jealous eye the husband bears,
Then is he out of quiet,
And she must fit her humor then
To stead his brain-sick diet.

Else round about the house she goes,
The holly wand must walk,
And though his words be reasonless,
Yet must she brook his talk.

Thus men do triumph like to kings,
And poor wives must obey;
And though he be a very fool,
Yet must he bear the sway.

Following the mock almanac came "Work for Armorers:
or the Peace is Broken. Open Wars likely to happen this
year 1609. God help the poor, the rich can shift." It was
written when, explains Dekker, play-houses stand empty, their
flags taken down, the players' comedies are changed to tragedies, and poets walk in melancholy. The only fairly innocent
mirth is at the Bear Garden, for, continues the cheerful punster,
"the pied Bull here keeps a-tossing and a-roaring, when the
Red Bull dares not stir." But he turns away from the folly
and cruelty of it, with pity in his heart for the " crushed " and
injured dogs and the bear whipped "till the blood ran down
his old shoulders": "methought this whipping of the blind
bear moved as much pity in my breast towards him as the leading of poor starved wretches to the whipping posts in London,
when they had more need to be relieved with food, ought to
move the hearts of citizens, though it be the fashion now to
laugh at the punishment." The bulk of the pamphlet is a sort
of undramatic prose morality in which Money and Poverty,
and their various counsellors prepare to make war. The plan
involves inconsistencies, and the reader is glad when a truce

is patched up between the leaders. Yet the book is written in a lively way, with considerable humor, and there is, as always, many an opportunity to look through the half-open door at some vividly drawn Jacobean character or custom.

In 1609 appeared "The Gull's Hornbook," probably Dekker's best known prose production, and certainly a masterpiece of its kind. It had its suggestion in "Grobianus," a Latin poem by Frederick Dedekind, which, writes Mr. McKerrow,[44] " is for the most part merely disgusting; it is concerned far more with such personal matters as the cleanliness and control of the body than with behaviour in society." In his general preface, Dekker gives the following account of his book: "This Tree of Gulls was planted long since, but not taking root, could never bear till now. It hath a relish of Grobianism, and tastes very strongly of it in the beginning: the reason thereof is, that having translated many books of that into English verse, and not greatly liking the subject, I altered the shape, and of a Dutchman fashioned a mere Englishman." A translation of Grobianus into English by R. F., in 1605, may have quickened Dekker's natural distaste for the subject. "Grobianism" appears in the first three of the eight chapters.

"The Gull's Hornbook" is the most entertaining and informing picture of early Jacobean days—a picture of times that were bad enough in many ways, but after all, of times when everybody wrote poetry and even a gull might be expected to produce an epigram or a satire. The chapters untouched by Grobianism advise a Gallant how to behave in Paul's Walks, in an Ordinary, in a Play-house, in a Tavern, and going home through the city late at night. Crammed with minutest detail, and full of wit and humor, they are the result of the keen, amused observation of a man that could look upon life's little ironies and foibles without any bitterness. Yet the brilliant journalist, the historian trained only by genius, was also a poet sensitive to the finger-tips; and this side of his nature comes to the surface in the passage I am compelled to quote, although it is well known.

" Present not yourself on the Stage, especially at a new play, until the quaking Prologue hath, by rubbing, got color into his cheeks, and is ready to

[44] *Introduction, The Gull's Hornbook,* De la More Press.

give the trumpets their cue that he's upon point to enter: for then it is time, as though you were one of the properties, or that you dropt out of the hangings, to creep from behind the arras, with your tripos or three-footed stool in one hand, and a teston mounted between a fore-finger and a thumb in the other: for if you should bestow your person upon the vulgar when the belly of the house is but half full, your apparel is quite eaten up, the fashion lost, and the proportion of your body in more danger to be devoured than if it were served up in the Counter amongst the Poultry: avoid that as you would the bastom. It shall crown you with rich commendation to laugh aloud in the midst of the most serious and saddest scene of the terriblest Tragedy: and to let that clapper, your tongue, be tost so high that all the house may ring of it: your lords use it; your knights are apes to the lords, and do so too; your Inn-a-court-man is zany to the knights, and, marry, very scurvily comes likewise limping after it: be thou a beagle to them all, and never lin snuffing till you have scented them: for by talking and laughing, like a ploughman in a morris, you heap Pelion upon Ossa, glory upon glory: As first, all the eyes in the galleries will leave walking after the players, and only follow you: the simplest dolt in the house snatches up your name, and when he meets you in the streets, or that you fall into his hands in the middle of a watch, his word shall be taken for you: he'll cry, *He's such a gallant,* and you pass. Secondly, you publish your temperance to the world in that you seem not to resort thither to taste vain pleasures with a hungry appetite: but only as a gentleman to spend a foolish hour or two, because you can do nothing else: Thirdly, you mightily disrelish the audience and disgrace the author: marry, you take up, though it be at the worst hand, a strong opinion of your own judgment, and enforce the poet to take pity of your weakness, and by some dedicated sonnet to bring you into a better paradise, only to stop your mouth.

. . . .

" Now sir, if the writer be a fellow that hath either epigrammed you, or hath had a flirt at your mistress, or hath brought either your feather, or your red beard, or your little legs, &c., on the stage, you shall disgrace him worse than by tossing him in a blanket, or giving him the bastinado in a tavern, if, in the middle of his play, be it Pastoral or Comedy, Moral or Tragedy, you rise with a screwed and discontented face from your stool to be gone: no matter whether the scenes be good or no; the better they are, the worse do you distaste them; and, being on your feet, sneak not away like a coward, but salute all your gentle acquaintances that are spread either on the rushes or on stools about you, and draw what troop you can from the stage after you: the mimics are beholden to you for allowing them elbow room: their poet cries, perhaps, *A pox go with you;* but care not for that, there's no music without frets.

" Marry, if either the company or indisposition of the weather bind you to sit out, my counsel is, then, that you turn plain ape, take up a rush, and tickle the earnest ears of your fellow gallants, to make other fools fall a-laughing: mew at passionate speeches, blare at merry, find fault with the music, whew at the children's action, whistle at the songs.

. . . .

" To conclude, hoard up the finest play-scraps you can get, upon which your lean wit may most savorly feed, for want of other stuff, when the Arcadian and Euphuized gentlewomen have their tongues sharpened to set upon you: that quality, next to your shittlecock, is the only furniture to a courtier that's but a new beginner and is but in his A B C of compliment."

"The Gull's Hornbook" was not like the Bellman books extraneous material collected for a special occasion, but the overflow of a full experience and extraordinary powers of observation passed through the sieve of a temperament equally alive to the absurd and the serious. Ten years before, Dekker had amused himself by adding to "Patient Grissill" an ignorant gallant, a gull, in the shape of Emulo, and later, in Asinius, we notice some of the same characteristics; in this book we have the complete picture.

From the point of view of Dekker's art and personality, no prose work possesses more interest than the imperfect book of prayers entitled "Four Birds of Noah's Ark," which also belongs to 1609. The preface to the reader indicates the scope of the four books:

" Under the wings of the Dove have I put prayers fitting the nature of the Dove, that is to say, simple prayers, or such as are fitting the mouths of young and the meanest people: and for such blessings as they have most need of. The Eagle soars more high, and in his beak beareth up to heaven supplications in behalf of Kings and Rulers. The Pelican carrieth the figure of our Redeemer on the cross, who shed his blood to nourish us, he being the right Pelican: with the drops of which blood have I writ prayers against all those deadly and capital sins, to wash out whose foulness our Saviour suffered that ignominious death. And lastly, in the spiced nest of the Phoenix, in which Bird likewise is figured Christ risen again, shalt thou find a book written full of thanks and wishes: of thanks for those benefits which grow unto us by Christ's death and resurrection: of wishes that he would in divers gifts bestow those blessings upon us."

It seems only natural that Dekker should have put into the most transparent and articulate form the fears and petitions of children, prentices, servants, prisoners, and other poor or unprotected persons. Very gentle in spirit and in rhythm is this book of the Dove; and the gentleness begins in the explanatory note that precedes the prayers:

" The Dove went out twice ere it could find an olive branch, which was the ensign of peace: so our prayers must fly up again and again, and never leave beating at the doors of Heaven till they fetch from thence the olive branch of God's mercy in sign that we are at peace with him, and that he hath pardoned our sins."

Very moving is the prayer for a child "before he goeth to his study, or to school," and equally so that "for a prentice going to his labor"; from the latter I quote:

" Let me not, O God, go about my business with eye-service; but sithence thou hast ordained that, like poor Joseph, I must enter into the state of a servant, so humble my mind that I may perform with cheerful willingness whatsoever my master commands me, and that all his commandments may be agreeable to the serving of thee. Bestow upon me thy grace that I may deal uprightly with all men, and that I may shew myself to him who is set over me a ruler as I another day would desire to have others behave themselves to me. Take away from him that is my master all thoughts of cruelty that, like the children of Israel under the subjection of Pharaoh's servants, I may not be set to a task above my strength: or if I be, stretch thou out my sinews, O God, that I may with unwearied limbs accomplish it. Fill my veins with blood that I may go through the hardest labors, sithence it is a law set down by thyself that I must earn my bread with the sweat of my own brows. Give me courage to begin; patience to go forward; and ability to finish them. Cleanse my heart, O thou that art the fountain of purity, from all falsehood, from all swearing, from all abuse of thy sacred Name, from all foul, loose, and unreverend languages."

Those who accuse Dekker of lack of dignity would do well to read the prayers comprised under " The Eagle," especially those for the council, the nobility, the church, the judges, and the two universities. The thought and diction are equally elevated, appropriate and direct. " A prayer to stay the pestilence" reminds us that Dekker was writing in the midst of death. It is full of pity and pain, and there are echoes from the Litany in it.

While " The Pelican" and " The Phoenix" sustain a high level, they are more general and less interesting than the first two books. The former concludes with a prayer for the evening that is full of beauty. I quote it in full:

"Thus, O God, am I nearer to old age than I was in the morning, but, I fear, not nearer to goodness: for he that strives to do best comes short of his duty. The night now stealeth upon me like a thief. O defend me from the horrors of it. When I am to lie down in my bed, let me imagine I am to lie in my winding sheet: and suffer me not to close mine eyes till my soul and I have reckoned and made even for all the offences, which not only this day but all the former minutes of my life I have committed against thy divine Majesty. Pardon them, O Lord; forgive me my sins, which are more infinite than the stars, and more heavy than if mountains lay upon my bosom; but thy mercy and the merits of my Redeemer do I trust in. In his name do I sue for pardon. Suffer, O Lord, no unclean thoughts this night to pollute my body and soul, but keep my cogitations chaste, and let my dreams be like those of innocents and sucking babes. Grant, O Lord, that the sun may not go down upon my wrath. But if any man this day hath done me wrong, that I may freely and heartily forgive him, as I desire at thy hands to be forgiven. Whether I sleep or wake, give thy angels charge over me that at what hour soever thou callest me I may like a faithful soldier be found ready to encounter death, and to follow the Lamb wheresoever he goeth."

Elsewhere I have said that to me it seems that much of Dekker's purity and clarity of phrase, at his best, sprang from his intimate knowledge of the Bible; in his prayers, biblical quotations are so interwoven with his own words as to appear a part of the very texture. Of course, if we seek deeper, the charm lies in the man himself, in his profoundly religious nature, in the temperament of an artist as sensitive to the beauty of holiness as to other forms of beauty. He had earlier attempted, on several occasions, to express his loyalty to Protestantism; but every attempt was a failure, for Dekker had no real interest in controversy and no power of invective. The gentleness of his genius, wasted in such work, had its way in the prayers, which, though essentially dramatic, are permeated with personality, not the expression of a temporary mood, though it is much to be capable of such a mood, but of a life-long fervor of faith and of sympathy with humanity. As a work of art, the prayer-book is almost flawless; it is nearly as impassioned as similar collections in Jeremy Taylor's "Holy Living," and it is more simple, tender, and unconventional.

CHAPTER VIII

We have already seen that about 1609 or 1610 Dekker stopped writing prose and returned to the theatre, and that the authors of "The Roaring Girl" hinted very plainly in 1611 by the motto on their title-page that they were in need of money. The same year is marked, it may be said parenthetically, by some commendatory verses of no great value, written for Taylor, the Water Poet. In 1612 Dekker's complaint of hard times grew still more pronounced: in the dedication of what was probably his next play, he wrote: "Knowledge and Reward dwell far asunder. Greatness lay once between them. But in his stead covetousness now. An ill neighbor, a bad benefactor, no paymaster to poets. By this hard housekeeping, or rather, shutting up of liberality's doors, merit goes a-begging and learning starves. Books had wont to have patrons, and now patrons have books. The snufft hat is lighted, consumes that which feeds it. A sign the world hath an ill ear when no music is good unless it strikes up for nothing. I have sung so, but will no more. A hue-and-cry follow his wit that sleeps when sweet tunes are sounding. But 'tis now the fashion. Lords look well; knights thank well; gentlemen promise well; citizens take well; gulls swear well: but none give well."[1]

In the Prologue to "The Roaring Girl" he or Middleton had written, partly, however, to excuse the "meanness" of the subject:

> " Tragic passion,
> And such grave stuff is this day out of fashion."

But of the three remaining plays that belong to the dramatic period 1610–1613, to be discussed in this chapter, one is a tragedy, if the death of the body and the manifold triumph of the soul constitute a tragedy; one is a tragicomedy with very little comedy of any sort in it; and the third is concerned with

[1] *If It be not Good,* P., III, 261.

the strife between human weakness and the powers of evil. As the date of the third play is certain, and as the subject and some details are connected with Dekker's prose, it may conveniently be considered first.

The full title is "If It be not Good, The Devil is in it. A New Play, as it hath been lately acted, with great applause, by the Queen's Majesty's Servants: at the Red Bull. Written by Thomas Dekker. *Flectere si nequeo Superos, Acheronta morebo.*" 1612.[2] It was written after May 14, 1610, for Ravaillac, who on that day murdered Henry IV, is a character in the epilogue in Hell.[3] Moll Cut-Purse is mentioned[4] as "late a sore tormented soul"—"at the Fortune," adds Fleay. It was a "new play" in 1612, and finally the dedication was composed shortly before "The White Devil" was acted, in 1611 or 1612. The date for the writing or the first acting of "If It be not Good," then, may be set down as 1611.[5]

The Fortune, to which Dekker had first offered the play, had rejected it, probably because it had in stock another play on the same subject:[6] in his kindly and generous recognition of the actors, "my loving and loved friends," to whom he dedicated the play, he writes: "When Fortune, in her blind pride, set her foot upon this imperfect building, as scorning the foundation and workmanship, you gently raised it up on the same columns, the frontispiece only a little more garnished."[7] Whether this garnishing refers to the prologue in Hell, as seems likely,[8] for it is a wretched piece of work and bears every evidence of hasty writing, or to other changes it is impossible to say, the more so as the text has come down to us in a corrupt state.[9] The Prologue, as well as the dedication, inveighs

---

[2] The running title is *If This be not a Good Play, the Devil is in it.*

[3] P., III, 354.

[4] P., III, 352–353.

[5] Fleay's argument for 1610 is not convincing.

[6] *Friar Rush:* Fleay, *Chr.,* I, 108. *Friar Rush and the Proud Woman of Antwerp:* Herford, 308.

[7] P., III, 261–262.

[8] This is Fleay's opinion.

[9] The Lurchall of the main play, as pointed out by Fleay, is usually Grumshall in the introduction: no pains were taken to reconcile the names. On

against the degenerate taste of theatre-goers and the "rudeness" of the plays then in vogue. But that mood does not last, and Dekker proceeds to draw a picture of the true poet. "Give me that man," he cries, who, when folly rules and the vast rooms of the theatre stand empty,

> " Can call the banished auditor home, and tie
> His ear with golden chains to his melody:
> Can draw with adamantine pen even creatures
> Forg'd out of th' hammer, on tiptoe to reach up,
> And from rare silence clap their brawny hands
> T' applaud what their charm'd soul scarce understands.
> That man give me, whose breast, fill'd by the Muses,
> With raptures into a second them infuses:
> Can give an actor, sorrow, rage, joy, passion,
> Whilst he again, by self-same agitation,
> Commands the hearers, sometimes drawing out tears,
> Then smiles, and fills them both with hopes and fears.
> That man give me: and to be such a one
> Our poet this day strives, or to be none;
> Lend not him hands for pity, but for merit:
> If he please, he's crown'd; if not, his fate must bear it."

The last lines exhibit the writer's usual independence, but in the Epilogue, a form of appeal to the audience he rarely employed, he intimates that "liberal" applause will be welcome. The Epilogue is interesting for other reasons; besides explaining the title of the play, it indicates that, in Dekker's conception of the matter, a drama was not a form of literature that might lightly be thrown off, impromptu, at any time. I quote the opening lines:

> " If't be not good, the Devil is in't, they say.
> The Devil was in't: this then is no good play
> By that conclusion; but hereby is meant,
> If for so many noons and midnights spent
> To reap three hours of mirth, our harvest-seed
> Lies still and rot, the Devil's in't indeed:
> Much Labour, Art, and Wit make up a Play."

---

p. 273, a comment of Jovinelli is put into the mouth of Rufman, who has not yet entered; on p. 310 a speech of the Sub-friar is given Friar Rush; on p. 281 a speech of one of the monks to Shackle-soul, the devil's name of Friar Rush.

In this play Dekker again brings continental folk-lore into English drama. His immediate source seems to have been "The Pleasant History of Friar Rush,"[10] well known in England as early as 1584, which tells the story of a devil sent by the Prince of Devils to a rich and dissolute monastery to complete the corruption of the inmates. The prologue in Hell, not borrowed from "Belphegor," as Herford shows, for it exists in the source,[11] seems to me, in the violent feebleness of its style, to depend upon Dekker's previous work of that sort, especially that essayed in "News from Hell," which was imitated from Lucian. As it was probably added only to attract the vulgar, it should not be read first by one who wishes to enjoy the play. In the main story, aside from the fact that Dekker merely hints at the licentiousness that bulks so largely in his source, his most important variation from the Friar Rush story lies in the fact that his devils attack virtuous persons or communities, not those already tainted with vice. "Dekker," writes Herford, "is thus brought back by sheer dramatic feeling to the original [Danish] conception of the story." He transforms a vicious sub-prior, at odds with the prior in the source, into a virtuous old man, who offsets the corruption of the body of monks in general and of the prior in particular. He further tones down the violence of the story by saving the cook, who in the "Pleasant History" is early cast into a kettle of boiling water, but in Dekker's version is only driven from the monastery by false accusation. In spite of these ameliorations, however, while the "Pleasant History" ends with repentance and salvation, Dekker's story ends for most of the monks in death and eternal punishment.

To the plot centering about Friar Rush, Dekker added two

[10] Registered 1567–8. The date of the first extant edition is 1620. *Literary Relations,* 303. Mr. Herford points out that Dekker by inadvertence retains the "Lucifer" of the legend instead of the Pluto of his own introduction in the scene in which the devils report their progress to their master.

In the discussion of the source and significance of the play I have drawn freely from Mr. Herford's book, 308–318.

[11] It is worth noting that in *Lanthorn and Candlelight* the devils hold a council to devise measures to regain their lapsing domain on earth, and finally send out one of their number to visit the world, G., III, 205–217. Similar material is employed in *A Strange Horse-race,* G., III, 346–350.

nearly parallel stories, one dealing with the court, the other with the business world, or, to be specific, with usurers. The first is admirably carried out; there is a good but inexperienced young king supported by two virtuous but not overwise old uncles; he falls a quick prey to the machinations of the clever devil Rufman, who is ably seconded by the young courtiers, especially the cynical Jovinelli; but when defeat in battle has brought him to the verge of suicide, to which he is urged by Rufman, his better soul suddenly awakes to see a heaven above the hell that yawns before him, and his kingdom and his bride are then restored.

Much less successful is the third plot. Towards the end it is needlessly complicated, and in the whole story there is absolutely no relief, for the third devil, Lurchall, has little to do but sit still and applaud his superior in villainy, Bartervile, the merchant and usurer;[12] in the first scene in which he appears, Lurchall says contentedly to himself:

> " Thou'st found
> A master, who more villany has by heart
> Than thou by rote. See him but play's own part,—
> And thou dost Hell good service. Bartervile,—
> There's in thy name a harvest makes me smile." [13]

In " If It be not Good," women have almost no part, and there is comparatively little of the humanity that one associates with Dekker's characterization. The chief exception is to be found in Father Clement, bold to condemn the sin of his superiors, compassionate of the weary pilgrims, very kindly to the cook Scumbroth, despising gold, discreetly holding down his head "as fast asleep" in the St. Anthony scene, and finally routing the powers of evil by his "holy spells." Scumbroth too is at first a genial figure whom Dekker had not the heart to damn; indeed he could not do it consistently, for in spite of the depredation wrought upon his life by the devil's gold, poor Scumbroth at least made an attempt to save the priory from

[12] Mr. Herford's interpretation of Bartervile seems to me unsustained by anything in the play.

[13] P., III, 295. In this plot Dekker uses some of the incidents of the story of Hans van Limericke and Joachim the Jew, already told in *The Raven's Almanac*.

Friar Rush. In the earlier scenes he has something of the simplicity and humor shown by Dekker's other servant clowns. That his speech becomes degraded after he has used infernal gold is certainly intentional and may be compared with the degenerate language spoken by Hircius and Spungius in "The Virgin Martyr." Even Friar Rush, at first, has a humorous spirit, exhibited in the long grace that enumerates the various heavy dishes forbidden to the friars, and in his argument, so convincing to his hearers, that "he that feeds well hath a good soul." Attractive, too, is the light and lyrical bill of fare promised under his management, which includes

> "Syrup of violets and of roses,
> Cowslip salads and kickchoses."

It may be added that in the St. Anthony scene there is another song that, as the singer is one of the tempters, sinks to licentiousness.

In spite of the outrageous prologue in hell, this play is one of serious intention; its evil spirits are not easily baffled or fooled, but, like Harpax in "The Virgin Martyr," are only too successful; even the epilogue in hell, with all its claptrap, contains some humor that is sufficiently grim. Bartervile's chief punishment is to stretch out his hands for his gold, only to find that it has become "air, shadows, things imaginary." Even the devils rather condemn the sins of the damned than rejoice in their fall. Here, as in the strange "Dream" written years later, Dekker permits his lost souls to ask the once unanswerable questions:

> "Why for a few sins that are long hence past
> Must I feel torment that shall ever last?"
> "Why is the devil,
> If man be born good, suffered to make him evil?"

Again, there is in this play considerable irony, unrelieved by humor or fantasy, that does not exist in Dekker's earlier or later plays and that seldom occurs in his prose. Conceived in an ironical spirit are the two devils that are Dekker's creation, especially Lurchall, who finds on earth a teacher. Pluto assumes a virtue in hell superior to that on earth, and Scumbroth murmurs, as he watches the devils embrace, "Sure these are no Christian devils, they so love one another." In an ironical sense too must be taken the speech on the salt tribute.[14]

Those who lay stress upon Dekker's tenderness, interpreting that beautiful and rare quality as weakness, should observe that he was capable of devising a drama more remarkable for power than for sentiment, an almost pitiless indictment of the court, the church, and the world of money-dealers, a play in which but one wrong-doer is allowed to repent, the rest perishing body and soul. "For boldly planned and all-embracing infernal machinery," writes Herford, "the play has no rival in the English drama." It is, to quote again, "the very idea afterwards carried out in Goethe's Faust,—the recasting of an old devil-story in terms of modern society. The polished urbanity of King Alphonso's guest, the ironical serviceableness of the merchant's clerk, already at isolated points recall the Mephistopheles of Goethe rather than that of Marlowe, and assuredly there is no scene in Marlowe's 'Faustus,'—the immortal opening and close always excepted—at all equal in conception to Dekker's pictures of the sudden transformation under temptation of a court of frail idealists and a convent of only half voluntary ascetics."

But if Dekker showed strength of an unexpected kind in the conception of the play and in some scenes, he lacked either the time or the ability to execute the greater part of his plan with any degree of adequacy. While the verse is not quite so super-humanly bad as Swinburne would have us believe, it offers few passages of any charm. Perhaps the King's speech at his lowest ebb of despair lends itself to quotation as well as any:

> " Fetch me, dear friend,
> An armed pistol, and mouth it at my breast:
> I'll make away myself, and all my sorrows
> Are made away."

It remains to be said, in the first place, that in the details of this play, as well as in some features of the scheme, re-appear

[14] P., III, 297. There is also an attack upon simony, p. 276, and upon the misuse of hospital funds, pp. 274–275.

elements that belong to the earlier stage: the echo dialogue, the pseudo-scholastic argument, the Golden head, the spectacular burning of the monastery, reminiscent of the catastrophe in "The Jew of Malta"; in the second place, we find what we have learned to expect,—pity for soldiers, for scholars, for the cheated and deceived, and something that we do not expect,—incidental slighting remarks about law, the best known of which is spoken by the King's councillor, who has put the laws enacted by Parliament into common language, and who will not hang them out of sight,

> "Like cobwebs in foul rooms, through which great flies
> Break through; the less being caught by th' wing there dies."

When Father Clement finally puts Friar Rush to flight, he exorcises him

> "by good men's prayers;
> The continence of saints, by which as stairs
> They ascend to heaven; by virgins' chastity;
> By martyrs' crown'd deaths, which recorded lie
> In silver leaves above,"—

words that may be taken as a sort of introduction to the play to be discussed next—"The Virgin Martyr."

There is no record of the early history of this play, which was already old in the first mention of it that has come down to us. On October 6, 1620, Sir George Buc, then Master of Revels, made a record of the reforming of "The Virgin Martyr" for the Red Bull, where the Queen's men were still playing. It was registered to print December 7, 1621, and was published the following year under the title: "The Virgin Martyr, a Tragedy, as it hath been divers times publicly Acted with great Applause, by the servants of his Majesty's Revels. Written by Phillip Messenger and Thomas Deker." On July 7, 1624, there was added a new scene that was never published. Fleay's guess that this play in its original form was the anonymous "Dioclesian" of the Diary, 1594, which he ascribes to Dekker, has nothing to substantiate it.[15] Aside from other

---

[15] The "rounce-robble-hobble," etc. (P., IV, 68), which he considers a vestige of primitive date is paralleled by "Bounce go the guns . . . romble,

considerations, the delicacy of characterization, on the one hand, and the vocabulary of Spungius and Hircius on the other, are approached by nothing in Dekker's known early work.

Critics are at one in assuming that Dekker and Massinger did not work together upon the play. The evidence seems to show that when the latter came to revise it, it was still in the hands of the Queen's servant, who had presented "If It be not Good" after the Fortune had refused it. Since Dekker is not known to have written for the theatre during his imprisonment from 1613 to 1619, "The Virgin Martyr" may reasonably be assigned to the dramatic period that preceded it. Some internal considerations strongly confirm this view. The most important lies in its close relations with "If It be not Good." Both plays deal with the same kind of material, the eternal struggle between the powers of good and evil, and both deal with it in the same way. In the first play there are three incarnate devils; in the second there is an incarnate angel as well as an incarnate devil, and besides the devil, there are two morality figures that likewise make evil seem incarnate. Instead of an old man, good and brave but powerless to rescue any besides himself, there is a saintly girl whom sin cannot approach, whose eyes are blind to all love but that of Heaven, and whose unwavering devotion to that heavenly love brings about the salvation of others. Although this play is called a tragedy, it is the story of a conquest: the powers of evil are beaten, the good prevail. In all this, but especially in the substitution of one lovely invincible figure for ineffective virtue, Dekker was making an advance or, in other words, "If It be not Good" was an unconscious preliminary study for "The Virgin Martyr." There are some minor correspond-

romble, go the waters" of *1 Honest Whore* (P., II, 82); and by a passage in Marston's *Antonio and Mellida* (II, 1) spoken by Catso: "But was't not rare sport at the sea-battle, whilst rounce robble hobble roared from the ship sides," etc. Such parodies of Harvey's hexameters might have been written at any time, especially by Dekker, who, as pointed out earlier, often reverts to the interests of his youth and who always remained on the side of Nash.

ences between the two plays: in both, for example, a ribald vocabulary is deliberately put into the mouths of the degraded; in " The Virgin Martyr " the British slave[16] speaks very much like the Soldier[17] in "If It be not Good "; and Harpax in the former play says of the devil, "He's more loving to man than man to man is,"[18] a speech that may be compared in general with the whole spirit of "If It be not Good," and in particular with an utterance of Scumbroth already quoted.[19] 1612, then, the year of the publication of the Friar Rush play, or possibly 1613, seems to be a probable date.

The source, pointed out by Koeppel,[20] is a Cologne Martyrology of the year 1576, "De Probatis Sanctorum Historiis," which contains the story of the persecution of Dorothea by Sapritius, the reconversion of two sisters by her persuasion, and the scoffing request of Theophilus that she should send from Heaven some of the fruit and flowers she had spoken of on earth. Dekker invented the hopeless love of Antoninus for Dorothea and that of Artemia for Antoninus. He added the devil Harpax and the two morality figures, and he developed from the mere mention of a boy bearing heavenly fruits and flowers the exquisite conception of Dorothea's child-servant who reveals to her his angelhood only at the hour of her martyrdom.

It is a great pity that the play has not come down to us untouched by Massinger's hand; yet doubtless for him too the subject had an appeal, for though he wrote no drama at all similar and created no characters at all comparable with Dorothea and the boy angel, he was interested in the soul's welfare, and in "The Maid of Honor" he substituted, at the end, devotion to God for devotion to earthly love. In spite of the irony of fate that impels some critics to discuss "The Virgin

[16] P., IV, 64.

[17] P., III, 291.

[18] P., IV, 57.

[19] To me, the very words of Father Clement, quoted above, p. 154, appear to show the direction that Dekker's thoughts were taking.

[20] Quellen-Studien zu den Dramen Chapman's, Massinger's, und Ford's. Quellen und Forschungen, 1897. See his note p. 83, for an indication that Dekker may have known some additional version of the legend.

Martyr" among his works, Ward is surely right in saying
that the greater part seems to have been contributed by
Dekker,[21] adding in the next sentence: "The action is simplicity itself; nor is there the slightest attempt at refining upon
the clear prose of the fable"—good evidence, if it were needed,
that Dekker was the author of the original plan, with its fine
climax of Dorothea's finishing her work on earth by rescuing
from eternal death the cruelest of her persecutors.[22] General
agreement has long assigned to him the most beautiful characters and poetry, together with the most degraded personages
with their talk. The pathos of Antoninus' love for Dorothea
seems to me in his manner, and so does the somewhat ineffective violence of the speech of Sapritius. Although the problem
is complicated by the circumstance that we have no unaided
Massinger play of about the same date as a basis for comparison, yet the frequent recurrence of Dekker's favorite
phrases and of his mannerisms of style make it likely that Massinger's work was mostly revision, not substitution, and that
the older poet's actual words are still, for the greater part,
retained. The first act, so highly praised by Coleridge, so even,
dignified and uninspired, is apparently an exception, for it
contains fewer evidences of Dekker's hand than any other act.
Of the rest of the play, Gifford assigns to Dekker all of the
second act, the prose of the third, and the first scene of the last.
To this I should add the greater part of the fourth act; clearly
his are the rather rude talk of Antoninus, first with the doctor and afterwards with his father, the episode of the British
slave, the scene in which Spungius, Hircius, and Harpax figure, and that in which the two first grow weary in beating
their mistress, and the greater part of the scene of Dorothea's
death.[23] Sometimes it is Dekker's fondness for iteration and
rhyme that help to decide his authorship, as in Angelo's words
to his mistress under torture:

[21] *Eng. Dram. Lit.,* III, 12–13.

[22] This is not Ward's opinion of the fifth act.

[23] Specifically p. 74 to the end of the act. Ward is doubtless right in
giving to Massinger Dorothea's long speech beginning "Thou fool," p. 73.
Dekker's Dorothea would not say "Thou fool."

"There fix thine eye still; thy glorious crown must come
Not from soft pleasure, but by martyrdom.
There fix thine eye still; when we next do meet,
Not thorns, but roses, shall bear up thy feet:
There fix thine eye still ";

and as in her dying speech.

"The distinguishing merit of this tragedy," writes Ward, "lies in the grandeur of the conception, which indicates a noble ambition to rise above the level of the themes to which the English tragedy of the age had accustomed itself and its audiences." No doubt he is right in saying that the execution fails to equal the conception, but I, at least, feel little inclined to cavil at a play that offers one of the most perfect and original scenes in the Elizabethan drama. Every student of poetry knows that dialogue of limpid loveliness between Dorothea and her servant, the boy-angel; it has the purity of sentiment and the purity of coloring of Fra Angelico, and there is not a breath to mar its beauty. The sustained gentleness of tone and rhythm and the artlessness of phrase remind one of Dekker's book of prayers, although these qualities are noticeable in smaller compass or less elevated in feeling in some of his other plays, and they appear again in "The Witch of Edmonton." Less fine but very moving is the scene in which Angelo returns to earth with the basket of celestial fruits and flowers promised by Dorothea, presenting it to Theophilus in language as gentle as that he has used in the colloquy with his mistress.

The prose scenes that have brought so much reproach upon Dekker's name must not pass without a word of comment. Hircius and Spungius are personifications, as Dekker took pains to state;[24] their names represent the two sins most abhorrent to the maiden purity of their mistress, and most in contrast with it. It is probable that as a secondary purpose they were intended to contribute humor, and occasionally, only occasionally, the humor is legitimate. But they were certainly not put into play in a spirit of immorality; the coarseness is superficial; it lies in the vocabulary that these morality figures use, not in the situations. Dekker everywhere uses the specific

[24] P., IV, 24.

and the concrete with remarkable ease, and in this partly lies the blame. While unable to see in the speech of these persons "the raciness and glow" that Lamb speaks of, I at least marvel much at the taste that can tolerate the tone and the situations in many of Massinger's plays, and balk at the prose dialogue of "The Virgin Martyr," which is as easily forgettable as Dorothea and Angelo are memorable.

The third play that gives evidence of belonging to this brief dramatic period is "Match Me in London." It was mentioned as an old play by Herbert, August 21, 1623, and had previously been licensed by Sir George Buc. It was first printed in 1631, with an epistle-dedicatory to Lodowick Carlell, but presumably Dekker did not supervise the editing, which is very badly done.[25] The title-page tells us something about its history: "A Tragicomedy Called Match Me in London. As it hath been often Presented; first, at the Bull in St. John's Street, and lately at the Private House in Drury Lane called the Phoenix." It will be remembered that "If It be not Good" was played at the Bull by the Queen's men in 1612, and that we first hear of "The Virgin Martyr" at the same theater. Internal as well as external reasons associate this play with the other two, especially with "If It be not Good." Like the latter, it contains allusions to "The Roaring Girl"[26] and to monopolies;[27] and in both Dekker employs a species of hunting the letter that he uses nowhere else. In "Match Me in London," we find Bilbo saying: "Be attentive. I will show you your Court Coranto pace; it consisteth of five bees and three cees; you

---

[25] Before printing the play had undergone revision. There is an isolated comedy scene (P., IV, 192–193) in which the names of the characters have been changed, for the "Clown" that "enters" becomes Bilbo after his first speech, and the "Coxcomb" is not to be found elsewhere in the play under that name, though he is doubtless identical with Pacheco, servant of John, and therefore "of the Court." In the stage directions of the second scene of the third act appears the name of Fuentes, not elsewhere mentioned. Revision may be also responsible for the fact that it is not clear how Tormiella was tricked into leaving her home the second time.

[26] P., IV, 141. Bilbo. "I am not the roaring girl you take me for." Pointed out by Fleay.

[27] *Idem*, 149. "Give him a Court loaf; stop's mouth with a monopoly."

borrow of any man, are brave on any terms, brag at any hand to pay, bellow at any that demands it, bite at any catchpole that fangs you, but carry neither conscience nor coin in your whole pockets."[28] With this may be compared Scumbroth's complaints after he has fallen from the black tree: " But two sins have undone me, prodigality and covetousness; and three pees have peppered me: the punk, the pot, and pipe of smoke."[29]

There is no obvious reason why we should not accept Fleay's date, " about 1611,"[30] but I incline to push it forward to 1612–1613. During the years that followed the publication of " The Roaring Girl " with its significant motto, Dekker's financial condition had been apparently getting worse, for in 1613, in the epistle prefixed to "A Strange Horse-race," he wrote: " The title of this book is like a jester's face, set, howsoever he draws it, to beget mirth: but his ends are hid to himself and those are to get money."[31] The same year Dekker entered upon his long imprisonment. These facts speak for themselves. I cannot dissociate from them the circumstance that "Match Me in London" has throughout an undertone of pain and bewilderment; and its total effect, upon me at least, is a piercing sense of the tragedy of life not found elsewhere in Dekker's writings except fragmentarily; it is most nearly approached by the ironical portions of " If It be not Good." Single passages hardly illustrate my meaning, but two speeches may be quoted; the first is spoken by the injured husband when the King asks what will content him, the second when he is driven from the church.

"Nothing, nothing. Why Sir, the powers above cannot please us, and can kings, think you? when we are brought forth to the world, we cry and bawl as if we were unwilling to be born; and when we are a-dying, we are mad at that." [32]

[28] *Idem,* 193.

[29] P., III, 329. See also P., IV, 190, where the figure about the law corresponds exactly to the figure already quoted in *If It be not Good,* P., III, 287.

[30] Fleay's identification of the play with the anonymous *Set at Maw,* 1594, based upon a few not unusual allusions to games of car ls, may be disregarded in view of the other evidence.

[31] G., III, 312.

[32] P., IV, 190.

" Dost thou tell me of thy proclamations, that I am banisht from the Court? That Court where I came to thee was none of thine; it belongs to a King that keeps open Court, one that never wrong'd a poor beggar, never took away any man's wife unless he sent his pursuivant death for her: oh thou daring sacrilegious royal thief, wilt thou rob the Church too as thou hast me? thrust me out of that house too in the sanctuary, turn'd devil in a crowd of angels ! " [33]

Somewhat similar in tone are the words of the base old father when the King orders him from the Court:

" Does the bell ring out? I care not. Your kingdom was a-departing too. I had a place in Court for nothing, and if it be gone I can lose nothing ; I ha' been like a lord in a play, and that done, my part ends."[34]

In the conception and carrying out of the two plots of the play is perceptible for the first time the influence of the romances of Beaumont and Fletcher.[35] How far, in his efforts to follow them, Dekker departed from his usual simplicity may best be pointed out by giving a rough outline of the play. The main plot is concerned with the attempt of a bad King of Spain upon the virtue of Tormiella, the young wife of a shopkeeper. The scene of action is first Cordova and then Seville. The play opens at midnight with Tormiella's suspicious father searching for her, at first alone, then with the aid of the suitor whom he would force her to marry; after the runaway marriage of the true lovers that very night, there follows a scene in the husband's shop, a reconciliation with the father, the revengeful lover's discovery of Tormiella, the visit to her of the disguised King conducted by an evil woman, the repeated wiling away of Tormiella from her home, the compliance of her father, the jealousy of the Queen who tries to make herself kill Tormiella, the strategy by which Cordolente secures an interview with his wife, the supposed murder of the Queen by the King and the supposed madness of Tormiella, who finally reveals her sanity to the revengeful lover now in the employment of the King. The sub-plot involves the King's brother and the Admiral, the Queen's father, who has

[33] *Idem,* 212.
[34] *Idem,* 215.
[35] Cp. Schelling, *Elizabethan Drama,* II, 235.

discovered the intended treason of the former, and who is apparently poisoned by him; but the Admiral comes to life and is supposedly made the executioner of the traitor. When the jealous lover has persuaded the husband to kill Tormiella at the altar, and Tormiella to kill the King on their wedding night, the final tragedy is averted by thunder and lightning in the church: this occasions the repentence of all the sinful except the unnatural father; the dead come to life and all ends happily.

Here we have a number of the characteristics that distinguish the romances:[36] the succession of highly improbable events, the mixture of tragic and idyllic matters ending in a happy dénouement, and the attempt to present a rapid succession of telling situations. Varied and violent emotion finds expression in short scenes and broken dialogue unusually swift and terse;[37] for example:

> *King.* Wilt venture for me?
> *Gazetto,* To the threshold of hell.
> *King.* May I trust thee?
> *Gaz.* Else employ me not.
> *King.* Did'st ever kill a scorpion?
> *Gaz.* Never; I ha' been stung by one.
> *King.* Did'st never bait a wild bull?
> *Gaz.* That 's the pastime I most love and follow.[38]

Or this:

> *Queen.* Out, crocodile. (*Spurns her.*)
> *Tormiella.* You will not murther me!
> *Queen.* I'll cure you of the King's evil. (*Draws two knives.*)
> *Tor.* To one woman
> Another should be pitiful; hear me speak.
> *Queen.* How dares so base a flower follow my sun
> At's rising to his setting?
> *Tor.* I follow none.
> *Queen.* How dar'st thou, serpent, wind about a tree
> That 's mine.

[36] See Professor Thorndike's *Beaumont and Fletcher*, pp. 107, 112–113, 124–128.

[37] In the whole play there are but three speeches over fourteen lines long and few over ten.

[38] P., IV, 205.

Tor. I do not.
Queen. Or to shake the leaves?
Tor. By Heaven, not any.
Queen. Or once to taste the fruit
    Though thrown into thy lap? If from a harlot
    Prayers ever came, pray, for thou dy'st.
Tor. Then kill me.[39]

In spite of his attempt to follow up the successes of Beaumont and Fletcher, so superbly carried on by Shakespere it is almost superfluous to say that Dekker acquired no particular command of the method of the romances, lacking as he did, the great constructive skill of his models, especially their power to work up to an ingenious climax. Yet the little play has for some readers considerable charm. If the King's repentance seems insincere, Dekker leaves the father, whose old heart was as corrupt in the first scene as in the last, both unrepentant and unforgiven. While yielding to influences alien to his nature, Dekker retained to some extent his unsophisticated way of dealing with his characters, thus partly atoning for the extreme improbability of the events. The central figure is Tormiella. She is so young, not yet seventeen, and so lovable that Bilbo runs away from her father's household, where, as he explains, he had had "man servants and maid servants under him," simply in order to serve her. Her kindliness towards her inferiors, her gentleness and her fierceness, the soft intensity of her love for Cordolente, are appealingly drawn. She belongs to a more protected class than "gentle Jane," with finer instincts, and she is not allowed to take any but a graceful part in the shop scene in which the disguised King bargains for gloves. This business is left to Bilbo, shrewd, faithful, and witty servant, at his best in a little war of wits, which he "of the City" wages with the Coxcomb, or Pacheco "of the Court," at the end of which they ceremoniously back away from each other with "dear signior," "delicious don."

Although the execution of the plot is, for Dekker, unusually

[39] *Idem,* 185–186. In both selections I have chosen the part of the scene that best illustrates the point, but a glance at almost any page will confirm the general statement.

even and unmarred by crudeness or coarseness, it contains few quotable passages of any length. Yet it is surcharged with emotion and the characters speak a highly metaphorical language, whether the King says of the weeping Tormiella,

> " What 's here?
> Why is this rose deni'd with a pearled tear
> When the sun shines so warm? "

or the bitter Gazetto comments as he catches sight of her, " I saw a dove fly by that had eaten carrion; it showed like a corrupted churchman"; or Cordolente complains in his homely words, " Oh sir, the smallest letters hurt your eyes most, and the least headache which comes by a woman's knocking hurts more than a cut to the skull by a man's knocking."

On the twenty-ninth of October, 1612, was presented a pageant devised by Dekker for the society of Merchant Taylors on the occasion of Sir John Swinerton's becoming Lord Mayor of London. It was printed the same year under the title: "Troja-Nova Triumphans. London Triumphing, or The Solemn, Magnificent, and Memorable Receiving of that worthy Gentleman, Sir John Swinerton, Knight, into the City of London, after his Return from taking the Oath of Mayoralty at Westminster, on the Morrow next after Simon and Jude's day, being the 29 of October, 1612." There is an epistle-dedicatory to the Mayor, in which Dekker, in his usual way, explains that while the "colors of this piece" are his own, the cost was borne by the Merchant Taylors: " to which nothing was wanting that could be had and everything had that was required." In the general introduction, Dekker speaks at some length of "our best-to-be-beloved friends, the Noblest strangers," meaning Frederick, Count Palatine of the Rhine, and his retinue. There were shows by water as well as by land, but, writes Dekker rather scornfully at the end of the piece, "Apollo having no hand in them, I suffer them to die by that which fed them; that is to say, powder and smoke. Their thunder according to the old gally-foist-fashion was too loud for any of the Nine Muses to be bidden by it." He mentions with pride the four "living beasts" upon which his

Tritons sat, not creations of painted cloth and brown paper but living creatures quaintly disguised "like the natural fishes, of purpose to avoid the trouble and pestering of porters, who with much noise and little comeliness are every year most unnecessarily employed." The verse does not require much comment: there is a welcome song with a well-managed refrain, a good phrase about Rumour and the "repercussive sounding" of her echoes, and some excellent democratic advice for the new Mayor.

The year 1613 is marked by the publication of "A Strange Horse-Race," already noticed. This must have been hackwork indeed, for aside from the contents which proclaim its character and the confession that its purpose was "to get money," Dekker hints that the book has been edited: "Yet the picture hath lost some of the colors I gave it."[40] And although the two prefaces contain a number of such sayings as, "It can be no shame to gather a violet growing close to the ground," or "The Titles of Books are like painted chimneys in great country-houses, make a show afar off, and catch travellers' eyes"; yet both are apologetic,—"a homely piece of work, neither so good as you deserve, nor so rich as I do wish it"; "bear with the hard-favouredness of the title"; and he closes the epistle to the Understanders with an abruptness and a note of strain and fatigue very unlike his usual easy "farewell" to his readers, and nowhere observable till now.

In 1613 began the real tragedy of Dekker's life, when as a climax to his money troubles he was thrown into the King's Bench Prison. Not all the independence of his spirit or the toil of his pen saved him from suffering much of the pain he had described with such sympathy some seven years earlier. In spite of the quiet dignity of his letters written in prison and the epigrammatic reserve of the prose also written there, we know from another source that he felt all the anguish that the heart of a poet could feel in such surroundings, not merely physical but the far crueler anguish of imagination, for in the "Dream" of Heaven and Hell that is the one poetic relic of those seven years, torment, horror, pain have a larger part than joy and rapture.

[40] G., III, 310.

When Dekker entered the prison walls, he was about forty-one years old. Neither letters nor personal utterance connected with the "Dream" mention wife or child. Of all the friends that might conceivably have come to his aid, we know of but one that did so. There may have been others, but no similar accident has preserved the record for us. This friend was Edward Alleyn, Henslowe's son-in-law and partner, a famous actor of majestic parts, the crowning act of whose life was the founding of Dulwich College—"College of God's gift," as he preferred to say. Such philanthrophy, designed to aid the destitute and educate the poor, was of the sort to rouse Dekker's keenest enthusiasm and in prison he set to work upon a poem to commemorate the College and its founder. Perhaps the consecration of the College chapel on the first of September, 1616, was the occasion that called forth his poem, for the letter with which it was enclosed is dated eleven days later. For personal reasons, it is a pity that the verses have not come down to us, but possibly the poet expressed in "The Wonder of a Kingdom" a more eloquent eulogy of "God's gift" than he could put into an occasional poem. Fortunately the letter that accompanied the poem has been preserved in the archives of Dulwich College.

"To my worthy and wor^{ll}-freind Edw. Allin, Esquier, at his house at Dullidge.

S^r

Out of that respect wch I ever caryed to yor Worth, (now heightned by a Pillar of yor owne erecting) doe I send theis poore testimonies of a more rich Affection. I am glad (yf I bee the First) that I am the first to Consecrate to Memory, (yf at least you so embrace it) So noble and pious a Work, as This, yor last and worthiest is. A passionate desire of expressing gladnes to See Goodnes so well delivered having bin long in labour in the world made mee thus far to venture. And it best becomes mee to Sing any thing in praise of Charity, because, albeit I have felt few handes warme thorough that complexion, yett imprisonment may make me long for them. Yf anything in my Eûlogium (or Praise) of yo^u and yor noble Act bee offensive, lett it be excused because I live amongst the Gothes and Vandalls, where Barbarousnes is predominant. Accept my will howsoever And mee
Ready to doe yo^u any service
Tho. Dekker.

King's Bench Sept 12. 1616."[41]

[41] J. P. Collier, *Memoirs of Edward Alleyn,* Shak. Soc. (1841), 131.

Alleyn soon sent assistance of some sort to Dekker, for an obviously later letter, undated and without the address, reads as follows:

" S^r.

I give you thanks for the last remembrance of your love. I write nowe, not poetically, but as an orrator, not by waye of declamation, but by petition, that you would be pleased, upon my lovinge lynes, to receave a yong man (sonn to a worthie yeoman of Kent here prisoner) able by his owne meanes to mayntayne himselfe, whose fortunes will answere itt. Hee is a yonge man lovinge you, beinge of your name, and desires no greater happines than to depend upon [you]. You shall doe mee much honor if you thinke him fitt to serve you as a servant, and him much love, because of your name, to receave. The yonge man is of good parts, both of bodie and mynd. I knowe you respect such a one, and I would not (upon that reputation I hold with you) offer a servant to bee unworthie of your attendance. If you please to receave him upon my commendation and your owne tryall, I shall thinck my selfe beholden to you, and you, as I hope, no waye repent the receavinge of such a servant of your owne name. Soe I rest

Your lovinge freind

Tho. Dekker."[42]

Comment upon these letters is hardly necessary. Yet how characteristic they are! the first " passionate " in its praise of one of the finer forms of charity, the second illuminating a practical and careful side of Dekker's proverbial kindheartedness that we have little chance elsewhere to observe. Characteristic too is the appropriate little apology for anything that may be " offensive in his poem," and the reserve with which he refers to the discomforts of his situation.

Dekker was in prison for about seven years; his own words leave no doubt upon the question:

" Out of a long sleep, which for almost seven years together, seized all my senses, drowning them in a deep Lethe of forgetfulness and burying me to the world in the lowest grave of oblivion: meeting in that drowsy voyage with nothing but frightful apparitions by reason, as now I guess, of the place in which I lay, being a cave strongly shut up by most devilish and dreadful enchantments, I did at last fall into a dream, which presented to my waking soul infinite pleasures commix'd with inutterable horrors."[43]

He mentions the same period of years in the epistle to

[42] *Memoirs of Edward Alleyn*, 186.
[43] *To the Reader*, prefixed to *Dekker, his Dream*, G., III, 11.

Endymion Porter.[44] These years might have been among the most productive of Dekker's lifetime; they were just preceded by a group of plays that in all probability included "The Virgin Martyr"; they were followed by another group represented by "The Witch of Edmonton." When we think of what might have filled that interval, pity for the poet is almost lost in pity for ourselves. Yet he was not wholly idle during these years. We do not know whether he tried to write plays. Besides the lost poem sent to Alleyn, there was another called "The Artillery Garden," a patriotic effusion, dated 1616. New editions of "1 Honest Whore" were called for in 1615 and in 1616, and "The Shoemaker's Holiday" was reprinted in 1618. More important was a new version of "Lanthorn and Candlelight." This had already run through four editions, the last, in 1612, under the following title, in part: "O per se O, or a New Cryer of Lanthorn and Candlelight. Being an addition or Lengthening of the Bellman's Second Night-walk. In which are discovered those Villanies which the Bellman, because he went i'th dark, could not see: now laid open to the world." It retained the preface of 1609 and added some new material, including the canting song that gives it the first member of its title. The issue of 1616 has a slightly different title, which I give in full: "Villanies discovered by Lanthorn and Candlelight and the Help of a New Cryer called O per se O. Being an addition to the Bellman's Second Night-walk: and laying open to the world of those abuses which the Bellman, because he went i'th dark, could not see. With Canting Songs and other new conceits never before Printed. Newly corrected and enlarged by the Author."[45] The preface is

---

[44] G., III, 7. The oft-quoted remark of Oldys reads, "From 1613 to 1616 and I know not how much longer."

[45] I have not seen this edition; but there is in the British Museum a copy of the 1612 edition, which has on the fly-leaf preceding the title-page a note by the former owner, Mr. Heber, from which I make the following extracts: "Another edition of this book was printed for John Busby in 1616 intitled 'Villanies discovered by Lanthorne and Candle-light, & the help of a new cryer called O per se O,' etc. On comparing it with the present one, I find it is increased by the addition of a whole section 'Of a Prison' occupying 6 chapters. . . . Ed. 1620 is an exact reprint of 1616."
I have used the edition of 1620. There is internal evidence that the

altered to permit the author to say, still keeping the figure of warring against rogues, "To furnish this army the better with soldiers have I opened a prison, out of which what troops issue and how practised in discipline, let but a drum beat to call up the rear; and thou shalt easily in one light skirmish know of what mettle they are." This promise is fulfilled by the insertion of a new section entitled "Of a Prison," made up of six chapters under the headings: Certain Discoveries of a Prison by way of Essays and Characters, written by a Prisoner; Of Prisoners; Of Creditors; Of Choice of Company in Prison; Of Visitants; Of Jailors.

Now one of Dekker's fellow prisoners in Kings' Bench Prison in 1617–1618 was Geffray Mynshul, of whom nothing is known except what is revealed in his one well-known volume called "Essays and Characters of a Prison and Prisoners," published in 1618 while he was still in confinement for debt. In this book he shows such keen appreciation of the prison tract of his companion in misfortune as not only to discuss the same subjects under similar titles and with but one exception in the same order, but also to borrow whole passages without change of figure or phrase.[46] The last third of the book which corresponds to nothing in "Villanies Discovered" is full of Dekker's favorite expressions or special ways of dealing with a subject, and the first of the three epistles, which is addressed to the "Young Gentlemen of Gray's Inn," though signed G. M., is in Dekker's liveliest manner, embellished with characteristic puns and pet figures.[47] As far as a distinction can be drawn, the essays avowedly by Dekker employ a style, that is rather more brief, pointed,

additions of 1616 remained unchanged, for Dekker speaks of his having made "more than a three years' voyage" to "these infortunate islands."

[46] For parallel passages proving this statement I must refer to an article, *Geffray Mynshul and Thomas Dekker* to be printed in *The Journal of English and Germanic Philology.*

[47] The wording of this epistle, dated June 6, 1618, indicates (1) that it was written for a second edition; (2) that the first edition was anonymous. The second epistle, dated January 27, 1617, speaks of the book as the author's "first-born" and is signed with Mynshul's name in full.

The mystery of Mynshul's method of using Dekker's material I shall not try to solve here.

abhoristic, couched in shorter sentences, and the tone is, on the whole, rather more Christian, the chapter on jailors, for example, being little more than an attempt to account for their "crabbedness" by the character of their occupation. Dekker allowed his section to remain in the 1620 edition, but when, in 1632, he brought out the book under a new name with changes, he replaced it by another prison-picture more carefully worked up and better integrated with the scheme of the pamphlet.

Since the portions of "Villanies Discovered" that Mynshul did not employ are not readily accessible, let Dekker speak for himself, first in an apology for his work:

"I make not an orchard but a private walk or rather a small garden-plot set with pot-herbs for the kitchen. The which I write is not a book, but a mere rhapsody of mine own disturbed cogitations. This fruit is no tree but a young plant new-budded, from whose tender branches thus much I gather: That imprisonment is a distillation, for at one and the same lymbec do we draw forth the bitter waters of men's oppression with our own sorrows and the sweet waters of patience if we can have the stomach to bear them."[48]

Passing over a contrast between the young and the old man in prison, I quote again from the same chapter:

"Art thou full of money in prison? Thou art a ship fraught full of wines in a tempest; it makes the Master Pilot and our[49] owner drunk, and then all is cast away. Avoid these draughts; for riot in a prison is dancing in shipwreck; it is blasphemy in thunder, and cursing in a time of pestilence. The name of a 'Good Fellow' is thereby gotten. But thou payest too dear to a Lapland Witch for a knot full of wind. The silver here saved is to thy wife a dowry, to thy children portions, to thyself a revenue. Prodigal expense in a jail is to call for more wine in a tavern when thou canst not stand."

In the chapter on prisoners, the philosophy of Shadow and Babulo re-appears:

"As for wants, hadst thou all things in the world, thou wouldst wish more, and lack much more than thou wishest for: no king hath always content, and no poor man is ever sad. . . . What want dost thou grieve at? It is no other sun shines on thee but the same; no other air breathes in thy face but the same; no other earth bears thee but the same, and in the same

[48] Ch. XI, unpaged.
[49] Her?

shalt thou be buried. That mother will never change her love; none in this portion are disinherited for bastards. But art thou in prison and do friends forsake thee; yet do not thou forsake thyself: the farther they fly from thee, the closer stick thou to thine own guard. Lie in an unwholesome bed, foul sheets, and with a loathsome bedfellow; there will be a lodging one day for thee where thou shalt have no cause to complain of these abuses. Art thou clapt in irons and thrown currishly into a dungeon out of which the sun is shut: Care not; mourn not. There is an eye that can pierce through locks and doors of iron to look upon and pity thee. And a hand which, without bribing the frozen palm of a jailor, can turn all keys, and through the narrowest grate can put in bread of comfort to feed thee whilst thou art drinking the waters of thine own affliction."

The chapter on creditors, while it opens with praise for the merciful, is chiefly an indictment of the merciless creditor written for the most part in a grave and reserved manner. I quote a single passage:

" I have heard of some pirates who carrying in their ships the rich vessels and vestments of the Church, broken and cut in pieces to make money of them: a storm hath risen and within eyesight of shore ship and men have been swallowed up in the sea: a quick and just trial for such thieves; distroyers of temples never die but by such vengeance. I protest before my Maker, I would not in scorn strike the picture of Christ, break in pieces the image of a holy martyr, no, nor spoil, or so much as deface the monumental grave of mine enemy. But more than sacrilege dost thou commit that ruinest a temple in which thy builder dwells. And how many of these temples dost thou lay flat with the earth in one year? nay, perhaps in one fatal term."[50]

The "choice of company in prison" must have presented problems. Yet, writes Dekker:

" Society is the string at which the life of man hangs; without it is no music; two in this make but an unison. Adam had his Eve. And every son of Adam hath a brother whom he loves.[51] . . . Since therefore thy companion must of necessity grow on the same tree with thee, it is fit he should be of the same color and taste, of which thou thyself art. Let him be like a die, even, square, smooth, and true, to run, so near as thou canst, neither higher nor lower than thou that art to run with him. If his fortunes be above thine, yet in the carriage of thy mind, lift it up to a height to equal

[50] The fine passage that follows is exactly reproduced by Mynshul. See *Essayes and Characters* (1821), published by Ballantyne and Co., p. 30: " Thou takest," etc.

[51] So far as in Mynshul, 38.

his fortunes. Is he bad whom thou takest by the hand? Do thy best to make him good. Is he good? be thou ashamed to be otherwise. Let him have some learning; he will be unto thee a winged hour-glass to send away the minutes of adversity merrily. Or if thou canst not get one with learning, be sure he comes furnished with wit; his tongue will be a sweet chime to rock thy cares and his own asleep. If he hath both wit and learning and yet want honesty, venture not, in a sea so dangerous, with him. . . . Lean not to a willow that bows every way nor lie in a nest where a swallow builds. It is a chattering bird and tells abroad what is done at home. And no man, I think, would dwell in a house full of nothing but windows for every eye to spy what he is doing."

Of "visitants"[52] Dekker says: "They that cheer up a prisoner but with their sight are robin-redbreasts that bring straws in their bills to cover a dead man in extremity; such acquaintances grow like strawberries in a barren country: you shall hardly in a day gather a handful."[53] He follows up this reflection with some excellent advice to the prisoner about borrowing money from his friends: "Let thy pen neither dig the mine too often nor in too many places." The chapter concludes abruptly: "How quickly is this maze of friends trodden out? Why should I wind any more upon this bottom when a whole kingdom can scarce afford stuff to do it? Of such pearl 'tis hard to make a bracelet to go about a man's arm; and therefore till I find a shell full of them, I will string no more."

The final chapter includes a sort of justification of the laws against debtors, an explanation of the unkindness of jailors, and some advice to prisoners who "go abroad" with their keepers. I quote some illustrative passages:

"To keep the sick from the sound were prisons invented, for a man in debt hath the sickness of the law upon him. If creditors had not iron nets to fish for their money, all men in the world would still borrow but never pay. . . . He that keeps a prison walks continually in a whirlwind and would lose his very cloak from his back, clap he not it close to his body. He must struggle and wrestle and blow, and all little enough to get through, and shall be sure evermore to be in a cold sweat. It is no wonder therefore if an inclination born with innated smoothness warp here and wax crabbed. He that sails to the Indies must look to be sunburned; and he that lives amongst the Goths and Vandals will smell of their hard conditions. . . . The prisoner cries out, he lies upon an ill bed; but upon what

[52] Ch. XV.
[53] The same figures are found, separated, in Mynshul, 46.

bed sleeps his keeper? I think he sleeps upon none: I think he can not sleep: for his pillow is not stufft with feathers but with fears. Every prisoner sinks under the weight of his own debts, but the keeper feels the burden of all."

As the passage about going forth with a keeper is, almost to the last syllable, reproduced by Mynshul,[54] it need not be quoted here, but we may remind ourselves in passing that imprisonment for debt permitted visits to the outer world, and that Dekker's confinement may have been thus relieved whenever his purse allowed so heavy a tax.

There still remains to consider the rugged, half-grotesque, half-terrible poem entitled "Dekker His Dream. In which, being wrapt with a poetical enthusiasm, the great volumes of Heaven and Hell were opened, in which he read many wonderful things." It was registered to print October 11, 1619, and published the followng year. The title-page is provided with a woodcut representing a man with mustachioes and pointed beard sleeping on a canopied bed. Halliwell and Grosart think there is no doubt that this picture is a genuine likeness of the poet. The epistle is addressed to Endymion Porter. Very much can be read between the lines, with their bald opening, devoid of compliment, their veiled personal allusion and their religious fervor:

"If you ask why from the heaps of men I pick out you only to be that *murus ahaenus* which must defend me, let me tell you—what you know already—that books are like the Hungarians in Paul's, who have a privilege to hold out their Turkish history for any one to read. They beg nothing, the texted pasteboard talks all; and if nothing be given, nothing is spoken, but God knows what they think. If you are angry that I thrust into your hands a subject of this nature, O good sir, take me thus far into your pardon: that it was impossible for me to beget a better: for the bed on which seven years I lay dreaming was filled with thorns instead of feathers; my pillow, a rugged flint; my chamber-fellows—sorrows that day and night kept me company—the very or worse than the very Infernal Furies. Besides, I herein imitate the most courtly revellings; for if lords be in the grand masque, in the anti-masque are players: so in these of mine, though the devil be in the one, God is in the other, nay in both. What I send you may perhaps seem bitter, yet it is wholesome; your best physic is not a julep; sweet sauces leave rotten bodies. There is a Hell named

[54] pp. 55–56, beginning "If thou walkest abroad."

in our creed, and a Heaven; and the Hell comes before: if we look not into the first, we shall never live in the last. Our tossing up and down here is the sea, but the land of angels is our shore. Sail so long as we can bear up, through honors, riches, pleasures, and all the sensual billows of the world; yet there is one harbor to put in at; and safely to arrive there is all the hardness, all the happiness. Books are pilots in such voyages: would mine were but one point of the compass for any man to steer well by."

The epistle closes with a would-be humorous attempt to keep up the figure used at the beginning: "If I hold the pen longer in my hand, I shall fall asleep again. But howsoever I wake or have mine eyes closed, I rest," etc.

Although the poem seems to me chiefly interesting as indicative of Dekker's unhappiness in prison and his pre-occupation with "the star-chamber of Heaven" and the "jails of Hell," yet it deserves more notice than it has received, for, in spite of its rough versification and a phraseology that is often inadequate, its scheme is large and not seldom imaginative. It embraces the destruction of the world, the last judgment, the joys of the blest, and at great length the pains of hell. The framework is a dream, waking from which the poet cries,

> "Yet my heart panted and my hair turn'd white
> More through the ghastly objects of this night
> Than with the snow of age."

There are interludes of prose and a marginal gloss, mostly explanatory and quoting as authorities the Bible, the Fathers, and the classics. Hell combines classical and biblical features, and Dekker's tenderness does not include the tormented spirits. Yet towards the end there is a dramatic monologue, written with considerable sympathy, in which a lost soul that had lived but thirty years on earth and had loved learning gives voice to the old complaint that finite sin should be punished with infinite pain. He accuses Adam, "man's master thief," but envies him his earthly happiness:

> "He lost a garden but an orchard found,
> Wall'd in with seas, with sun-beams compass'd round;"

and especially the gift of Eve:

> "A woman, in whose face more beauties shone
> Than all the beauties after made in one";

and complains, as he compares his own lot:

> " God's holy hunger though it oft did kill me
> God's holy banquet yet did never fill me."

The whole passage is interesting and in some ways recalls the Earl's soliloquy in " Westward Ho."

In the account of the " signs before the last day," the following lines are quotable:

> " The father stabb'd the son, the son the brother;
> Man was not man till he destroyed another ";

and space may be permitted for a few others on the torment of wind-tossed spirits:

> " Here I beheld, methought, souls, scarecrow-like,
> Some bound, some hang by th' heels, whose heads did strike
> The icy-knobbed roof, toss'd to and fro
> By gusts implacable, able down to throw
> Rampires of brass; which still beat out the brains
> And still renewed them with plangiferous pains ";

and for

> " The hyperborean wind, whose rough hand flings
> Mountains for snowballs,"

and finally for such a phrase as

> " the Egyptian
> Caliginous black vapor."

But the poet we know best is not here; even the joys of the redeemed are described without charm. In the account of Christ's sufferings, however, there is a lyrical and intimate note that makes one feel again that Dekker had a staff of comfort to lean upon in his dark hour. I quote three couplets with the biblical references:

> " That face, whose picture might have ransom'd kings,
> Yet put up spettings, baffulings, buffetings.
>   Esa. 50. Jerem. 3. Math. 26. Mark 14. Luk. 22.
> That head which could a crown of stars have worn,
> Yet spitefully was wrench'd with wreaths of thorn.
>   Math. 27. Mark 15. John 19.

. . . .

That body, scourg'd and torn with many a wound
That his dear blood, like balm, might leave us sound.
Luk. 23. Psal. 129. Zach. 13."

This poem contains the familiar pity for wounded soldiers, and a passage in which one possibly can read hurt pride and indignation:

" Or when thin, pale-cheek'd scholars held but forth
Their thread-bare arms, and did beseech their worth
To pity hapless learning once so much
As not to see her beg: no, they 'd not touch
A poor book's cover though within it lay
Their soul's wealth."

Yet whatever may have been Dekker's sufferings and privations in prison, and they must have been great to have so nearly stopped that long industrious pen, and keenly felt, for, as he wrote in his early picture of a prisoner, "Calamity [is] most irksome to the gentle nature," the man was guarded from the worst effects of misfortune by something childlike and sweet in his character, and neither despair nor cynicism, not even bitterness in any deep sense, was among his companiors in that "cave" of horrors.

CHAPTER IX

The Last Years

Dekker was set free in 1619, and by January of the following year he was once more established in the theatrical world. It was not the same world. Two of the poet-dramatists had died, the greatest, and the one who perhaps stood next to the greatest. Dekker's former enemy was about then setting forth his opinions of matters and persons in a quarter where they were received only too hospitably for the good name of either guest or host. His former friend Marston, playwright become priest, was now reading the service in Christchurch, Hampshire. Middleton had turned from debased comedy to powerful but debased tragedy and was occupying intervals with the devising of city pageants. Webster was not writing plays in 1620. Heywood was pursuing the industrious and even tenor of his way that led, if we can trust his word, to two hundred and twenty dramas. With a productiveness too gay for so prosaic a term as industry, Fletcher was pouring forth play after play as if dimly forewarned that he had but five years to live. Among Fletcher's collaborators was Massinger, who, on the title-page of "The Virgin Martyr" two years later first saw his own name in print. John Ford was wasting his energies on a moral treatise, needing, it may be, the impulse of another mind to set him about the true business of his life. John Day, too, Dekker's early collaborator and friend, had not been writing plays for some years. Perhaps it is not an accidental coincidence that both Ford and Day felt the renewed desire to write for the stage when they began to work with Dekker. Certainly, so far as we have opportunity to judge, the genial poet-journalist was still the leading spirit, as he seems to have been in every single case of his collaboration with others that has come down to us.

The last period of Dekker's dramatic activity covered five years. It includes six known plays, two collaborated with

177

Day: "The Life and Death of Guy of Warwick," registered to print January 15, 1620, but apparently never published, and "A French Comedy of the Bellman of Paris," licensed to act July 30, 1623, for the company at the Red Bull;[1] three with Ford, first "The Witch of Edmonton," then "The Fairy Knight,"[2] licensed June 11, 1624, as a new play for the Prince's company at the Red Bull, and finally "The Bristow Merchant," licensed October 22, 1624, for the Palsgrave's men at the Fortune. The sixth play, "The Wonder of a Kingdom," seems in its present form to be Dekker's work alone. At this point may as well be mentioned two other plays, whose loss we owe to Warburton's incredible carelessness: "Jocundo and Astolfo" and "The King of Swedland," both registered as Dekker's on June 29, 1660. The second of these plays would seem to belong to this decade rather than to an earlier. It is very unfortunate that but two of these eight plays have come down to us; for although the period is sometimes absurdly labeled as one of decadence and of revamping old plays, it is commonly agreed that to Dekker "The Witch of Edmonton" owes much of its beauty of characterization and its intelligent humanity. The fact that the lost plays were not printed proves nothing as to their value, for the authors did not print the play last named. It will be recalled that Dekker apparently left to others the printing of plays upon which he had merely collaborated, and that Ford did not publish his refashioning of "The Sun's Darling," although it was a court play, and "while the stage flourisht . . . lived by the breath of general applauses."

The full title of the first play on which Dekker and Ford worked together runs as follows: "The Witch of Edmonton: a known true Story. Composed into a Tragi-comedy by divers well-esteemed Poets; William Rowley, Thomas Dekker, John Ford, etc. Acted by the Prince's Servants, often at the Cockpit in Drury Lane, once at Court, with singular applause. Never printed till now. 1658." It was written in 1621 between April 27, when the account of the trial of Mother Sawyer was regis-

---

[1] Fleay: for the Revels, which then dissolved, and the play passed to the Prince's players at the Curtain.

[2] Fleay queries *Huon of Bordeaux,* then an old play.

tered to print, and December 29, when it was performed at Whitehall by the Prince's men.[3]

The name of the Witch, her compact with the Devil in the guise of a black dog, and her fate, together with some hints as to her previous history, were derived from " The Wonderful Discovery of Elizabeth Sawyer, a Witch, late of Edmonton, her Conviction and Condemnation and Death. Together with the relation of the Devil's Access to her and their Conference together. Written by Henry Goodcole, Minister of the Word of God, and her Continual Visitor in the Gaol of Newgate. Published by Authority."[4] But the minister of the gospel had less pity and less knowledge of the human heart than the playwright, who in a few brief powerful scenes shows us how the deformed ignorant old woman, beaten, abused and hounded on by her superstitious neighbors, goes wild with fury, and giving herself up to evil passions, becomes that which she is suspected of being. While it was no part of Dekker's purpose to announce his belief or disbelief in the power of witches to use the magic of hell, his intention to lay upon cruelty the chief guilt in the process of witch-making is made perfectly clear in the opening speech of Mother Sawyer:

> " And why on me? Why should the envious world
> Throw all their scandalous malice upon me?
> 'Cause I am poor, deform'd and ignorant,
> And like a bow buckl'd and bent together
> By some more strong in mischiefs than myself?
> Must I for that be made a common sink
> For all the filth and rubbish of men's tongues
> To fall and run into? Some call me Witch;
> And being ignorant of myself, they go
> About to teach me how to be one: urging
> That my bad tongue (by their bad usage made so)
> Forspeaks their cattle, doth bewitch their corn,
> Themselves, their servants, and their babes at nurse.
> This they enforce upon me; and in part
> Make me to credit it."

[3] J. T. Murray, *English Dramatic Companies* (London, 1910), II, Ap. F.
[4] Reprinted in Bullen's edition of *Ford's Works,* I. The relations of the play to its source are discussed by F. Bielefeld in a dissertation called *The Witch of Edmonton . . . Eine Quellenuntersuchung.* Halle, 1904.

The whole conception of Mother Sawyer, pitiful, abject, terrible, uttering a speech commensurate with her misery and her crimes, is sufficient evidence that Dekker's dramatic powers were still developing. Pity and tenderness had always been his, but terror, though found in his prison utterances, received dramatic expression in this play only.[5]

Dekker here reverts once more to the old Marlowe motive, though profoundly humanized by its fresh and original application. The villain is the Devil, who makes an agreement with his first victim, the Witch, by a sealing with blood. The same agent suggests to Frank Thorney the immediate murder of Susan, although the thought had already risen in his own soul:

> " The mind's about it now. One touch from me
> Soon sets the body forward."

The Devil is likewise associated with Cuddy Banks in the comedy scenes, but with no serious outcome, for, says the evil spirit,

> " We meet his folly
> But from his virtues must be runaways."

In this play it is made very clear, as it is not in " If It be not Good," that it is only human sin or weakness that gives to the powers of evil their opportunity to enter in and take full possession of the heart. But the characterization is so powerful and so true to life that the Devil is not, to the reader, a prominent personage; the double tragedy seems to be less the consequence of direct external influence than the concomitant result of hereditary weakness, bad environment, and brutal ignorance —the modern equivalent for the devil.

The horseplay of the comedy scenes, which is not at all like

[5] Although there has been general agreement that the conception of the part played by the Witch belongs to Dekker, some few voices have of late been vaguely raised for Rowley. Aside from stylistic considerations, which are greatly in Dekker's favor, his advanced humanitarian sympathies are so strongly expressed elsewhere that it would require a great deal of evidence to deprive him of the credit due to the treatment of witchcraft in this play. This treatment receives proper relief only when compared with such an appeal to superstition as *The Late Lancashire Witches* of Heywood and Brome.

Dekker's unaided work, should probably be assigned to Rowley, yet one familiar with the sympathies of the former is inclined to see his hand in Cuddy's affection for the black dog, which in return uses him " doggedly not devilishly," and in his simple inquiry, after he has learned its true nature, whether it were not possible for him " to become an honest dog yet."

The domestic tragedy that constitutes the rest of the play is divided between Ford and Dekker. All agree that to the former belongs the long opening scene—situation, characters, and poetry; and perhaps a part of the second, though honest, homely Old Carter with his hearty ways and his racy speech should probably be given to Dekker.[6] To the older poet too Swinburne, who takes no note of Rowley, assigns the greater part, or all, of the second, third, and fourth acts, and the opening scene of the fifth. There seems to be no reasonable doubt[7] that Susan, the innocent victim in the web of crime, is one of Dekker's women. This heroine of the homely name such as he preferred to give to his English girls, has a character almost as transparent and direct as Dorothea's, and her speech is sometimes almost as gentle; indeed, in her relations with the unworthy Frank, she is gentleness and humility incarnate, whether she explains her tears:

> " You, sweet, have the power
> To make me passionate as an April day:
> Now smile, then weep; now pale, then crimson red.
> You are the powerful moon of my blood's sea,
> To make it ebb or flow into my face,
> As your looks change;"

or begs to be allowed to accompany him farther:

> " That I may bring you through one pasture more
> Up to yon knot of trees; amongst those shadows
> I'll vanish from you, they shall teach me how."

After Frank has mortally wounded her and explained that he had never intended to return, she has no reproaches to make:

[6] Creizenach: to Dekker or Rowley.

[7] Ward's tentative assignment to Ford is so phrased as to be an excellent argument for Dekker.

> " Why then I thank you more;
> You have done lovingly, leaving yourself,
> That you would thus bestow me on another.
> Thou art my husband, Death, and I embrace thee
> With all the love I have;"

and a moment later:

> " Now heaven reward you ne'er the worse for me.
> I did not think that death had been so sweet;
> Nor I so apt to love him. I could ne'er die better,
> Had I stay'd forty years for preparation:
> For I'm in charity with all the world.
> Let me for once be thine example, Heaven;
> Do to this man as I him free forgive,
> And may he better die and better live."

" The part of Susan," writes Swinburne, " is one of Dekker's most beautiful and delicate studies; in three short scenes he has given an image so perfect in its simple sweetness as hardly to be overmatched outside the gallery of Shakespeare's women. The tender freshness of his pathos, its plain frank qualities of grace and strength, never showed themselves with purer or more powerful effect than here; the after scene where Frank's guilt is discovered has the same force and vivid beauty."

In this after scene Dekker's presence is felt in the poignant homeliness of the events, the kindliness of Katherine, and in a sweetness and downright honesty in Winnifred not at all visible in the first act. It is Dekker's Winnifred who remains by her husband's side after she becomes acquainted with his guilt, but bluntly reproaches him for his peculiar meanness towards Old Carter: " Your sin's the blacker, so to abuse his goodness." Dekker's hand is likewise seen in the father's awful punning when he presents the bloody knife to Frank: " What say'st thou to this evidence? is't not sharp? does't not strike home? Thou canst not answer honestly, and without a trembling heart, to this one point, this terrible bloody point "; and in Frank's fear when the spirit of Susan and the living Winnifred come at the same time to his bedside: " How dar'st thou come to mock me on both sides of my bed? . . . out-face me, stare upon me with strange postures: turn my soul wild by a face in which were drawn a thousand ghosts leap'd newly from their graves to pluck me into a winding-sheet."

The second play preserved from the period under consideration is "The Wonder of a Kingdom." It was registered to print May 16, 1631, but was probably not then a new play, for the prologue speaks of it as having

> "Won grace
> In the full theatre."

It was printed in 1636 as "written by Thomas Dekker"; its title-page bears the following motto: "*Quod non dant proceres, dabit histrio.*" Thirteen years before its publication, there was licensed for a company of strangers at the Red Bull a new comedy by John Day under the somewhat similar title, "Come See a Wonder." Before considering the possible relations between these plays, it is necessary to speak at some length of the first, which, besides being a puzzle, is a medley. Even the title might be of doubtful application if it were not for the hint conveyed in the Latin quotation on the title-page, which, as Fleay intimates, seems to clinch his plausible identification of the "Wonder" with Dulwich College.[8] There are three plots, two of which are closely connected. The first tells the romantic love story of Fiametta and Angelo, who except at the first behave like a pair of puppets and who do not deserve the happiness they finally attain; Fiametta's nurse was possibly drawn with Juliet's nurse in mind, and Angelo, disguised as a French doctor, recalls Andelocia in the same rôle.[9] To this story, feebly conceived and executed without charm, is joined the second plot, a double intrigue in which a sister, in order to further a brother's base design, puts herself into a compromising position. It was undoubtedly written after Fletcher[10]

[8] The only reason for a different interpretation lies in Tibaldo's words to his sister, "I beg it at thy hands that, being a woman, thou'lt make a wonder." P., IV, 239.

[9] It is in this plot that Fleay finds the allusion to cards, p. 286, that leads him to identify what he calls "the original Dekker play" with the anonymous *Mack* of the Diary, 1595. But there is no reason for separating this plot from the Tibaldo plot, which, as shown in the pages following, is modeled on Fletcher.

[10] Cp. Schelling, II, 235–236.

had pointed out the way: the general idea of a heroine's dally-
ing with evil, yet coming off safe, the types of character represented by Alphonsina and the slightly sketched Alisandra, the
situation brought about by the disguise of Tibaldo as a girl, the
surprise of the dénouement, are all foreign to Dekker's usual
method. Like Fletcher's also seems to me the dialogue with
its swiftness, smartness and looseness.

The third plot has the merest thread of a story and is arti-
ficially joined to the rest of the play.[11] It contrasts the prodigality, at once mean and magnificent, of Signior Torrenti with
the boundless hospitality of Jacomo Gentili, who has built as
" a gift to charity " a palace with seven gates, twelve vast rooms
and three hundred and sixty-five windows. However fanciful
appear some aspects of his philanthropy, he is very explicit in
his purpose:

> " My heirs shall be poor children fed on alms,
> Soldiers that want limbs, scholars poor and scorned;
> And these will be a sure inheritance,
> Not to decay: Manors and towns will fall,
> Lordships and parks, pastures and woods be sold,
> But this land still continues to the lord;
> No subtle tricks of law can me beguile of this.
> But of the beggars' dish I shall drink healths
> To last forever; whilst I live my roof
> Shall cover naked wretches; when I die
> 'Tis dedicated to Saint Charity."

The story of the " noble house-keeper " and that of the
" riotous lord " are bound together by the adventures of the
poor sailor brother of the latter, who, cruelly rebuffed by him,
turns to the hospitality of Gentili. These three characters,
together with some of the minor ones, are drawn with considerable power. Gentili is the least distinct, not unnaturally if
it was the playwright's object to celebrate the founding of
Dulwich College without being personal.[12] Aside from his

---

[11] Fleay, besides pointing out that few of the characters of the Gentili
plot are named in the *dramatis personae,* indicates the links that connect it
with the rest of the play: (1) " We shall your will obey," p. 223, to
" Meantime we'll hence," p. 224; and (2) " No more of compliment," p.
280, to " 'Tis nobly spoke," p. 281.

[12] See below, p. 196, for what seems to me a possible prose portrait of
Alleyn.

charity and hospitality, his only notable features are an unwillingness to marry and a pride in his hale old age, including the
boast,

> " My kitchen is my doctor, and my garden
> Trusty apothecary."

Torrenti's prodigality is highly poetical, whether he talks " as
if he grasped the Indies in each hand," or would give

> " A prince's ransom now to kiss
> Black Cleopatra's cheek."

His brother, " a brave boy all elemental fire," possesses a swift
indignant eloquence, and when Gentili would force his friends
to come to his aid he proudly refuses " to steal compassion
from them like a thief."

This interesting little Gentili-Torrenti play is so in conso-
nance with Dekker's known affection for Alleyn and his recognized social sympathies, and the poetry, whether imaginative,
crude, or pedestrian, is so similar to his work elsewhere that
it is difficult to imagine that a second hand had any share in
its composition.[13] The chief reason for supposing that this is
the case is to be found in the fact that after the publication of
Dekker's play and probably after his death, Day wrote " The
Parliament of Bees," a rhymed masque-like play, in which large
portions of the Gentili-Torrenti story are incorporated with
few changes except those necessary to secure rhyme.[14] He
likewise used in his " Bees " certain portions of " The Noble
Spanish Soldier," a play registered as Dekker's, published as

---

[13] It is hardly necessary to add that the one-legged soldier is very similar
to the maimed soldier in *If It be not Good* and to the British slave in *The
Virgin Martyr,* and that hale old men abound in Dekker's plays. Bullen
calls attention to the likeness between Gentili's programme for each day of
the week and that of the King in *If It be not Good.* See *Introd., Works of
John Day,* 26; see also his note prefixed to *The Parliament of Bees.*

[14] Character 2, the Hospital Bee, is Gentili; char. 3, the Plush Bee, is
Torrenti; char. 7, the Gathering Bee, is Lord Vanni; char. 9, the Quack-
salving Bee, is the apothecary; char. 10, the Usuring Bee, is the broker
(Henslowe, remarks Fleay). Char. 4 and 5, the Field Bee and the Poetical
Bee, are taken from " The Noble Spanish Soldier."

This note gives no idea of the ingenuity of Day's transference; it merely
identifies the chief characters.

Samuel Rowley's (S. R.), and exhibiting the handiwork of both. Fleay adopts the easy solution of assigning to Day all that he appropriated, but in view of the internal evidence it is more reasonable to suppose that Dekker was an unnamed collaborator upon "Come See a Wonder," for which he wrote the Gentili-Torrenti sub-plot, and that later he reclaimed it for a play entirely his own. There remains always the possibility that Day helped plan this little social play or that some of his lines have been retained. To the question of honesty that thus arises, Bullen would seem to give the most satisfactory reply when he says: "As Dekker and Day were on more than one occasion collaborateurs, it is open to a generous critic to assume that one of the two writers put his work at the disposal of the other";[15] that is, to re-phrase the quotation from my point of view, that in those days of loose collaboration and loose ownership of plays, Day, in writing the "Bees," selected whatever material suited his purpose, whether written by Dekker or himself, from a play to which in its original form both had contributed; and that he did it without any sense of dishonesty. This view is strengthened by the fact that the most charming part of "The Parliament of Bees" was written for the occasion and could not be mistaken for the work of any one except Day.

But before we leave "The Wonder of a Kingdom," a specimen must be given of Torrenti's raptures, that, as Bullen truly says, "remind us more of the frolic exuberance of Old Fortunatus than of Day's dainty courtliness."

> " I'll pave my great hall with a floor of clouds,
> Wherein shall move an artificial sun,
> Reflecting round about me golden beams
> Whose flames shall make the room seem all on fire;
> And when 'tis night, just as that sun goes down,
> A silver moon shall rise, drawn up by stars,
> And as that moves, I standing in her orb,
> Will move with her, and be that man i' th' moon
> So mock't in old wives' tales; then overhead
> A roof of woods and forests full of deer,
> Trees growing downwards, full of singing choirs.
> And this I'll do that men with praise may crown
> My fame for turning the world upside down."

[15] Note prefixed to *The Parliament of Bees.*

A word must be added about Dekker's share in "The Noble Soldier," already referred to under its running title "The Noble Spanish Soldier."[16] It was registered to print in 1631 as by "Thomas Decker," and again in 1633; but when it was finally published in 1634, the title-page bore the initials S. R., commonly interpreted as Samuel Rowley. A printer's note tells us that the author was then dead. Bullen's suggestion that the play had undergone some revision at Dekker's hands seems to me reasonable.[17] The language of the King and more frequently of Baltazar, the honest soldier, recalls Dekker's violence of phrasing in connection with similar characters, and some of Cornego's puns have a weakly Dekkeresque flavor. The style, in so far as it is Dekker's, reminds one of "Match Me in London" more than of any other single play.[18] Such a working over of speeches and dialogue adds nothing to Dekker's fame; for he seems to have been unable to put any heart into the work. The use of his name when the play was registered may have been unwarranted, or an explanation may be found in the desire of author or publisher to secure a larger sale.

Except for the probably slight work on this play, Dekker's last recorded drama is the lost "Bristow Merchant." It was written together with Ford, and the supposition that it was

[16] Fleay identifies this play with *The Spanish Fig* written for Henslowe in 1602, but he has the only significant fact wrong: the king is not poisoned with a Spanish fig but with wine prepared for some one else; however, in the poisoning scene "Spanish figs" are mentioned as a usual agent for producing death.

[17] *Introd.* to his edition of the play, in *Old Eng. Plays,* I. (1882.)

[18] The enumeration of nations, p. 302, is similar, as Bullen points out, to that in *Match Me,* P., IV, 180, and it occurs in a scene assigned to Dekker by Fleay. Both plays use figures drawn from the animal kingdom in a somewhat similar way; compare, for example, the following passages:

"I do not love to pluck the quills
With which I make pens, out of a Lion's claw."

Noble Spanish Soldier, p. 293.

"I do not like
To see a Bull to a wild fig tree tied
To make him tame."

Match Me, P., IV, 202.

the revamping of an old play is impertinent. It has lately been suggested[19] that there may have been some connection between this play and a short novel written by Dekker at some date previous to December 17, 1630, when it was registered to print under the title "Penny-Wise, Pound-Foolish." It was published the following year anonymously. Its sub-title is as follows, "A Bristow Diamond set in two Rings, and both Crack'd. Profitable for Married Men, pleasant for young men, and a rare example for all good Women." It tells the rather dreary story of a "Bristow" merchant, who after an extended career of profligacy and an attempt at murder, is finally ransomed and lovingly received by the wife he has twice betrayed —"a rare example for all good Women." He repents, and reduced to poverty, they live in a small shop until the wife's penny, which was all the venture she would entrust to her husband in his pound-foolish days, and which he had given to a subordinate, returns with an increment of many pounds and is the means of restoring prosperity to them. We are told that the story is true but that the names of the characters have been changed.[20]

The address to the reader is cheerful, moralizing, and not without humor. I quote a few lines:

"The discourse is hid, like our ladies' heads in taffeta pursenets, under the masques of Ferdinand and Annabell. Their lives and their loves are enclosed in this nutshell, which, if you crack without hurting your teeth, the kernel is sweet in the chewing. The apples plucked from this little tree may serve to turn in the fire in your Christmas nights, and not much amiss all the winter after. So fall to, and farewell."

Following this address is a brief discourse on "The Excellent Worth of a Penny," from which I make two characteristic extracts:

"A Penny is a very faithfull messenger, and the best errand it goes upon is when a rich man sends his commendations by it to a beggar. The rich man gives and the poor man takes; no, the poor man gives and the rich

[19] By Professor W. Bang in his preface to the edition of "Penny-Wise, Pound-Foolish," printed in *Materialien zur Kunde des älteren Englischen Dramas,* 1908.

[20] *Materialien,* etc., 185.

man takes, for the prayers of the poor increase the blessings of the rich.
. . . A Penny had wont to pay for a Pot of nappy Ale: but now a Pot of
Ale defies the company of a Penny."

In 1625 London was swept by the great plague which carried
away among its victims the dramatist Fletcher. Doubtless thus
deprived of the incentive to write plays, and feeling anew the
terrible interest of the subject, Dekker once more took up the
work of the contemporary historian and gave the world a
detailed account of the plague at its worst in his "A Rod for
Runaways. In which flight of theirs, if they look back, they
may behold many fearful Judgments of God, sundry ways
pronounced upon this City and on several persons both flying
from it and staying in it. Expressed in many dreadful Examples of sudden Death, fallen upon both young and old,
within this City and the Suburbs, in the Fields and open
Streets, to the terror of all those who live and to the warning
of those who are to die, to be ready when God Almighty shall
be pleased to call them. With additions of some new Acci-
dents. Written by Tho. D."[21] The brief epistle, appropriately
addressed to a surgeon and adorned with several puns and the
writer's favorite figure, shows no such signs of personal pain
or money difficulties as are discernible in the works written
just before and after his long imprisonment.

The tone of the general preface is impersonal and somewhat
tragic, but not without verbal tricks. "It is a picture," writes
Dekker, "not drawn to the life, but to the death . . . of above
23,000 in less than twelve weeks." "Be sure you have hung
strong padlocks upon your doors," he advises the absentees,
"for in many streets, there are none to guard your goods but
the houses themselves. If one shop be open, sixteen in a row
stand shut up together, and those that are open were as good
to be shut, for they take no money." "Few woollen drapers
sell any cloth," he goes on grimly, "but every churchyard is
every day full of linen drapers: and the earth is the great
warehouse, which is piled up with winding-sheets. To see a

[21] G., IV, 267–310. It is clear that this edition is not the first, an infer-
ence borne out by the text, p. 284, which shows a careless manipulation of
dates.

rapier or feather worn in London now is as strange as to meet a Low-country soldier with money in his purse. The walks in Paul's are empty: the walks in London too wide, (here's no jostling), but the best is, Cheapside is a comfortable garden where all physic herbs grow. We wish that you, the runaways, would suffer the market-folks to come to us (or that they had hearts to come), for the Statute of Forestalling is sued upon you. We have lost your companies, and not content with that, you rob us of our victuals: but when you come back, keep open house (to let in air) and set good cheer on your tables, that we may bid you welcome."

The point of view is that of the moralist: "God must have fair play," he urges; and again, "The Gospel and God's heralds, preachers, have a long time cried out against our iniquities, but we are deaf, sleepy and sluggish; and now there is a thunder speaks from Heaven to wake us." Mixed with the admonitions is the old passionate love and pity for London, mother of his life, nurse of his being. As in the first plague book, written over twenty years before, stories, mostly tragic, make up a large part of the pamphlet. As we might expect, there is a "happy" story or two, but for them he apologizes: "Neither do I this out of an idle or undecent merriment, for jests are no fruit for this season"; and after a tale relating how a company cheated their hostess out of her pay by showing what seemed to be tokens of the plague, he adds, "It is not safe to kiss lightning, mock at thunder, or dally with divine judgments." There is no space to speak of the other stories unless perhaps that of the plague-stricken mother; while she called for aid, her child, likewise stricken, "leaning to her cheek, immediately departed," and, as the incident ends "so her child and she went lovingly together to one grave." Although this second plague-book, written by one who had lived through many a year of such horrors, is less luxuriant, poetical, dashing, than its predecessor, there is perhaps a gain in simplicity; the tone of the whole is more evenly and earnestly religious, and it closes with a prayer of mellow charity for all, even the "runaways" against whose selfishness the pamphlet was avowedly written.

Except for a fourth edition of "Canaan's Calamity" in 1625, there is no record of any other work until 1627, when Dekker wrote the lost pageant for Hugh Hammersley's mayoralty. We know this, for he says so in a small volume called "Wars, Wars, Wars," printed in 1628, but now apparently lost; it was dedicated to Hammersley and the two sheriffs of London and Middlesex for the year, and its body consists of a praise of war and of the aldermen then in office and closes with " some vigorous and, doubtless, acceptable applause of the twenty City Lieutenants." If we are to judge from Collier's remarks, the "tract" is a poem; it contains the lines about his old age quoted in the second chapter of this study.[22]

For 1628 and for 1629 Dekker also wrote the mayoralty pageant. The first, entitled "Britannia's Honor: Brightly Shining in several Magnificent Shews or Pageants, to Celebrate the Solemnity of the Right Honorable Richard Deane," was presented October 29, "at the particular Cost and Charges of the Right Worshipful, Worthy, and Ancient Society of Skinners." It was printed the same year and presumably brought the maker the "golden gains" he mentions in his dedication. Of the uninspired verse of the speeches, unbroken by a single lyric, the following are among the best lines:

> " There the poor Bee, the sweating tradesman, flies
> From flower to flower, and home with honey hies,"

one of the many passages that show that Dekker as well as Day had a fondness for bees used allegorically. But to the lover of Dekker the interest lies in the outburst of love for London expressed in the opening pages, and in the modest and kindly little note at the end, equally characteristic, commending the architecture of the pageant, unmatched for years and executed by " Mr. Gerard Christmas, the father, and Mr. John Christmas, the son."

In " Britannia's Honor," the glory of furs had necessarily been a part of Dekker's theme. He would seem to have found iron a more interesting subject, for the following year he wrote

[22] For a reprint of Collier's article, which contains all that is known about *Wars*, see G., V, Ap. 1.

a much better pageant for the Society of Ironmongers. Possibly the personality of the Mayor had something to do with the matter, for his dedication to James Campbell, the new mayor, contains a warm little recognition of the circumstance that his father had worn the robe of scarlet before him. Neither date nor publisher's name appears on the title-page, but if Dekker followed his usual custom, he had the pageant printed soon after it was produced. Both the title, "London's Tempe," and the sub-title, "The Field of Happiness," refer to Campbell's name; and the fifth pageant is an arbor furnished with trees, flowers, and fruits, "reflecting upon the name of Campe-bell or Le Beu Champe, a fair and glorious field." The praise of iron is vigorous and ingenious, and skillfully inserted in the little dramatic scene between Vulcan and Jove. In the same show is found the most durable thing in the play, a song sung by the Cyclops "in praise of iron, the anvil and hammer" —a little lyric[23] that gives one a new idea of Dekker's versatility and the conviction that his singing days were not yet past.

In 1630 the "2 Honest Whore" appeared in print for the first time, and the same year saw a third edition of "The Bachelor's Banquet." To this year belongs, also, "Penny-Wise, Pound-Foolish." Although "Match Me in London" was registered to print in 1630, November 8, it was not published until the following year. Its epistle-dedicatory is addressed "To the Noble Lover (and deservedly beloved) of the Muses, Lodowick Carlell"; and it reads as follows:

"That I am thus bold to sing a dramatic note in your ear is no wonder, in regard you are a chorister in the choir of the Muses. Nor is it any over-daring in me to put a play-book into your hands, being a courtier; Roman poets did so to their emperors; the Spanish, now, to their grandees; the Italians, to their illustrissimoes; and our own nation, to the great ones.

"I have been a priest in Apollo's temple many years; my voice is decaying with my age, yet yours, being clear and above mine, shall much honour me if you but listen to my old tunes. Are they set ill? Pardon them; well? then receive them.

"Glad will you make me if by your means the King of Spain speaks our language in the Court of England; yet have you wrought as great a

[23] Included by Schelling in his *Seventeenth Century Lyrics*.

wonder; for the nine sacred Sisters, by you, are there become courtiers and talk with sweet tongues, instructed by your Delian eloquence. You have a King to your master, a Queen to your mistress, and the Muses your play-fellow. I to them a servant," etc.

Since this preface is one of the last personal utterances of the poet, now nearly sixty years old, it is pleasant to observe how serene it is, how free from anything that could connote disappointment or pain; full of graceful appreciation for the work of another, but quietly confident of his own past service to poetry.

From 1632 has come down to us a merry little lyric commending the "Northern Lass,"[24] a play written by Richard Brome, servant and "son" of Jonson, who evidently saw no impropriety in claiming his master's former adversary as a second literary father. I quote all but the last two lines.

"TO MY SON BROME AND HIS LASS.

Which, then, of both shall I commend?
Or thee, that art my son and friend;
Or her, by thee begot? A girl
Twice worth the Cleopatrian pearl.
No: 'tis not fit for me to grace
Thee who art mine, and to thy face.
Yet I could say, the merriest maid
Among the Nine for thee has laid
A garland by; and jeers to see
Pied idiots tear the Daphnean tree,
Putting their eyes out with those boughs
With which she bids me deck thy brows.
But what I bring shall crown thy daughter,
My grandchild, who, though full of laughter,
Is chaste and witty to the time,
Not lumpish cold, as is her clime.
By Phoebus' lyre, thy Northern lass
Our Southern proudest beauties pass."

These lines were written by one who had not lost the zest for living and who was not ground down by unusual poverty or suffering. The same state of mind is to be seen in some additions to his most popular prose pamphlet, probably written

[24] Entered S. R., March 24.

at about the same time, for in 1632 was once more published
in altered form and under a new title, the "Villanies Discovered" of 1616 and 1620. As I have not seen this very rare
edition or even its full title[25] I must fall back upon the edition
of 1638, which I agree with Fleay is a reprint of that of
1632.[26] The dedications of 1638, as noted earlier in the study,
could not have been written as late as 1638, for in the first
Dekker speaks of his "threescore years," and in the second
more vaguely of its being "now about twenty years past, since
a bed of strange snakes were found . . ." and of Candlelight's being "the first that discovered that cursed nursery of
vipers."[27] The full title, then, in 1638 runs as follows: "English Villanies seven several times Prest to Death by the Printers;
but (still reviving again) are now the eighth time, (as at the
first) discovered by Lanthorn and Candlelight; and the help of
a new Cryer called O-per-se-O: whose loud voice proclaims to
all that will hear him, another Conspiracy of Abuses lately
plotting together to hurt the Peace of this Kingdom; which
the Bellman (because he then went stumbling i' th' dark) could
never see till now. And because a company of Rogues, cun-
ning, canting Gypsies, and all the Scum of our Nation fight
here under their Tattered Colors, at the end is a Canting Dic-

[25] Lowndes is contented with "English Villanies six several times prest
to death, but still reviving again, and now the seventh, etc." He speaks of
an imperfect copy sold for 18 shillings.

[26] The only reason for thinking that it is not a reprint lies in the fact
that the table of contents and the body of the tract do not correspond:
there are three additional chapters on prison life, not named in the table
of contents; and one chapter there named—"The Infection of the
Suburbs"—is omitted. The table of contents does not correspond with that
of the edition of 1620 either, for, besides omitting the six chapters on
prison life earlier discussed, it has two new chapters: "The Abuses of
Keepers, Nurses, or Char-women," and "The Abuses of Alehouses," retained in the body of the 1638 edition. Fleay's assumption that the edition
of 1637 (i. e., 1638, the last page bears the inscription: Febru. 27, 1637,
Recudatur. Matth. Clay) is "spurious" rests apparently upon some such
discrepancies as I have indicated, increased perhaps by his desire to assign
to Dekker some anonymous plays in the Diary, a desire which has an
obvious connection with the date of the poet's birth.

[27] It was actually twenty-four years since Candlelight had discovered that
"nursery."

tionary, to teach their Language: with Canting Songs. A Book to make Gentlemen Merry, Citizens wary, Countrymen careful. Fit for all Justices to read over because it is a Pilot by whom they may make strange Discoveries. 1638."

The epistle-dedicatory addressed to the Justices for the Peace of the county of Middlesex exhibits the usual regard for law and for justice tempered with mercy, and inserts, in a character of the true magistrate, a little hint to the effect that all magistrates are not possessed of the same notions of equity. The epistle to the reader is not important except for the aid it affords in establishing the date. The additions to the pamphlet are dovetailed into the original plan[28] and take a generally narrative form. After a vivacious and vivid account of meal-time and locking-up time in prison, which closes with the story of the infernal messenger's stealing a "Discovery" written by a prisoner,[29] the Bellman is made to pursue the journey into another prison, where he heard "the sound of tunes more tragical, more serious: here was another manner of noise, new terrors, new shrieks, new condolements. No, no, they were not new, the air is filled with them every day; they are not strange because they are common." In the midst of his account of the "ululations" and "deplorations," Dekker pauses to name the five debtors' prisons on the south side of the Thames and the nine on the north side; he then continues, falling into the pointed style of the earler prison section:

"A prisoner is a bird in a cage; when he sings, he mourns: a bear at a stake baited for money: a horse in a pound; be his courage never so great, there 'tis lost: a Daniel in the lion's den, but where his Abacuc?

[28] The visit of the Devil's mesenger to prisoners, at the end of ch. 11, may have been added to the 1616 edition, for I have not seen the corresponding chapter.

The opening sentence of ch. 12, which immediately follows is: "Albeit I have done with prison-keepers, I must not take such an abrupt leave of prisoners." This sentence must have immediately followed the last chapter of the 1616 prison section, which closes with a discussion of keepers. It is without meaning in its present position, where it must have been retained carelessly.

[29] End of ch. 11. Unpaged.

. . . If a gentleman keeps a wretch in prison, he deserves to be degraded, for gentry is bound to honor, to defend the oppressed. If a citizen bars a man of his liberty, he himself is not free but hazards the danger of being a foreigner in Heaven, for disfranchizing his brother on earth."[30]

The next chapter[31] gives a picture of the politic bankrupt, "not the honest bankrupt undone by suretyship, casualties or losses at sea; but a politic bankrupt, a noble-in-the-pound bankrupt, a five-shillings bankrupt, nay, a ten-groats-in-the-pound bankrupt, a voluntary villain, a devouring locust, a destroying caterpillar, a golden thief." The law-loving and law-conversant poet cites the laws of recent monarchs against these "anthropophagi," who even in prison are "brave in clothes, spruce in ruffs, with gold-wrought nightcaps on their heads."

In the last chapter[32] of these additions, the Bellman persuades "the better sort of prisoners who had the true feeling of sorrow indeed" to draw up a supplication to Conscience; and the narrative continues:

"At length she was entertained and welcomed into a worthy citizen's house: a gentleman that by her assistance had risen to great wealth, by her argument grew strong in religion; by her persuasions embraced scholars, loved soldiers, made much of all men.

"His soul was a garden beautifully planted; his mind a palace rarely adorned; his body a temple of such admirable building that people passing by would do it reverence.[33]

"In this grave citizen's company was sweet society of other noble spirits, sitting at a table, all of them taking honor from the city to be called her sons and she as much glorying by them to be saluted by the name of mother.

"At the very first sight of Conscience, they all rose up, receiving her with all the graceful compliments that were due to so divine and excellent a creature: every one of them hasting with a kind of grave ceremony to take her by the hand and seat her highest at the board.

"Then all being silent and their eyes fixed only upon her face with an expectation of some speech from her, she drew out of her bosom the prisoners' supplication, read it openly, and repeating the particular numbers of all such miserable men as lay in prison, she fetched a deep sigh,

[30] Ch. 12.   *The Abuses done to Prisoners by Over-cruel Creditors.*
[31] Ch. 13.   *The Villanies and Abuses Committed by Politic Bankrupts.*
[32] Ch. 14.   *The Prisoners' Supplication.*
[33] Margin: *The picture of a noble citizen.*   Edward Alleyn? Alleyn had died in 1625.

and then brake into this passionate abruption: ' O,' quoth Conscience, ' if amongst you (but I hope you are none of them) there be any under whom men suffer the cruelty of English execution (worse than the German wheel), imprisonment: let Conscience yet persuade you to send Mercy to speak to them at their iron grates. . . . The omnipotent builder of the heavens oftentimes squares out his platforms by your lines and your measures: for if man commiserates man, the Master and chief Almoner of mercy extends compassion to him; if not, not. It is one of the main petitions which you tie your souls to every morning: dally not with the great Treasurer of heaven and earth, to ask one thing and mean another:[34] so your own turns be served, you care for nobody else: not to forgive when you are forgiven is to tell a lie to Him that is all truth; you make a promise and break it, you beg a blessing and take up a curse: such equivocation runs hand in hand with condemnation.

" ' Be men, be Christians, be citizens. Citizens possess generosity, affability, meekness, love, piety, pity; this is the blazon of a noble coat: make it the escutcheon of your arms: mercy is the best motto, clemency a crest; no herald can give a braver. Release men made captives to you by the laws of this kingdom, and the laws which are set down in the Upper House of the Celestial Parliament will make you free denizens in a more glorious kingdom. A kingdom where there is no change of kings, no alteration of state, no loss of peers, no wars, no revenges, no citizens flying for fear of infection, none dying of them that stay, no prisoners to write petitions to Conscience, yet Conscience sits there in glory: there is true majesty, true honor, true peace, true health: there is all life, all happiness, all immortality.'

" She ended; they arose, and one of the company, who was a well-willer to prisoners, hastened home to write down what he heard Conscience utter."

Here the story of Dekker's life must close. Nothing is known about him after 1632. The following year his sometime collaborator William Rowley borrowed the prologue written for "The Wonder of a Kingdom" to use with his own play, "All's Lost by Lust," but this incident fails to lighten in any spot the shadow that falls, gently enough, on the poet's last months or years.

[34] Marginal note: " Forgive and be forgiven."

CHAPTER X

CONCLUSION

Born in London, almost certainly in 1572, of unknown parentage, Thomas Dekker lived into the fourth decade of the seventeenth century. He was solely a man of letters. His preparation for his calling lay in a grammar-school education or its equivalent, wide reading, probably a brief campaign in the Netherlands, association with "scholars" and writers, one of whom was Nash, and in attendance at the theatres, where he was most delighted by Lyly and most deeply moved by Marlowe. This education was supplemented by the university of life in a great city and by an unusually intimate acquaintance with the charms of the country. At a date unknown, perhaps about 1596, he began to write for Henslowe, and the connection, which covered a period of prodigious productiveness, lasted to the end of 1602, possibly a few years longer. It was interrupted by Jonson's spectacular attack upon Marston and the rest, an attack that Dekker answered reluctantly and to the destruction of an unfinished tragedy of great promise. These years brought him success and fame, many and warm friendships, and the tolerable sort of poverty enjoyed by most men in his position. About 1606 he broke with the stage and turned to pamphlet-writing, but in spite of the popularity of some of his books and a half-hearted appeal to the patronage he had at first disdained, he seems to have served a more capricious and less appreciative mistress. His return to the drama was marked by three plays tragic in spirit and expression. But neither prose nor plays paid his debts, for in 1613 he entered King's Bench prison. That "terror" of almost seven years seems to have maimed his creative powers for the time, but immediately upon his release we find him once more writing plays, chiefly in collaboration with Day and Ford; one of these plays unites a deepened sense of tragedy with all his early sweetness of temper. The plague of 1625 may have

198

ended his work for the theatres. Our few glimpses of his last years show him busy and serene: he wrote two new prose pieces, edited several plays that had not yet been published, and for three years held the honored and well paid office of city poet. His last known poetical utterance was gay and enthusiastic; and his last known prose simple and elevated. He had a special affection for Nash, Marston, Webster and Alleyn, and he collaborated with every important dramatist of his day except Shakespere, Chapman, Beaumont, and Fletcher; with Massinger he did not collaborate, but one of his tragedies was subjected to the younger playwright's blameless and uninspired pen. Although he was reserved in his personal utterances and singularly modest, he did not when he was old feel that his life had been a failure. He had spent the greater part of it in doing what he most enjoyed. He had had, as he well realized, the pageantry and the spectacle of life and the visions of the idealist without money and without price; and his humor and his religious faith had shielded him from the evil effects of poverty and imprisonment that might have been experienced by a nature less richly endowed. There is many a sadder story in the history of the Elizabethan stage.

Besides the warmheartedness, the sincerity, the piety and the patriotism with which Dekker is usually with justice credited, he possessed a manly and independent spirit that despised servility and resented injustice, a democratic breadth of sympathy more in accordance with the twentieth than the sixteenth century, a keen and wise interest in matters of good citizenship, and that other modern virtue of a generally optimistic outlook upon life. He loved all sorts of beauty; most of all, the beauty of music, poetry, and religion, and disillusion never came to brush off its bloom. We know less about the habits of the man: he probably did not escape the personal grossness that seems to have prevailed equally among bohemians, citizens, and gentlemen.

Born with the temperament of the idealist and the seeing eye of the realist, endowed with a two-fold gift for poetry and prose, and possessed of unusual wit and humor, Dekker was bound in the nature of the case to scatter his powers. The necessity of rapid production very likely conduced towards the same end, although this seems to me less certain, for ease has seldom been a nurse to literature, and Dekker, like most of his fellow playwrights, wrote primarily to make a living.

Of his non-dramatic work only a few words need to be spoken. A duly weighed appreciation of his lyrics must wait for a collection that shall include all the floating songs; but it may now be said of the best that they have upon them the freshness and spontaneity of the early days, and of the one that Palgrave has made familiar, that it ranks with Shakespere's, but it could not have been written by Shakespere, for it is a song of the people.

Dekker's prose is once more coming into its own. Although the books most popular during his lifetime have the least enduring value, yet all possess interest, for they afford us luminous glimpses into the past and they reflect the personality of the author, upon whom city scenes exercised so potent a fascination, and who loved, pitied, and laughed with and at the people who thronged them. Always clear and idiomatic, he commanded a variety of styles, often swift, gay, exuberant, nearly always picturesque, but at will whimsical, dramatic, ironical, or epigrammatic, and rising at his very best to a noble simplicity that may have had its origin in his susceptibility, moral and aesthetic, to the rhythm of the English Bible. He also possessed an admirable gift as raconteur. Modern prose had not to wait for Dryden.

Any attempt to estimate Dekker's dramatic achievement is at the outset almost paralyzed by the fact that about half the plays he wrote alone and the great majority of those he wrote with others have been lost. We must further remind ourselves that, yielding to a temptation presented to few, he gave up some four years to prose alone and that nearly seven of what should have been his best years were spent in prison. During a career that, thus interrupted, lasted from about 1594 to the end of 1624, he tried his hand, alone or with others, at almost every variety of play except the tragedy of blood, though examples of some species have perished. He was most successful when he set up a new type, as in " The Shoemaker's

Holiday," or greatly modified an old type, as in "Old Fortunatus" or "The Virgin Martyr," or a prevailing type as in
"The Honest Whore." He retained a taste for allegory and
a vital interest in the strife between good and evil, but he
showed little subtlety in depicting the inner struggle against
temptation. Since the romantic is seldom absent from his
plays and since his most beautiful poetry was composed for
romantic scenes, we may assume that his permanent sympathies lay in that field; but with a sort of fore-feeling for
the direction literature was to take in the distant future, he
realized the artistic possibilities in the unsophisticated life of
the humble, and he represented it upon the stage with more
fidelity to fact, humor, grace, and sympathy than any other
Elizabethan. While his conceptions were often large in their
scope, they were usually simple and treated with simplicity;
and though he used spectacle freely, and surprise not infrequently, he depended for effect rather upon faithfulness to life
than upon involved or startling stories. He therefore seldom
uses Italian motives; even the pastoral did not attract him.
He avoided the violent, the unnatural, the disgusting, the unwholesome; his only intrigue plays were collaborated with
others and exhibit none of his gifts except goodnatured satire.
He shows a marked preference for the gentler virtues: to his
lovers, love is a sacrament—there is no passion except in connection with lust, and his plays offer us no villains worth mentioning; his most heroic figures are gentle in their heroism
rather than sublime, and he was but obeying an instinct of his
genius when he gave to Dorothea a child angel as attendant
and protector and when he made Bellafront climb a slow and
painful path to salvation. Whether conditioned by the bent
of his own mind or by the composition of the companies he
was writing for, he was fond of depicting elderly or old men,—
Old Fortunatus dominated by hunger and thirst after experience, mad Simon Eyre by a different sort of Elizabethan rapture, Gentili by the passion of hospitality. But after all,
Dekker's characters do not readily classify themselves: not
all his women are gentle nor all his lovers mad.

Dekker must early have learned to depend upon his humor

for a part of his success. At its best it finds expression in the creation of character, and there he showed a modern tendency to temper the humorous with the serious, the pathetic or the strongly likable: it is so with Orlando, with Eyre, his wife, and his band of shoemakers; even with the "high-flying" Matheo, and it is so with his servant-fools. He also drew well simple, rather naïve persons—not clowns, but a knight and his wife or an eligible widow. He had no aptitude for the comedy of humors. His use of dialect—Dutch-English and Welsh-English—is the most convincing on the Elizabethan stage and it is so used as to seem to reveal racial character- istics in the speakers. He kept his early fondness for puns and Lylyisms, and his love of the unexpected often makes his humor flash with wit. What has been called the Hogarthian quality in some of his comedy scenes is perhaps not based wholly upon desire to please the vulgar, for elsewhere a note of grimness or of irony is heard in the speech of that keen observer of life. Against him, however, must be reckoned a limited volcabulary of innuendo and "scrurrility" of the sort not wholly unemployed by the greatest. Though more than annoying, for it gets into one's way, it does not affect an im- portant character or enter into a situation, and ro one can remember it.

Dekker's greater faults as a dramatist are well known: the two most serious are a considerable unevenness of execution, although this is not found in all the plays; and a more con- siderable weakness of structure, though even here one play usually described as incoherent would assume form with proper editing. His own words and the evidence of care- ful workmanship in other matters forbid us to assume that he had no fitting sense of the dignity of his art. Perhaps the explanation may be sought for in the circumstances of his life and in his temperament: his long collaboration with men of inferior talent during his formative period must have worked him injury, perhaps even his precocity if he actually began writing at twenty-two; his humor, poetry and naturalness probably obscured to himself and to others his generally poor technique; the long interruptions suffered by his dramatic work were also against him. But possibly a genius that was essentially lyrical and bound to attain its most nearly perfect expression in a scene, a mood, sometimes a mood lasting through a whole play, was more capable of producing unity of sentiment or of character than any other unity. As there seems to me some evidence that he did not produce rapidly his greatest work—with the possible exception of his songs—I am inclined to ascribe to temperament that other fault of a descent to slovenly verse so astounding to the reader; for no amount of industry quite answers the stubborn demand for the time and the place and the right mood " all together."

It is often said that Dekker showed no evolution, no development. In the absence of so much of the evidence, late plays as well as early, this is a difficult problem to face. Yet I venture to think that dramatically and psychologically " The Honest Whore " is an advance upon " Old Fortunatus " and " The Shoemaker's Holiday "; that the finest scenes in " The Virgin Martyr " show a more exquisite perception of the power of language to reveal character than any previous play; and that in tragic power " The Witch of Edmonton " surpasses all earlier work.

Dekker's positive contributions to the drama have been partly indicated: power of varied humor, power of pathos and the most delicate sentiment, not even shadowed by sentimentality; power to make the everyday aspects of life seem as attractive as they really are; power to create character,—a power based on sound psychology, for he was, to employ one of his own phrases, " deep read in the volume of a man "; hence we have no violation of human nature, no treacherous friend is made hero or heroine, no nice girl is compelled to marry a newly converted ruffian, no woman falls, repents, and promptly dies without any special reason, as in Heywood's most famous tragedy, and there are few unmotivated conversions. At Dekker's very best he was able to create, also, brief scenes of surpassing beauty, as when he suggests with poignant and haunting phrase a thing so elusive as the charm of a girl's being when she awakes from sleep, or with unmatched purity makes poetry, in diction and melody, a translucent garment for young angelhood and young sainthood. And he had command, not only of fresh, racy, natural prose dialogue, but also of beautiful poetical dialogue, whether to set forth the ardors of hopeless love or the frail and dying beauty of spring.

Many and varied gifts go to the making of a great dramatist, and from the fame of every one of Shakespere's contemporaries large deductions have had to be made: from Dekker's too they must be made. But his best work has remained unhurt by changing tastes and manners. Whatever he wrote is touched with the artistic and spiritual grace of sincerity, and not even the form of the drama can conceal from us the personality of the most poetical and the most lovable of the group that surrounded the master.

BIBLIOGRAPHICAL NOTE

Bibliographies of Dekker are to be found in Bullen's article in the *Dictionary of National Biography*, in Minto and McKerrow's article in the *Encyclopaedia Britannica*, in Morley's *English Writers*, in Schelling's *Elizabethan Drama*, in the *Cambridge History of English Literature* and in W. Scheffler's *Thomas Dekker als Dramatiker*. A list of works, extant, non-extant, and conjectural, is given by Fleay in his *Biographical Chronicle of the English Drama*. Complete titles of original editions of the plays and pageants are given in the *Cambridge History of English Literature*, vol. VI ; the titles, not always complete, of the long poems and prose works in vol. IV. All the authorities mentioned above, except Schelling, give lists. A list of extant works corrected from the point of view of the writer of this study may be found in the *Table of Contents*.

The only large collection of Dekker's plays and pageants is Pearson's reprint, *The Dramatic Works of Thomas Dekker*, in 4 volumes, London, 1873. The Mermaid *Dekker* edited with *Introduction* by Ernest Rhys includes : *The Shoemaker's Holiday, The Honest Whore, Old Fortunatus*, and *The Witch of Edmonton*. Three plays partly written by Dekker are not in Pearson's collection: *Patient Grissill*, found in vol. V of Grosart's prose collection and elsewhere; *The Noble Soldier*, reprinted in Bullen's *Old English Plays*, vol. I (1882) ; and *The Weakest Goeth to the Wall*, found in W. C. Hazlitt's edition of *Webster*, vol. IV.

Single plays have been repeatedly reprinted. The plays collaborated with Webster, Middleton, Massinger and Ford appear also in the works of these writers. Three of the pageants have been reprinted: *The Magnificent Entertainment* in John Nichols' *Progresses, Processions, and Magnificent Festivities of King James the First; Troja Nova Triumphans* and *London's Tempe* in F. W. Fairholt's *Lord Mayors' Pageants*. Four of the plays have received careful critical editing: *The Shoemaker's Holiday*, by Warnke and Proescholdt, 1886 ; *Patient Grissill*, by G. Hübsch, *Erlanger Beiträge*, vol. 15, 1893 ; *Old Fortunatus*, by H. Scherer, *Münchener Beiträge*, vol. 21, 1901 ; and *Satiromastix*, also by Dr. Scherer, *Materialien zur Kunde des älteren englischen Dramas*, vol. 20, 1907.

The standard edition of Dekker's long poems and prose works is Grosart's *Non-Dramatic Works of Thomas Dekker*, in 5 volumes, 1884. It does not include the following pieces: *A Knight's Conjuring* (altered from *News from Hell*), which has been reprinted by E. F. Rimbault for the Percy Society, *Publications*, vol. 5 ; *Penny-wise, Pound-foolish*, reprinted by W. Bang in his edition of Ford's *Works, Materialien*, 1908 ; and the two important *Prison* sections, added respectively to the 1616 and the 1632 editions of *Lanthorn and Candlelight*. *The Gull's Hornbook* and *The Seven Deadly Sins of London* have been repeatedly reprinted.

CRITICAL COMMENTARY

The following list does not include such general works as those by Collier, Fleay, Ward, Schelling, Courthope or Creizenach, or the useful introductions and notes belonging to the editions mentioned above. Nor does it include, except in a few cases, articles on Webster, Middleton, Massinger or Ford, although such articles usually discuss Dekker in some aspect of his work.

Bang, W. *Dekker-Studien.* Englische Studien, vol. 28.

Bielefeld, F. *The Witch of Edmonton . . . eine Quellenuntersuchung.* Halle, 1904.

Boyle, Robert. *Introduction* to F. A. Gelbcke's translation of *Old Fortunatus* into German. *Die englische Bühne zu Shakespeare's Zeit.* Leipsic, 1890.

Bullen, A. H. *Thomas Dekker.* Dictionary of National Biography.

————. Much valuable material scattered by way of notes and introductions through his editions of Middleton, Day, and Ford, and his reprint of *The Noble Soldier.*

Collier, J. P. *Memoirs of Edward Alleyn, Founder of Dulwich College.* Shakspere Society Publications, vol. I. 1841.

Disraeli, Isaac. *Quarrels of Authors.*

Dixon, W. M. *Chapman, Marston, Dekker.* Cambridge History of English Literature, vol. VI, ch. 2.

"Dramaticus." *The Players who Acted in " The Shoemaker's Holiday."* Shakspere Society Papers, vol. IV, p. 110 (1849).

Fritsche, Hermann. *Notes* appended to his edition of *The Shoemaker's Holiday.* Thorn, 1862.

Goodcole, Henry. *The Wonderful Discovery of Elizabeth Sawyer, a Witch, late of Edmonton, her Conviction and Condemnation and Death.* Reprinted in Bullen's *Ford,* vol I (1896).

Greg, W. W. His edition of *Henslowe's Diary, Part II,* has an article on Dekker, a table of the plays written for Henslowe, and notes on the plays.

————. *Henslowe Papers.* The index is a guide to further notes on Dekker.

————. *On the Authorship of the Songs in Lyly's Plays.* Modern Language Quarterly, vol. I. Cambridge, 1905.

Hazlitt, William. *Lectures on the Dramatic Literature of the Age of Elizabeth.*

Herford, C. H. *The Literary Relations of England and Germany in the Sixteenth Century.* Cambridge, 1886.

Koeppel, E. *Quellenstudien zu den Dramen Chapman's, Massinger's und Ford's.* Quellen und Forschungen zur Sprach und Culturgeschichte, no. 82. Strassburg, 1897.

————. *Studien über Shakespeare's Wirkung auf zeitgenössische Dramatiker.* Materialien, 1905.

On this subject, see also *Fresh Allusions to Shakspere*. New Shakspere Society, 1886.

Kupka, Paul. *Über den dramatischen Vers Thomas Dekkers*. Halle, 1893.

Lamb, Charles. *Specimens of English Dramatic Poets.*

Lange, A. F. *Introduction* to his edition of Thomas Deloney's *Gentle Craft* (source of *The Shoemaker's Holiday*). Palaestra, vol. 18. Berlin, 1903.

Lázár, Béla. *Über das Fortunatus-Märchen*, pp. 79–88. Leipsic, 1897.

McKerrow, R. B. *Thomas Dekker* in the Encyclopædia Britannica (with W. Minto).

Minto, W. See above.

Penniman, J. H. *The War of the Theatres*. Boston, 1897.

Pierce, F. E. *The Collaboration of Webster and Dekker*. Yale Studies in English, 1909.

Routh, V. R. *London and the Development of Popular Literature*. Cambridge History of English Literature, vol. IV, ch. 16.

Scheffler, Willibald. *Thomas Dekker als Dramatiker.*

Schmidt, F. W. V. Critical remarks in connection with his translation of *Old Fortunatus* into German. Berlin, 1819.

Small, R. A. *The Stage Quarrel between Ben Jonson and the So-called Poetasters*. Forschungen zur englischen Sprache und Literatur, vol. I. Breslau, 1899.

Smeaton, O. *Preface* to his edition of *Old Fortunatus*. Temple Dramatists.

Stoll, E. E. *John Webster, the Periods of his Work*. Boston, 1905.

———. *The Influence of Jonson on Dekker*. Modern Language Notes, vol. 21.

Swinburne, A. C. *The Age of Shakespeare* (contains the well-known essay on Dekker, and also essays on Webster and Middleton). Harper and Brothers, 1908.

———. *Essays and Studies* (contains essay on Ford). Chatto and Windus, 1888.

Whipple, E. P. *The Literature of the Age of Elizabeth*. Cambridge, Mass., 1886.

INDEX.

The Index contains the titles of works, and the names of authors and of a few other persons important in Dekker's history—whether found in text or notes. It does not cover the Bibliography, nor include the names of scholars and critics, which, for the greater part, are given in the Bibliography. Long quotations are indexed under the titles of works.

Alleyn, Edward, 13, 88, 166–167, 168, 184n, 185, 196n, 199

All's Lost by Lust, 197

Amends for Ladies, 110n

Antonio and Mellida, 155n

Antonio and Vallia, 28n

Antony and Valia, 28

Anything for a Quiet Life, 100

Arches of Triumph, The, 83, **89–90**

Arden of Feversham, 49

Areopagitica, 131

Arraignment of Paris, The, 34n

Artillery Garden, The, 168

Awdeley, John, 136

Bachelor's Banquet, The, 8, 86, 87, 103–104, 115, **123–124**, 192

Bad May Amend, 47n

Bear a Brain, or Better Late than Never, 51

Beaumont, Francis, 115, 161, 163, 177, 199

Bellman of London, The, 110, **135–137**

Bellman of Paris, A French Comedy of the, 178

Belphegor, 150

Bible, The English, 17, 51, 146, 200

Birth of Merlin, The, 29n

Black Book, The, 128

Blind Beggar of Alexandria, The, 92

Blurt, Master Constable, 93, 96, 134

Bristow Merchant, The, 178, **187–188**

Britannia's Honor, 15, 191

Brome, Richard, 180n, 193

Caesar's Fall, 47n, 83, 90

Canaan's Calamity, 9, **52**, 117, 191

Canterbury Tales, The, 5

Carlell, L., 119, 159, **192–193**

Case is Altered, The, 57n

Caveat for Cursitors, A, 136–137

Chamberlain, John, 110

Chance Medley, A, 49

Chapman, George, 75, 82, 92, 96, 102, **105**, 199

Chaste Maid in Cheapside, A, 95

Chaucer, 5, 49

Chettle, Henry, 6, 42n, 48, 50, **59–60**, 64, 69n, 74, **75–76**, 79–80, **84**

Christmas Comes but Once a Year, 49, 75, 83

Christ's Tears over Jerusalem, 52

Civil Wars of France, Introduction to the, 47n, 51, 79

Come See a Wonder, 183, 186

Connan, Prince of Cornwall, 49

Crack Me This Nut, 31n

Cynthia's Revels, 66, 68n, 72

Day, John, 26, 50, **63**, 75, **82–83**, 109, 110, 111, 116, **177–178**, 185–186, 191, 198

Dead Term, The, 17, 41, 123, **134–135**

Dedekind, F., 14, 142

Dekker His Dream, 15, 17, 152, 165, 167, **173–176**

Dekker relationships, Conjectural, 13, 78n

208

Deloney, Thomas, 52, 56n, **57**, 82, 137

De Probatis Sanctorum Historiis, 156

Devil's Answer to Pierce Penniless, The (see *News from Hell*)

Devil's Law Case, The, 92

Dioclesian, 154

Doctor Faustus, 7, 31, 32–33, 153; Dekker's conjectural part in, 33n

Double P. P., The, 123n, **127–128**

Drayton, M., 50, 82

Dutch Courtezan, The, 106

Earl Godwin, 49

Eastward Ho, 102, 106, 107

Edward the Second, 16

Englishmen for My Money, 63

English Villanies, 12, **194–197**

Essays and Characters of a Prison and Prisoners, **169**, 171n

Every Man in His Humor, 74

Every Man out of His Humor, 53n, 62

Exhortation of London unto Her Children, The, 8n

Faerie Queene, The, 5, 36

Fair Constance of Rome, 49

Fair Maid of the West, The, 114

Fair Quarrel, A, 93

Fairy Knight, The, 17, 178

Family of Love, The, 111

Famous Wars of Henry I and the Prince of Wales, 85

Father Hubbard's Tale, 9

Faust, 153

Fawn, The, 106

Field, N., 110n

Fletcher, John, 115, 161, 163, 177, 183–184, 189, 199

Ford, John, 13, 20, 29, **53–54**, 82, 177, 178, **181**, 187, 198

Fortune's Tennis, 51

Four Birds of Noah's Ark, The, 14, 15, 19, 117, **144–146**

Fraternity of Vagabonds, The, 136

French Doctor, The, 28n

Friar Rush, 148n

Friar Rush and the Proud Woman of Antwerp, 148n

Gentle Craft, The (see *The Shoemaker's Holiday*)

Gentle Craft, The (by Deloney; see Deloney)

Goethe, 153

Golden Ass and Cupid and Psyche, The, 49

Goodcole, Henry, 179

Greene, Robert, 6, 8

Greene's Ghost Haunting Conycatchers, 136

Grobianus, 14, 142

Groundwork of Cony-catching, The, 137

Gull's Hornbook, The, 6, 9, 15, 120–121, 123, 131, **142–144**

Guy of Warwick, The Life and Death of, 178

Hamlet (the early), 5, 39n

Hamlet, 18, 101n

2 Hannibal and Hermes, 47n

Harington, Sir John, 16, 118

Harman, T., 136–137

Harrison, Stephen, 83, 89

Harvey, Richard, 9

Hathaway, Richard, 50

Haughton, William, 48, 50, 59, **60**, 63

Henry V, 31

Henslowe, Philip, 45, 79–80, 82, 114, 166, 198

Henslowe's *Diary*, 28, 29, 38, 47–52, 53, 64, 75, 79, 80, 85, 93, 183n, 194n

Heywood, Thomas, 50, 75, 82, 83, 84, 177, 180n, 203

Hoffman, 42n, 76

Holinshed, 16, 76

Holy Living, 146

Honest Whore, The, 7, 47, 51, 52, 60n, 81, 90, 91–92, **93–101**, 103, 109, 114, 117, 155n, 168, 192, 201, 203

Humorous Day's Mirth, A, 92
Huon of Bordeaux, 178n
If It be not God, the Devil is in It, 7, 8, **147–154**, 155–156, 159, 160, 180, 185n
If You Know not Me, You Know Nobody, 39n
Isle of Dogs, The, 10
Isle of Gulls, The, 37, 102n
Jephthah, 49, 50, **51**, 85
Jests to Make You Merry, 80, 115, 122, 123, **133–134**, 135; see also *The Misery of a Prison and a Prisoner*
Jew of Malta, The, 63, 154
Jew of Venice, The, 28–29n
Jocundo and Astolfo, 178
Jonson, Ben, 15, 48, 50–51, 57n, 62–63n, **65–75**, 79, 82 87–88, 91, 102, 106, 177, 198
Jourdan, S., 17
King Sebastian of Portugal, 49, 64
King of Swedland, The, 178
Knight's Conjuring, A, 1, **4–5**, 8, 55n, 117, 129n, **130–131**
Kyd, Thomas, 5
Lady Jane, 75, 83; see *Sir Thomas Wyatt*
Lanthorn and Candlelight, 2, 12–13, 83, 118, **135–139**, 150n, **168**; for ed. of 1616 and 1620, see *Villanies Discovered;* for ed. of 1632 and 1638, see *English Villanies*
Late Lancashire Witches, The, 180n
Lenten Stuff, 9n
Locrine, 19n
London's Tempe, 192
Look about You, 51n
Love's Metamorphosis, 9, 32n
Lust's Dominion, 63
Lyly, John, 6, 31–32, 33, 38–39, 53–54, 64, 112, 198; for songs formerly attributed to, 54n
Machiavelli, 16
Mack, The, 183n

Mad Pranks of Merry Moll of the Bankside, 109
Mad World, My Masters, A, 95
Magnificent Entertainment, The, **87–89**, 90
Maid of Honor, The, 156
Maiden of Confolens, The, 84n
Malcontent, The, 106
Marlowe, Christopher, 6, 7, 16, 32–33, 82, 153, 180, 198
Marston, John, 20, **66–67**, 69n, 70, 73, 75, 79, 84n, 91, 102, 106, 155n, 177, 198, 199
Martin Mark-all, 13, 74n, 136
Mary Frith, Life and Death of Mistress, 110n
Massinger, Philip, 28, 154, 155, **156–157**, 159, 177, 199
Match Me in London, 107n **159–164**, 187, 192–193
May Day, A, 92
Measure for Measure, 92, 95
Medicine for a Curst Wife, 51, 75
Meres, F., 12, 28
Merry Wives of Windsor, The, 92, 104
Michaelmas Term, 95, 96n
Midas, 32n
Middleton, T., 9, 20, 48, 50, 52, 54n, 82, 90, **92–93**, 94, **95–96**, 100, 106, **109–111**, 113, 116, 128, 134, 177
Midsummer Night's Dream, 18, 36, 38, 39n
Milton, 131
Misery of a Prison and a Prisoner, 18–19; see *Jests to Make You Merry*
Mother Bombie, 6
Munday, Anthony, 42, 49n, 50, 51, 66, 79, 83, 84
Mynshul, Geffray, **169**, 170, 171n, 172n, 173
Nash, Thomas, 4, 5, 7, **8–9**, 10, 18, 21, 52, **128–129**, 130, 155n, 198, 199

News from Hell, 4, 8, **128–130**, 150

Noble Soldier, The, 185–186, **187**

Noble Spanish Soldier, The (see *The Noble Soldier*)

Northern Lass, The, 193

Northward Ho, 16, 60, 83, 90, **91–92**, 101, **102–103**, **105–108**, 109, 114, 115

Ode prefixed to *The Arches of Triumph*, 90

Ode to Munday, 84

Old Fortunatus, 7, 8, 25, 28, **29–35**, 39, 45, 46, 48, 61n, 117, 201, 203

Old Law, 93

Old Wives' Tale, The, 8

Orestes' Furies, 51

Othello, 94, 101n

Overthrow of Rebels, The, 75n

Page of Plymouth, 48, **50–51**

Palmerin of England, 83, 84

Parliament of Bees, The, 185–186

Patient Grissill, 6, 16, 23, 33, 39, 48, 50, 51, **59–63**, 76, 144

Patient Grissell, The Play of (by John Phillips), 59n

Peele, George, 6, 7, 8

Penny-Wise, Pound-Foolish, **188–189**, 192

Phaeton, 29, 79; see *The Sun's Darling*

Philenzo and Hypollita, 28n

Philipo and Hippolito, 28

Phoenix, The, 100, 111

Pierce Penniless, His Supplication to the Devil, 4, 128

Piers Plowman, 17

Pleasant History of Friar Rush, The, 150

Poetaster, The, **66–67**, 68n, **69–73** *passim*

Pontius Pilate, 49, 75

Porter, Endymion, 168 173

Quinze Joyes de Mariage, Les, 15, 124

Raven's Almanac, The, 120, **139–141**, 151n

II Return from Parnassus, 67n

Richard II, 39n

Roaring Girl, The, 90, 92, 103, **109–114**, 147, 159, 160

Robert II, King of Scotland, 66

Rod for Runaways, A, 189–190

Romeo and Juliet, 18, 45, 101n

Rowlands, Samuel, 9, 13, 74n, 135–136, 138

Rowley, Samuel, 185–186, **187**

Rowley, William, 56n, 57n, 178, 180n, 181, 197

Sale, Antoine de la, 124n

Sapho and Phao, 32n

Satiromastix, 9, 18n, 49n, 60, 63, **64–75**, 103, 114, 117, 120

Set at Maw, The, 160n

Seven Deadly Sins of London, The, 17, **40–41**, 116, **119–120**, 123, **131–133**, 139

Seven Wise Masters, The, 49

Shakespere, 3, 9, 18, 53, 59, 67, 75, 82, 91, 92, 93, 115, 163, 182, 199, 200, 204

Sharpham, Edward, 75

Shoemaker's a Gentleman, A, 57n

Shoemaker's Holiday, The, 16, 19, 33, 39, 45, 56–59, 106, 117, 168, 200–201, 203

Sir John Mandeville's Travels, 17

Sir John Oldcastle, 75

Sir Thomas Wyatt, The Famous History of, 50, **75–78**; see also *Lady Jane*

Smith, W., 50, 75

Spanish Fig, The, 187n

Spanish Moor's Tragedy, The, 49n, **63**

Spenser, 5, 10, 16, 38, 75, 134

Stewtly, 49n

Stow, 16

Strange Horse Race, A, 5, 15n, **139**, 150n, 160, 165; for song in, 27

Stukeley, The Famous History of the Life and Death of Captain Thomas, 49n

Sun's Darling, The, 26, 29, 39, 52–56, 81, 178

Tamburlaine, 7, 33

Taming of the Shrew, The, 59n

Tasso, 75

Tasso's Melancholy, 75

Taylor, Jeremy, 146

Taylor, John, 147

Theatrum Poetarum, 42

Titus Andronicus, 63

Trick to Catch the Old One, A, 95, 111

Triplicity of Cuckolds, The, 51–52

Troilus and Cressida (by Dekker and Chettle), 49; possible plot of, 49n

Troja Nova Triumphans, 14, 164–165

Truth's Supplication to Candlelight, 38, 47n, 51

Two Harpies, 47n

Two Shapes, 47n

Villanies Discovered, 168–178, 194

Virgin Martyr, The, 7, 28, 152, 154–159, 168, 177, 185n, 201, 203

Wars, Wars, Wars, 191

Weakest Goeth to the Wall, The, 16, 42–45

Webster, John, 26, 50, 75, 76–78, 82, 83–84, 89, 92, 106–108, 116, 177, 199

Westward Ho, 31n, 45, 75, 83, 90, 91–92, 101–108, 114, 115

What You Will, 70

White Devil, The, 83, 148

Whore of Babylon, The, 14, 19, 21, 24n, 29, 36–42, 45, 46, 51, 76, 103, 114, 117

Wilkins, George, 134

Wilson, Robert, 50

Wisdom of Solomon Paraphrased, The, 52

Witch of Edmonton, The, 3, 53, 158, 168, 178–183, 203

Women beware Women, 93

Wonder of a Kingdom, The, 166, 178, 183–186, 197

Wonderful Discovery of Elizabeth Sawyer, The, 179

Wonderful Year, The, 1, 3, 8, 40, 86–87, 115, 117, 121–122, 123, 124–127

Work for Armorers, 18, 81, 115–116, 118, 141–142

Worse Afeard than Hurt, 47n

Yorkshire Tragedy, The, 49n